ASSIGNMENT RUSSIA

OTHER BOOKS BY MARVIN KALB

Eastern Exposure

Dragon in the Kremlin

The Volga

Roots of Involvement
(with Elie Abel)

Kissinger
(with Bernard Kalb)

In the National Interest
(with Ted Koppel)

The Last Ambassador
(with Bernard Kalb)

Candidates '88
(with Hendrik Hertzberg)

The Nixon Memo

One Scandalous Story

The Media and the War on Terrorism
(co-edited with Stephen Hess)

Haunting Legacy

The Road to War

Imperial Gamble

The Year I Was Peter the Great

Enemy of the People

ASSIGNMENT RUSSIA

BECOMING A FOREIGN CORRESPONDENT
IN THE CRUCIBLE OF THE COLD WAR

MARVIN KALB

BROOKINGS INSTITUTION PRESS

Washington, D.C.

The Brookings Institution is a private nonprofit organization devoted to research, education, and publication on important issues of domestic and foreign policy. Its principal purpose is to bring the highest quality independent research and analysis to bear on current and emerging policy problems. Interpretations or conclusions in Brookings publications should be understood to be solely those of the authors.

Library of Congress Control Number: 2020952502
ISBN 9780815738961 (hc)
ISBN 9780815738978 (ebook)

9 8 7 6 5 4 3 2 1

Typeset in ITC Cheltenham

Composition by Elliott Beard

CONTENTS

PREFACE

Eric Larson, the best-selling author of a recent Churchill biography, defines his book as "a work of nonfiction." He then defines nonfiction as "anything between question marks [that] comes from some form of historical document, be it a diary, letter, memoir, or other artifact," as well as "any reference to a gesture, gaze or smile, or any other facial reaction, [that] comes from an account by one who witnessed it."

This book is also a work of nonfiction, but I cannot swear to the absolute accuracy of every quote, gesture, or smile. I wish I could. This book is a memoir, and memoirs often live in the hazy mist of memory. I have a good memory, but not a perfect one, and therefore my recollection of an event or a conversation may not conform to someone else's. But I've done the best I could. Memoirs, by definition, are not works of history—no footnotes, no bibliography.

Please consider *Assignment Russia* as a long letter home after an unforgettable personal adventure. It's the story of a few very important years in my life as a young reporter trained in the crucible of the Cold War. In the 1950s, I pursued one professional goal with an unflinching determination—to become CBS's Moscow correspondent. It took three years for me to get to Moscow, but it was worth the effort. In May 1960, I finally got there, arriving in the Soviet capital shortly after the collapse of the Paris summit and starting a Moscow assignment that lasted until January 1963 and included such stories as the opening up to Mongolia, the building of the Berlin Wall, and the Cuban Missile Crisis. Those were stories and years packed with professional excitement and personal growth, the rich fodder for my next memoir.

But for this memoir, buckle down for the story of my midnight arrival to CBS in early July 1957, the last recruit hired by the legendary broadcaster, Edward R. Murrow, and then my deeply gratifying ascent through the ranks of a growing and talented news department to become the network's Moscow correspondent at a dangerous moment in the Cold War. It was a major, important assignment for me and CBS, and I hoped that I would be able to perform in the Murrow tradition of serious, fearless, and enlightening journalism, so essential for the functioning of American democracy.

October 15, 2020
Chevy Chase, Maryland

ACKNOWLEDGMENTS

So many helped me, friends and family alike. To avoid unnecessarily lengthening the book, I shall mention only a few.

I start with the warm and wonderful people at the Pulitzer Center on Crisis Reporting, where the inspiration for this memoir was sparked. Jon and Kem Sawyer, who run the center, created the environment for serious research and fun exchanges. They got me started, and I am deeply grateful for their help, encouragement, and friendship.

In the spring of 2019, I moved to the Brookings Institution, which had been my unofficial home for years. There, among outstanding scholars of public policy, I continued my research and writing and eventually finished this memoir. I am especially indebted to John Allen, president of the Brookings Institution, for his kindness and understanding, as well as for setting an example for courageous, sensitive leadership during a time of national crisis that is widely appreciated. To all of my Brookings colleagues, thank you for your invaluable help, offered often without my even asking: to William Finan, Yelba Quinn, Elliott Beard, Cecilia González, Robin Ceppos, and their other very able colleagues at the Brookings Institution Press, including Janet Walker, who copyedited the manuscript;

to Holly Cohen, who helped with the research; to Cy Behroozi, Sara Chilton, and Laura Mooney of the Brookings Library; and to Emilie Kimball and Andrew Sanders—bless you for always being there when I had a question or needed assistance.

Among my friends, who helped tirelessly with editing and lengthy consultations, Garrett Mitchell, who writes the elegant *Mitchell Report*, and Walter Reich, a professor of medicine and expert on the Holocaust who teaches at The George Washington University (GWU), stand at the top. They were there from the beginning and stayed loyally to the end. For whatever it's worth, they have my eternal gratitude.

Also, with dignity and understanding, a constant source of encouragement was my friend, Michael Freedman, president of the National Press Club, executive producer of *The Kalb Report*, and a media professor at GWU. He knows his contribution to this memoir, from title to content, and the depth of my gratitude.

Always my family: First, to Mady, my wife for the past sixty-two years and a key character in this memoir, who has always been my Number One adviser; our daughters, Deborah, an author and editor, and Judith, a professor of Russian language and literature at the University of South Carolina; our sons-in-law, scientist David Levitt and professor Alex Ogden; our grandchildren, Aaron and Eloise, phenomenal fountains of pride, love, and amazement; and my brother, Bernard, a model and inspiration to me and everyone else lucky enough to bask in his love, example, and friendship—to all of you, my thanks and love.

I have now at age 90 reached a time in my life when I appreciate not just the big things, but the small things too, like a smile, a gesture, or even, in pre-pandemic times, a handshake or a note. So, in that spirit, I extend my hand in friendship to every reader, hoping that together we can build a better world where kindness, compassion, and understanding become the recognizable ingredients of a normal day in American politics.

ASSIGNMENT RUSSIA

JOINING A "BAND OF BROTHERS"

It was certainly not what I had imagined.

In my mind's eye, as I arrived at the global headquarters of CBS News in late June 1957, a raw recruit only recently hired by the legendary Edward R. Murrow, I envisaged a news room bustling with energy, of immense influence and power, with dozens of desks arranged in clusters (one for national news, another for Europe, a third for Asia, and a fourth for local news), each desk cluttered with at least one telephone, a type-writer, a pile of newspapers, and an abandoned cup of coffee, reporters writing, editors yelling, producers in pained anguish for copy, walls covered with maps and bulletin boards, banks of tickertape machines tagged "Associated Press," "United Press International," "Reuters," and "Agence France-Presse," all standing side-by-side, like soldiers on parade, belching forth news and information about this, that, and everything else—in other words, the normal noisy chaos of a news room, only more so. This was, after all, CBS News, the home base for the "Murrow Boys," a special "band of brothers" formed during the bitter days of World War II to provide solid, reliable

1

news and information for network viewers and listeners. And, on this night, on the seventeenth floor of 485 Madison Avenue, as the hallway clock inched toward midnight, I was joining this "band." I was thrilled.

On the train ride from my parents' home in Queens, where I had spent the weekend, to midtown Manhattan, where I was now to start a new chapter in my life, I thought about the steps that had brought me from my pursuit of a PhD in Russian history at Harvard to the midnight-to-8 a.m. shift at WCBS Radio. Of crucial importance, without doubt, was my brother's advice years before to major while in college not in English literature, which was tempting, or American history, which was equally tempting, but in a subject of burning contemporary relevance—one that offered me a realistic shot at an interesting job after graduation, no small consideration for someone raised during the Great Depression. Bernie thought, given my interest in journalism and the Cold War, that the subject might be "Russia," meaning the language, the history, the literature, the politics, the culture of the country that at the time posed a set of crucial strategic challenges to the United States. Not for the first time, Bernie was right, and, while a senior at City College and a graduate student at Harvard (and while serving in Army Intelligence during the Korean War), I plunged into the grim, but rich and fascinating history of America's principal adversary during the Cold War. When the State Department urgently needed a Russian-speaking attaché at the American Embassy in Moscow in January 1956, I was one of a small number of candidates who had a top-secret clearance, was unmarried, and could leave in a week. After a few interviews at the State Department, I was one of two selected for the job. For the next thirteen months, I worked as a translator, interpreter, and a kind of press attaché at the embassy, met many Russians, including a number of Soviet leaders, among them Communist Party chief Nikita Khrushchev, who nicknamed me Peter the Great (I was, he laughed, almost as tall as the noted tsar), and traveled, most of the time by myself, from one end of this vast country to another. It was the equivalent of a crash course in modern Russian history.

On my way back to Cambridge, where I picked up my pursuit of a PhD, even though, in a corner of my mind, I always considered journalism to be a more promising prospect, I detoured to Southeast Asia where Bernie was covering the rise of anti-imperialist nationalism in Indochina and Indonesia for the *New York Times*. My visit to Vietnam ignited an interest in that remarkable country that has never left me. Back at Harvard, I resumed my studies, absorbed at the time with the subject of my dissertation, a biography of Sergei Semyonovich Uvarov, the nineteenth-century classicist who authored the populist Russian slogan, *Orthodoxy, Autocracy, and Nationality*. Though busy with research and teaching, I still found time to write essays and book reviews about Russia for the *Saturday Review of Literature* and occasional articles for the *New York Times Magazine*. One of those had obviously caught Murrow's eye. It focused on Soviet youth. The famous broadcaster, much to my surprise, called and invited me to his New York office, where we engaged in an impromptu seminar on Russia. He, like an eager graduate student, asked many questions, and I, like an equally eager professor, tried to answer them. Toward the end of a three-hour conversation, which was supposed to run a half hour ("he's a very busy man," his secretary reminded me, unnecessarily), Murrow offered me a job at CBS News. I thought for a moment that I had arrived in heaven.

The reason was that for a few years I had played with the far-out possibility of becoming the Harry Schwartz of CBS News. Schwartz was a scholar, a specialist on Soviet affairs, who worked for the *New York Times*, and he deepened the paper's daily coverage of America's major adversary by adding his analysis to the paper's hard news coverage from Moscow. Let us say, the Kremlin announced a shakeup of leadership. The story would obviously be reported from Moscow, and

Schwartz would often add a "what does this mean?" analysis. Might CBS be interested in a similar analysis from me? Though I never raised this idea with Murrow, the possibility of a Schwartz-like assignment at CBS News suddenly seemed to shimmer on the not-too-distant horizon.

Bye, bye scholarship; hello journalism!

So, in June 1957, a new adventure beckoned—but, only to acknowledge the obvious, it entered not with clashing cymbals but on cat's paws, so quietly and unobtrusively that you would have been excused for thinking CBS News was, at least on the night of my arrival, a monastic retreat rather than an elite, trend-setting news operation.

Maybe I should have noticed the distinction the moment I walked out of the elevator onto the seventeenth floor at the beginning of my early morning shift. No one was there, no one leaving, no one arriving, except me. The arrow to the main newsroom pointed to a long, dimly-lit corridor—office doors shut and dark on my left, an editing room and Studio 9, also dark, on my right. As I walked into the newsroom, a chubby man with graying hair hurriedly pushed past me, grunting what sounded like a "hello" but not stopping, nor looking back. He was gone before I could respond. The newsroom, at first glance, was no larger than my mother's living room. It had half a dozen desks, as I recall, one of them placed in front of a window covered with a Venetian blind hanging at an odd angle. The tickertape machines were all standing, one next to another, like robots, on the right side of the room, but they were uncharacteristically silent, as though nothing was happening anywhere in the world. Which could not be true, I told myself. Separating the newsroom from Studio 9 was a large rectangular window, which looked as if it had not been washed in months. If the original idea was to flash signals of late breaking news from the newsroom to the studio, I doubt that anyone in the studio could have seen them. An unnatural, ghostly silence seemed to have settled over the newsroom. Strange, I thought, that no one was manning the phones, no one barking orders, no tickertapes ticking, no bustle—no nothing.

What I'd confronted was the midnight stillness of an empty newsroom. In the dead of night, there is probably nothing more still than an empty newsroom.

I was alone, and I was a bit puzzled.

I knew I was to write a string of early morning news broadcasts—the 5 a.m., the 5:30, the 6, and the 6:30 a.m. newscasts for WCBS Radio, the local outlet of the CBS radio network, but I was never told how to write a radio newscast. I guess CBS management had simply assumed that anyone who was a PhD candidate from Harvard could write a radio newscast, a local one at that. John Day, the news director of CBS News, an ambitious, grouchy ex-newspaperman from Louisville, Kentucky, had clearly made that assumption when, at Murrow's suggestion, he hired me and gave me my marching orders—"your job will be to write the morning newscasts" for WCBS, he told me on the phone a week or two earlier; and I did not have the wit, nor did I wish to display my inexperience in daily journalism, to ask how does one write a morning newscast. After we agreed on when I would start (as I write now, I'm not absolutely certain, but it was a week or ten days before the July Fourth weekend—of that I'm sure!), what my shift would be (midnight to 8 a.m., at the beginning), and my salary ($7,600 a year), Day mumbled "good luck," and quickly got off the phone. Aside from his hurried order about writing the local newscasts for WCBS Radio, he imparted no further insight into my new responsibilities. Worse, I didn't ask. I learned later that I was not his choice for this job at CBS News. He wanted a reporter with lots of ink-stained experience. I was Murrow's choice. He wanted someone who knew about Russia. Learning to write a local newscast, in his judgment, could and would come later. Murrow won this contest, and I was to ride his coattails through my time at CBS, which lasted twenty-four years, even though Murrow himself resigned in January 1961, four years after I had come on board. I later learned that he had become disillusioned with broadcast news (was it "merely lights and wires in a box?" he wondered) and accepted President John F. Kennedy's offer to head the United States Information Agency. Murrow left behind an unparalleled legacy of professionalism, decency, and integrity, a banner for every journalist to hold high, a model for every student of this challenged craft.

Since there was no one in the newsroom to point me to a desk I could call my own, I took the one closest to the news tickers. For the better part of an hour, maybe longer, I just sat there in a state of wonder and disbelief. I knew I could write a dissertation. But a newscast? I was not at all sure. Occasionally I would get up to look at an incoming story on the Associated Press or check the other tickers, some of which had finally begun to clatter with their reports. Also, figuring there might be some elaboration of my responsibilities, tagged to a bulletin board, or left on the cluttered desk near the window (the editor's, I assumed), I walked around the newsroom, reading one CBS memo or another, many dated, some new, learning little to nothing about the organization or my job. Carefully I combed through CBS's impressive collection of newspapers, from the *Times* to the *Daily News*, available on a long table, certain that in this harvest of print I'd find a gem I could hijack for my morning newscasts. I didn't want my newscasts to sound like the morning newspapers, but in time I came to rely on the newspapers more and more.

Then, back to my desk. Sometime between 1 and 2 a.m., with the newspapers having been read and the ticker tape machines having been scoured for nuggets of news, I checked my watch and realized, with a start, that I could wait no longer. I would have to begin what was for me the uncharted task of writing my first radio newscast—the one that was supposed to air at 5 a.m. But I really did not know how to write a radio newscast. I knew the length—three minutes and fifty seconds. But, for a local newscast, what was to be my lead? How would I select it? I needed help, but none was available at the time. I knew an editor would have to review the copy—but when would he arrive? And who was the announcer who would actually read the script? I began to worry like my mother, the apple having fallen not too far from the tree. Suppose the editor got sick, or the announcer had an accident? What would I do? To whom would I turn? I looked up from my desk, feeling flushed and thinking I was seeing the walls closing in on me. I needed to splash some iced cold water on my face. I went to the bathroom.

On the way, I passed a few of the offices of CBS's top brass. First, Day's office, which looked small and scruffy, like the man himself. Day, in a huff, would later quit CBS in 1961, when he was not promoted to be president of the network, a job he thought he deserved. Then Sig Mickelson's spacious, orderly office. His responsibility was television news at a time when radio was still CBS's main moneymaker. In the early 1950s, Mickelson brought Walter Cronkite to New York, named him "anchorman," and changed the format of all evening news shows. Then Robert Skedgell's office, warm and pleasant as the man himself proved to be. Skedgell, once a copy boy at fledgling CBS News, was now director of Radio News, but he earned his wings a few years earlier when he helped set up the network's first TV news studio on the fifth floor of the Grand Central Station building on 42nd Street. "Hell," he said at the time, "I hardly know what television is."

The water in the bathroom was warm but still welcome, and, feeling only slightly better but, ready or not, realizing I could no longer procrastinate, I hurried back to the newsroom, sat down at my desk and looked up at the clock: "2:47 a.m.," it mercilessly screamed.

I slipped a sheet of paper into my typewriter and wrote an

identifying preamble, "June 27 [as best I recall], 1957, 5 am, WCBS Radio, Kalb." At that instant, as though ordered by a cruel, distant deity, my fingers froze: I had no idea what my lead sentence would be.

I had options, of course. Because I had recently returned from the Soviet Union, my interests naturally flowed toward foreign news. Rumors had circulated in Moscow about a pending change in Soviet leadership. Affecting Khrushchev? No one was certain. Columnist James Reston of the *Times* wrote about President Eisenhower's concern about a possible agreement with the Soviet Union on banning or limiting atomic weaponry. The Senate was deliberating another increase in defense spending. And two local stories seemed interesting: a subway train had jumped the tracks at 108th Street in Manhattan and delayed more than 50,000 commuters on their way to work, and twenty-one people were injured, none seriously, when two buses crashed into a parked car.

Which of these was to be my lead?

It was, I noticed, 3:32 a.m.

For what seemed like an eternity, I looked at my typewriter, then at the newspapers, and finally at the unusually quiet ticker tape machines; and then back at the typewriter, urging the keys, on their own, to type out a story. Suddenly, the British news agency, Reuters, shattered the nighttime quiet with bells ringing a bulletin. I jumped from my seat like a rocket shot from a silo, rushed to the Reuters machine, and, yes, there was a bulletin. It was from New Delhi, India, and it reported that twenty-seven people had just been killed when their boat capsized in the Ganges River.

Twenty-seven people dead!

"Thank God," I shouted.

Quickly, as if I had been writing radio newscasts for decades, I dashed off my lead. "Bulletin from New Delhi, India," it began. "Twenty-seven people died today, according to the British news agency Reuters, when their tourist boat capsized in the Ganges River. The director of the tourist agency expressed sorrow for the loss of life, adding his agency would start an immediate investigation. This was the second time a tourist boat had capsized in the Ganges in the last four years. Meantime, in Moscow," I continued, writing one news story after another in descending order of importance—in my judgment anyway—until I reached the two essentials of local news: sports and the weather. My Moscow story was speculation about an upcoming Kremlin shakeup, then Ike's reservations about a ban on atomic weapons, then possible increases in the military budget, before I concluded with the two traffic accidents in Manhattan. I was (and am) a devoted Yankee fan and would, most contentedly, have written a long story about that day's Yankee-Cleveland game. The Yankees were pitching Johnny Kucks, the sinker-balling righthander who had shut out the Brooklyn Dodgers in the concluding game of the 1956 World Series. The weather was warm and humid, typical for New York in late June.

I read and reread the script. I wanted to see lyrical lines leaping off the pages, lilting melodies of news and information resonating like Mozart in a Viennese newsroom.

I looked up at the clock. "4:45," it shouted.

"Where the hell is the editor?" I asked myself, feeling my anxiety mushrooming into panic. At which point, the gods sent a jolly warrior to my rescue. Harold (Hal) Terkel bounced into the newsroom, a round man with a broad smile on his face, a Yankee hat perched on his balding head, a lunch box in his right hand and a crumpled newspaper in his left. "Ah," he grinned, "you must be Kalb." Carefully, he placed his lunch box on the editor's desk and then extended his hand in a warm, very friendly way. "I'm Hal Terkel," he said in an accent that had never left the Bronx. "In case you were wondering, I'm your editor." Terkel, I later learned, was a relative newcomer to

CBS, having joined the network in 1955 as a writer and editor after years with two small radio stations, WLIB and WHLI, and briefly with the New York office of the Voice of America.

I was relieved, but still quite uncertain about whether I had written a script bound for the wastebasket or one good enough to be read on air. Though Terkel had not yet sat down at his desk, I handed him my script and quietly withdrew to watch and wait.

It was 4:50 a.m.

Terkel, though clearly overweight, moved with surprising lightness. He took my script, smiled again, and, now comfortably seated, read through it very swiftly.

"Very nice," he sighed, resorting to this utterly meaningless expression to avoid saying what he really thought. "Very nice." Then, casting a quick glance at the clock, he asked, "Were there any Americans on board?"

"Any Americans?" I echoed.

"Yes, you know, on the tourist boat, the one that capsized."

"Let me doublecheck." I raced to my desk, read the Reuters copy, and shouted back, "No, Mr. Terkel, no mention of Americans."

"Hal," Terkel said, "and thanks."

He waited only a second or two before putting a fresh sheet of paper in his typewriter and banging out a radio script for the 5 a.m. newscast. He was rewriting my script. It had not measured up. I'd failed. Terkel, on the other hand, resembled a remarkably explosive bundle of energy and spontaneity. It took him less than five minutes to rewrite the script, finishing at 4:56 a.m., when a short man in a seersucker suit walked into the newsroom and gingerly made his way to Terkel's desk, ignoring me en route. Hal handed him the script. He softly whispered, "Mornin', Hal," and made his way to Studio 9, where, a few minutes later, he delivered the 5 a.m. news with a smooth professionalism that suggested CBS was, as always, an efficient, smooth-running news organization.

Terkel was listening intently to the newscast. When it ended, the seriousness on his face melted into a warm smile of satisfaction. "Well, did it again." He pumped his right fist. I could not share his satisfaction. The script was not mine, and I must have looked as I felt, an unhappy rookie who, when tested, had flunked. Terkel approached me and, placing his right hand gently on my shoulder, said, "Marvin, please don't worry. You're a good writer—that's clear. You just don't know how to write a local newscast." He paused before adding, "and it's my job to help you."

Again, looking up at the clock, a constant reminder of the time left before the next broadcast, Terkel plunked himself down behind his desk. "Look, we have about twenty-eight minutes before the next broadcast. Let's talk for a few minutes, and then I'll write the top of the 5:30, and you write the weather and sports. I want to know what you think about Johnny Kucks. I think he's over-rated."

"Yes, of course," I replied. "Let's talk."

Terkel steepled his fingers, a sign he was engaged in serious thinking. "Suppose you were a mailman, and you lived in Queens," he began. "You get up at, say, 4:30 in the morning, you shave, shower, and then put on the 5 a.m. news." He looked at me, wondering if I was seeing the picture he was painting. "What do you think I'd be interested in?"

"I don't know. What?"

"Well, do you think I'd really be interested in that boat capsizing in the Ganges? Especially when there were no Americans on board? I doubt it. Maybe the accident yesterday, holding up people getting to work? You know, no one was killed, no one really hurt, but if you have nothing else, maybe you could lead with that. That's what I did."

"I'm not sure I agree," I objected. "Twenty-seven people were killed, and if not that story, then surely the shakeup in Moscow. Seems to me that's more important than an accident in Manhattan."

"It's a judgment call, I agree," Hal replied. "But my gut tells me that for a *local* newscast, I've got to go with local news. That's why my mailman turns to WCBS. For local news. If he wanted network news, national or world news, he'd go to CBS. Right?"

I still had a question mark on my face. I was not sure I did get it.

Terkel, again glancing at the clock, abruptly dropped his teacher pose and became an editor with a broadcast on his near horizon. No nonsense in his voice or manner, he repeated, "I'm doing the top stories. You do the weather and sports, and add some analysis about starting Kucks today. OK?"

"OK," I replied.

It was 5:24 a.m.

I went back to my desk and quickly wrote the weather report and then an analysis of the Yankee-Cleveland game, stressing, "Among Yankee fans, there appears to be a difference of opinion about today's starting pitcher for the Yankees. On the one hand, those believing right hander Kucks has shown he's a great pitcher, but among more traditional Yankee fans, an equally strong feeling that Kucks may be overrated. Yes, he pitched a great game during last year's World Series, but so far this year he has been disappointing."

Terkel and I finished our assignments at roughly the same time. I read Hal's contributions to the 5:30 newscast, noticing he did add a brief item about the Ganges accident. He read mine, sporting an especially big grin when he came to the Kucks item.

It was 5:28 a.m.

At that moment, the man in the seersucker suit returned, carrying a container of coffee. He appeared to be remarkably tranquil. Terkel, with a smile, handed him the script. He made his way to Studio 9, where once again he delivered a smooth rendition of the local news.

"What about the 6?" Terkel asked. "Game to try it yourself?"

"Yes. Game indeed."

For the 6 and again the 6:30, I wrote the whole script, modeling both on Terkel's 5 a.m. masterpiece and his informal teaching class, which I appeared to pass. Terkel seemed pleased. I was too. From Terkel, I had learned how to write a local newscast, and I had met my first real friend at CBS. He had heard that I was Murrow's "boy," a reporter-in-the-making who had recently returned from a year in the Soviet Union. He apparently shared Murrow's belief that CBS needed someone on its staff who knew about the Soviet threat and challenge. After the 6:30 newscast ended, a few other writers and editors began showing up to prepare the 7 a.m. local newscast and then the network's 8 a.m. *World News Roundup*, CBS's pioneer radio news program dating back to 1938, when Murrow and his colleague, William Shirer, started reporting regularly on Hitler's relentless march toward World War II. Terkel, as though taking a cue from an invisible director, took me protectively by the arm and steered me into an empty, nearby editing room. Just as Murrow had done during our first meeting, Terkel asked me a series of questions, most especially about Soviet youth: their schooling, upbringing, their outlook on life, religion and marriage, their approach to parenting.

An hour passed quickly. Terkel had opened his lunch box and was nibbling on a sandwich when, looking at me like a solicitous parent, he put his hand on my knee and pronounced, "Marvin, you look beat. On your way." At which point he swooshed me out of the room. "Get some sleep," he added unnecessarily. "I'll see you tomorrow morning."

Though I had entered CBS at midnight, imagining a busy newsroom but finding an empty one, I left a little after 8 a.m. the next morning, just as the newsroom was beginning to fill up, feeling more attuned to the reality of broadcast news and determined, if at all possible, to persuade CBS that what it really needed at the height of the Cold War was another Harry Schwartz. And his name, I hoped, would be Marvin L. Kalb.

CBS'S "SPECIALIST ON SOVIET AFFAIRS"

If, in the 1920s and 1930s, you ever thought about journalism, you probably imagined a journalist to be someone like Hildy Johnson, the cocky, wisecracking reporter who dominated the action in the 1928 play, *The Front Page.* Written by two former Chicago reporters, Ben Hecht and Charles MacArthur, the play, which attracted standing-room-only crowds on Broadway, focused on Johnson's playfully unprincipled approach to getting a story. He lied to his newspaper colleagues. He misled the mayor. But, no matter, he got his scoop. Journalistic ethics, if such existed then, be damned!

Edward R. Murrow was Hildy Johnson's polar opposite. His speech was what linguists called "great American," sounding like it came from no one part of the country, but all parts; his suits were handmade on Saville Row; and his code of professional ethics was fashioned in war, hot and cold. There was no room for games or affectation, except, critics say, for the use of his middle initial. With friends, it was always Ed or Edward

Murrow, but, on air or in any formal setting, it was Edward R. Murrow. A number of his wartime colleagues also used their middle initials—William L. Shirer, for example, or Howard K. Smith, or Richard C. Hottelet. It was their way of endowing the new business of radio and television news with a measure of respectability and legitimacy. John *Charles* Daly was the reporter who broadcast the news of the Japanese attack on Pearl Harbor. Charles? Later on, when network news achieved a higher degree of popular acceptability, Dan Rather did not need a middle initial or a middle name; nor did Tom Brokaw or Ted Koppel.

But, in the late 1950s, when I entered CBS News, the middle initial was still considered a badge of honor, a link to the greatness of Murrow's World War II reporting, and for several years, like many other aspiring journalists, I toyed with a byline that included an *L*, for my middle name, Leonard, but I ignored it as often as I used it. For a few years, my byline at the *Saturday Review,* the *New York Times*, and other publications was Marvin L. Kalb, but the *Times*, for some reason, dropped the *L*, and soon thereafter, when I began to appear regularly on CBS Radio and TV, I too dropped it. It suddenly seemed superfluous.

On July 1, the start of my second week at CBS, I met a brilliant, beautiful redhead from South Orange, New Jersey. Eleven months later, we were Mr. and Mrs. We met under the clock at Grand Central Station, a blind date—she coming in from New Jersey, I from Queens. I was dazzled and fell in love. I must have made a favorable impression on her, because that night in her diary she wrote that I was "warm" and "natural."

Madeleine (Mady) Green was a Phi Beta Kappa graduate from Wellesley College, and in September 1957, she was starting a PhD program in Soviet studies at Columbia University. From date one, we always had much to discuss, and now, 62 years later, we still do.

I stayed on the midnight-to-8-a.m. graveyard shift for more than three months, Terkel providing a course in radio news every morning. Among many other things, he expounded on the differences between local and network news and the importance of writing for the ear (radio) as opposed to writing for the eye (newspapers). "People don't read radio," he'd explain. And he would advocate the occasional use of a phrase rather than a whole sentence for dramatic effect, and, perhaps most important, the need to "talk" to the listener rather than "lecture" to him or her. You need "to have a conversation, to respect his intelligence," he would urge. Terkel would have been a superb professor—he taught as much by example as by word. I will always remember his rewrite of my first attempt at a radio script. No one could have introduced me to CBS and journalism more effectively, more appealingly, than this thoughtful Yankee fan from the Bronx, who in later years was the editor who taped my broadcast reports from Moscow, making suggestions along the way to improve their "listenability," a word Terkel made up and one that still makes sense to me.

Whenever he had a chance, Terkel would tell stories—he loved to tell stories about the "business," his way of saying journalism-as-practiced-by-CBS. "Have I ever told you," he'd often begin a story with a mischievous grin, "how we had to break into a Lowell Thomas newscast with a news bulletin?"

"What's that?" I asked, bewildered. "Break into a newscast with a news bulletin?"

Thomas was one of CBS's most fabled personalities. He was, in addition to being a successful newscaster, an actor, a writer, a businessman. Most notable, Thomas was the reporter who discovered and publicized "Lawrence of Arabia." Success haunted his every move, almost.

Toward the end of an illustrious career, Thomas decided that it would be more comfortable for him to do his evening newscast from his home in Pawling, a New York City suburb, than from a studio at 485 Madison Avenue, and no executive at CBS had the courage to object. What Thomas wanted, Thomas got, even if that meant his newscast would be taped, not live, when aired—not the most desirable way of producing a news program.

Terkel explained how this system was supposed to work—that is, until one day when it didn't. A team of writers in the New York newsroom would write Thomas's script and then transmit it by modern-day Pony Express to his home in Pawling, where Thomas had built an impressive studio. Thomas, a genuine pro who had been broadcasting the news since 1930, would practice reading the script once or twice, and when he was ready, he would contact a radio producer in New York, who had one major responsibility—to arrange the taping of the Thomas newscast, usually an hour or so before it was actually broadcast to the nation. "Good evening, everybody" was Thomas's distinctive opening, known to millions of listeners who trusted him more than any other newscaster. Among his many awards was a Presidential Medal of Freedom.

"One day," Terkel recounted, giggles between words, "something really big happened in the middle of his newscast. Really big. I forgot what it was, but we had to get it on the air real fast. I wrote a bulletin, gave it to one of our announcers, who went into Studio 9 and broke into whatever was on the air at the time. Well, it happened to be one of Thomas's taped newscasts. 'We interrupt this newscast,' the announcer said, 'to bring you the following news bulletin.' Everyone in the newsroom, realizing what they had just heard, burst into laughter, at which point the phone rang. It was Thomas, and he was furious. He didn't think it was funny at all, interrupting his news program with a news story." Terkel shook his head. "We did."

Most of the time, Terkel and I were, of course, absorbed with our immediate responsibility—which was preparing the scripts for the four radio newscasts (5, 5:30, 6, 6:30) that welcomed New York's early risers to the glories of Gotham;

but for the others who soon after 6 a.m. began to join us on the dawn patrol, their focus was, understandably, on the crown jewel of the CBS Radio Network, namely, the CBS *World News Roundup* (WNR), which, in 1938, started a tradition of timely and reliable news that survives to this day. The WNR staff was small, dedicated, no-nonsense: two writers, a producer, and an anchor. It seemed as if they rarely exchanged a word, each knowing by instinct and experience what the others were thinking and expecting. They occupied four scruffy desks in the middle of the newsroom. They were constantly shuffling newspaper and teletype clips back and forth, pointing at this one or that. When they spoke, it was generally in short bursts, the anchor suggesting his preference for the story that should lead the broadcast, raising his head and his bushy eyebrows as if to ask, "What do you think?," the writers often nodding in agreement, then shifting their excitement to their typewriters, which somehow managed to survive the fury of their one-finger-here-one-finger-there assault, until, magically, a good script emerged. Relentlessly, the clock ticked its way, minute by minute, toward 8 a.m., everyone in the newsroom by now accustomed to casting a frequent, respectful glance in its direction.

At just the right time, the editor handed the script to the anchor, who gave it what could only be described as a "quick read" before rushing into Studio 9, where the mood abruptly changed from the contained chaos of the newsroom to the calm professionalism of a broadcast studio.

At exactly 8 a.m., as the second hand brushed past the number 12, the anchor, a tall, fullback of a man with a booming voice, "talked" to his listening audience: "Good morning," he said. "This is the CBS World News Roundup. I'm Dallas Townsend." For the next fifteen minutes, he took his listeners on a global tour with stops in Washington, Chicago, London, Moscow, and Cairo, picking up reports from CBS correspondents at each stop. If Townsend had the time (again, the clock—

he'd often be looking up at the clock), he would conclude his roundup with a feature story designed to elicit a sympathetic nod or smile from his listeners. When, sliding a finger across his throat, the director would signal the end of the broadcast, Townsend would lean back, his face in a broad childlike grin. "How'd we do?" he'd ask, knowing the answer. "How'd we do?"

Townsend, an old timer who'd joined the network in 1941, had been a writer and editor on the WNR for many years before becoming its principal anchor in 1956, by which time he was recognized at CBS and beyond as a major star. During the 1948 presidential campaign between President Harry Truman and his GOP challenger, New York governor Thomas E. Dewey, Townsend anchored all of CBS's radio coverage. He had the same responsibility in 1952. It aroused no look of surprise when he was selected to anchor the WNR.

Once a week or so, I would deliberately delay my departure from the newsroom at 8 to talk with Townsend, and he would always stop for a brief chat about journalism in general or an aspect of Soviet policy that he had just reported. He was the gracious gentleman, willing to talk and, when he considered it appropriate, ask questions about Russian policy. Like Terkel, he too had heard that I had only recently returned from the Soviet Union. In those dangerous days of the Cold War, Russia was a natural takeoff point for almost any conversation about foreign affairs, especially among reporters. Many wanted to know about the unpredictable Soviet leader, Nikita Khrushchev. Was he really as reckless in his actions as he seemed to be in his rhetoric? they asked. What would it take for the Cold War to become a hot war? Because a number of my recent articles had focused on Soviet leaders and policy, they wanted to know my opinion, and I was only too happy to oblige. If I could come to be seen at CBS as a ready and willing resource on Soviet affairs, I would be one happy fella.

One Sunday, under my mother's rather relentless pressure, I reluctantly started the long-delayed chore of combing through bulging boxes of books, trinkets, and papers packed in Moscow and shipped to my parents' home in New York, where they had been stacked in the basement untended for months. No sooner had I started than a surprise popped out of the first box I opened. In two large unsealed embassy envelopes were dozens of typed and written notes I'd kept during my Moscow assignment—notes defined as anything from a scrap of paper to a discarded napkin to an 8-by-11 page of embassy paper. These notes contained names, phrases from a conversation, even a sentence every now and then. Together, if one is blessed with a generous spirit, they might be described as a haphazard diary—but only if you were willing to stretch the definition quite a bit. They were notes of interesting conversations I'd had with Russians, including peasants I'd met in villages or Communist Party chieftains I'd been introduced to at Kremlin functions or at embassy receptions. Or notes of my general impressions of places I'd visited during my many trips through the vast Soviet countryside, from Bukhara and Samarkand in central Asia to Tbilisi in Georgia or Kiev in Ukraine.

On this Sunday, reading one note only led to my reading another, and then another, until I realized, after many hours had passed, that there might have been a point to keeping my "diary"—maybe, I had thought, these notes, efficiently strung together by sympathetic editors, might one day be packaged into a book about a young American's adventures in the Soviet Union during the Cold War. But maybe not. A book might have been a dream too far. I had to be honest with myself: if I had been a serious diarist, I would have been more responsible and surely more systematic, composing my thoughts in whole sentences, collecting tourist books of every place I'd visited, new Russian novels, interesting magazines, copies of newspapers, history books—the ingredients of a society stuck at the time in the mud of Marxist totalitarianism.

Still, the idea of a book kept reappearing in conversations with friends, family, and my new colleagues at CBS, and it intrigued me. I had my notes; maybe I had a book. But in the cultivated world of book publishing, as practiced in New York, the heart of the industry, no one could get anywhere without an agent. With a respected agent, publication was not only possible; it was probable. Without an agent, publication was impossible.

One day, sitting in the CBS newsroom, a friend told me about an agent with a special interest in foreign affairs, particularly in U.S.-Soviet relations.

"Contact her," I was advised. "What have you got to lose?"

The agent's name was Edith Haggard, and she'd been working at Curtis Brown Ltd., a prominent literary agency, since the late 1930s. Later that afternoon, my courage summoned to the task, I called, and, much to my surprise, she, not a secretary, picked up the phone. Another surprise: she knew my name, probably because she read the *Saturday Review*, a magazine devoted to books. I'd been writing for the *Saturday Review* since 1953, when I was still a graduate student at Harvard. My brother, Bernie, had introduced me to editor Ray Walters, who needed a reviewer with some knowledge of Russian affairs. As a student, I had "some knowledge," and Walters gave me the opportunity to review first one book and then another and then another; and I must have been doing these reviews well enough to satisfy Ray, because this arrangement continued for many years. It was an assignment I treasured. It kept me up to date on new books. It helped build my reputation in the field. It added to my file of published work.

"Do you have a book?" Haggard asked, an obvious question.

"I have a kind of manuscript," I replied.

"A kind of . . . ?"

I tried to describe my collection of notes, my effort at composing a diary, but she cut me off. "Can you stop by at 11 tomorrow morning?" she asked briskly.

"I'll be there."

"And don't forget to bring your notes," she added, a drop of sarcasm in her voice.

In person, Haggard was small, charming, and so delicate she was often compared to Chinese porcelain. "So what have you got?" she wanted to know. I gave her "my notes." She smiled when I explained my sloppy but determined approach to note taking. By the time I left, an hour later, a warm and wonderful hour spent sharing stories about Tolstoy, Turgenev, and Chekhov, Haggard said she would read my notes, and if she liked them, she already had a publisher in mind, who was also strongly inclined toward books about Russia.

A few days later, she called. "Marvin," she said, a touch of excitement in her voice, "your notes need a lot of work, but I love what you have written, what you have discovered in Russia. I love the conversations, the humor, the Slavic sadness. It needs a lot of editing, but I think we have a terrific book here, and Roger agrees with me."

"Roger?" I asked.

"Yes, Roger Strauss of Farrar, Strauss and Cudahy. It's a good house, and I recommend we go for it."

Who was I to argue? "Thank you, thank you," I said, making no effort to disguise the excitement in my voice. "I could not be happier."

Pause.

"When will they publish it?"

"Next November 1958. Roger's aiming to put it out as quickly as he can."

"Fantastic!" I said.

Haggard then wanted to discuss the advance, but I was too excited to listen. Besides, I had an hourly newscast to write.

In early October, John Day informed me that my position at CBS would change. I had been a "writer for WCBS radio," in other words, a writer for a local station. I would now become a "writer for CBS News." I would be joining the network. A year later, on my speedy ascent, I would be named a "CBS News reporter" and, when I was assigned to Moscow shortly thereafter, a "CBS News correspondent." My work shift would also change: from midnight to 8 a.m. to 4 p.m. to midnight. The immediate advantage was both personal and professional. I would be able to see Mady at more convenient times, and I would be able to meet a few more of my new colleagues. Aside from Murrow, two were especially friendly and helpful— Robert Trout and Blair Clark.

I had already read and heard a great deal about Trout, once described as "the voice of CBS News." His family name at birth was Blondheim, which, Trout thought, sounded German at a time when German-sounding names were becoming unpopular in the United States. So, in 1932, as he launched his remarkable seven-decade career, most of the time with CBS, he dropped it—Blondheim became Trout, and Trout became a household name.

For many years, Trout's voice was associated with major events, such as presidential inaugurations, political conventions, wars, even the Kentucky Derby. During the Great Depression, when President Franklin D. Roosevelt used the relatively new technology of radio to talk to the American people, Trout was the reporter who often introduced the president, in the process coining the term that made its way into history— "fireside chat."

It was then only natural that, on March 13, 1938, it was Trout who interrupted regular programming on CBS Radio to introduce a new concept in broadcast news, the CBS *World News Roundup.* "The program *St. Louis Blues* will not be heard tonight," Trout announced. A "special program" would take its place, including "pickups direct from London, Paris, and such other European capitals as, at this late hour abroad, have communications channels available." Shirer reported from London, Murrow from Vienna, having just arrived there from Warsaw and Berlin. Thus was born a great broadcast—and an even greater industry.

During World War II, on D-Day, Trout did thirty-five newscasts in twenty-four hours, earning him the title "Iron Man." For two years, he shared the London beat with Murrow. He tried teaching the swiftly rising star of CBS News to consider the microphone a metallic friend, someone with whom he could easily communicate, with or without a script. Trout had proved to be a superb ad-libber; Murrow never so. Though he became an exemplary broadcaster, indeed the pioneer of broadcast news, Murrow was never on a first-name basis with a microphone. During newscasts in Studio 9, for example, he would often break out in a sweat, opening his collar, even his trousers, to ease his anxiety. Trout, on the other hand, could probably not have imagined a story he could not broadcast with absolute ease and grace.

Yet, on the day I first met Trout, a day of unusual warmth in early October, perfect weather for a World Series game, the legendary broadcaster entered the newsroom wearing a long, woolen scarf wrapped carefully around his neck. Twice. I was taken aback. Was he trying to be funny? His reputation as a comic had already spread through the industry. But though the newsroom was warm, Trout made no effort to unwrap his scarf. He sat down behind a desk, smiled or waved at the writers and editors in a most friendly, relaxed manner—he was very popular with everyone. When a writer (not me) handed Trout his script for an hourly newscast, the broadcaster did unwrap his scarf once, but kept the rest of it firmly around his neck. He read the script in a barely audible voice, a kind of private practice session, and then, satisfied, he walked into

Studio 9, his old haunts, and read the script without a hitch, as he had done with thousands of other scripts throughout his career.

Just as everyone in the newsroom stopped to marvel at the master, I turned to the editor, who had cleared Trout's script. "Why is Mr. Trout wearing a scarf?" I asked, puzzled.

"Why don't you ask him?" he replied.

I laughed. "Because I don't want to lose my job."

"No," he said, "he'll tell you."

"I'd rather you tell me."

"Ask him," the editor repeated. "He's really a very nice guy."

So encouraged, I greeted Trout one day as he left Studio 9. "Mr. Trout," I said, but words suddenly failed me. "That was a very nice broadcast," I added limply. I could think of nothing else to say.

"You're Kalb," Trout remarked, sparing me further embarrassment. "Ed said you'd be joining us, and we ought to talk. About Russia. Right?"

"Yes, Sir."

"It's Bob, OK?"

"Yes, Sir," I repeated.

We both walked back into the newsroom. I couldn't wait any longer. "May I ask you a question, Sir?" A long pause followed. Trout, a tall, thin man with sharp features on a very angular face, knew where I was going.

"You want to know about my scarf?"

"Yes, Sir."

Trout laughed. "I wear a scarf now quite often," he said, pointing to his throat, "to protect my biggest asset, my throat, my voice. It's what pays the rent." He laughed and sat down, waiting for me to join him. "I've become highly susceptible to colds lately," he said. "My doctor thinks a scarf might help me avoid them."

A question mark must still have been on my face, because

Trout added, "Even my wife thinks he may be right." His wife had just entered the newsroom. She often accompanied Trout to the office.

Over the next few months, we talked many times—about the highlights of his career, about London during the blitz, about Stalin and Russia, about Roosevelt, whom Trout admired enormously, and about Murrow, whom he admired even more, if that was possible. Though he had never attended college, not even for a single course, Trout was a walking encyclopedia. He knew a little about a lot. He was also, as his editor often reminded me, a "very nice guy," who just happened to wear woolen scarves on warm days.

No star at CBS News burned more brightly than Murrow's, even though at the time he was beginning to feel disillusioned with television news, a fact he probably confided to very few others except his wife, Janet, and his executive producer, Fred Friendly. Whenever he walked into the newsroom, usually after lunch, wearing no jacket, his head down, his tie loose, a cigarette in his hand, looking like a man carrying the weight of the world on his shoulders, the writers and editors would stop talking and instinctively pull back, opening a path for him to the tickers. It was like a scene from the Bible, Moses making his way to the Red Sea. As the new kid on the block, though one whose job at CBS Morrow, more than anyone else, had helped create, I too would pull back, as ignorant of his deepening unhappiness as everyone else in the newsroom.

I was to learn of it only a year later, on October 15, 1958, when he addressed the annual convention of the Radio Television News Directors Association (RTNDA) in Chicago. And he made news. "This nation is in mortal danger," he began, stunning the audience with this startling message, stating in public what he had feared in private—that television, though profitable and in many ways satisfying, was actually failing to do its job, not helping a nation trapped in the global challenges of the Cold War. He painted a grim picture: if you watched prime-time television for one solid week, he posited, you would find only "evidence of decadence, escapism, and insulation from the realities of the world." He respected the potential of television. "This instrument can teach, it can illuminate; yes, it can even inspire," he noted. "But it can do so only to the extent that humans are determined to use it to those ends." (Murrow had his doubts, and he was now prepared to express them.) "Otherwise," he concluded, using a phrase many others would later echo in their criticisms of television news, "it is merely wires and lights in a box."

Murrow was not one for small talk, and he often fell into bouts of depression. But if, on those occasions, he felt a need for instant reassurance, he always knew he could find it in the CBS newsroom, where he was always held in the highest esteem, admired and loved, a warm reverence enveloping the reporter who, more than any other, had turned radio into broadcast news. Literally a hush would fall over the newsroom whenever he appeared. Would he say something? Or just read the tickers, and leave, his normal routine?

Every now and then, on these midday visits, he would have a word for me. "Enjoying your new life as a journalist?" he'd ask, a gentle pat on my shoulder. But, before I could answer, he would already have moved on.

Still, a few months later, as a result of a rush of troubling news from the Middle East, Murrow invited me to write a number of his radio commentaries. They all focused on Khrushchev's policy toward Egypt. But even before Murrow could offer his invitation, Blair Clark had already offered me the opportunity to write commentaries about Soviet policy for his own newscast.

Blair Clark was the producer and anchor of the *World Tonight*, a fifteen-minute roundup and analysis of the day's news, which aired weekdays at 8 p.m. Occasionally, Clark would stop me in the corridor and ask about a Khrushchev speech. Was the Soviet leader signaling a possible shift in policy? Clark might have read something on the wires, or in a book, and he wanted to talk about it. Unsolicited, I had been sending short memos on different aspects of Soviet policy to a small number of producers and correspondents, hoping they'd be helpful in shaping the evening newscasts. Was the news from Moscow that day truly significant, important enough to lead the newscast, or just interesting and therefore worthy of mention, or was it, in my opinion, merely another dollop of Soviet propaganda? I tried, with the memos, to answer such questions.

Apparently, Clark thought the memos were helpful, and once or twice a week he would arrange the equivalent of a brief seminar on the latest news from Moscow—the two of us meeting in his small office overlooking the midtown traffic on 52nd Street. In this respect, Clark reminded me of Murrow. Thoughtful, always curious, he had a way of turning a newsroom into a classroom, and I was, in those early months at CBS, thrilled to be able to talk to him; and if I was able to help him, even more so. Very quickly, it seemed, we became really good colleagues.

If America had an aristocracy, Clark would have been a member of it. He looked like my image of an aristocrat. Tall and handsome, elegant and soft-spoken, he was born into the riches of Long Island, raised in New England, and educated at Harvard. There he met an ambitious Bostonian named John Kennedy, and the two quickly became good friends. Clark served in the military during World War II, and he was a successful newspaper editor after the war. In 1953, while reporting from Paris, he joined CBS and, within a few years, rocketed through the reporter ranks to become the anchor of the *World*

Tonight. A few years later, he replaced John Day as vice president of CBS News.

What would distinguish his broadcast from the *World News Roundup*, aired at 8 a.m., CBS's other fifteen-minute newscast? Between the two broadcasts were eleven hourly newscasts, all focused on hard news. What had happened from one hour to the next? By 8 p.m., Clark reasoned, the CBS listener would be ready for a broadcast that placed the hard news of the day into a more analytical context—in other words, the listener would be ready for what would soon become known as "news analysis." His reasoning proved to be prescient. Listeners did want to know not only what happened during the day, but why. Just as the *World News Roundup* satisfied the needs and desires of an America waking up to another day of excitement and danger, the *World Tonight* satisfied their yearning, after a tough day at work, for a sensible explanation of what it all meant, perspective on the news added like whipped cream on a sundae of hard news. Because Russia was almost always a major story, whether morning or night, it followed that the zigs and zags of Russia's policy and personality would find a home on the evening broadcast.

After a few months of office seminars and an occasional drink at Colbee's bar, a CBS favorite near the main entrance to 485 Madison Avenue, Clark one day suggested that, in addition to my regular responsibilities, I undertake another—that, when asked, I write about Soviet policy for different broadcasts. Clearly he had the *World Tonight* in mind. Maybe he had checked with Murrow, maybe not, but sometime in mid-March, he took his own suggestion to a new level—he started to read my analyses on air, often without changing a word, sometimes giving me name credit. The subject was often the budding, problematic relationship between Khrushchev and President Gamal Abdul Nasser of Egypt.

"You don't mind?" he'd joke.

Understatement of all time: I was delighted.

I remember what happened the first time he informed me that he was going to read one of my commentaries.

As Clark entered Studio 9 shortly before 8 p.m., I raced into News Director Bob Skedgell's empty office (Bob had left for the day), shut the door, called Mady, my mother, and brother with the news ("Yes, the program starts at 8 p.m.," I reminded them), flicked on the radio, sat back, and listened, and waited. Finally, toward the end of the show—*there it was!*—my analysis of recent Soviet moves in the Middle East. For a moment or two, I sat motionless, staring at the audio console, perhaps a tear or two in my eyes. I was trying to absorb what had just happened—Blair Clark had read my analysis on CBS radio. Thousands had heard it, probably many more. (Ratings must have spiked when my mother began boasting to her family and friends.) Most gratifying was that it was Clark's initiative to read it on air—his voice, my words, CBS's stamp of approval. In this way, unofficially, I had become one of his writers, focusing on Soviet policy. In a few weeks, this arrangement widened to include pieces on communist activities and actions around the world. With no fanfare, I had taken a small step toward becoming the Harry Schwartz of CBS News. I was obviously in the right place at the right time.

———

As helpful as Blair Clark was in advancing my career, so too, following a circuitous route, was the unlikely romance of Khrushchev and Nasser. Both of these leaders, for different reasons, engaged in a dangerous conspiracy in the mid-1950s that not only threatened Western interests in the Middle East but almost led to war. It was, however, a conspiracy that was a godsend to journalists: a compelling story likely to make every front page and every hourly newscast. CBS had to cover the story; and even if I were not a budding specialist in Soviet affairs, I still would have been following it.

For the first time, Russia was sending arms to Egypt, challenging the West's once dominant position in the Middle East. Russia was also using Radio Cairo to expand communist propaganda into other Arab capitals. Nasser, a charismatic Egyptian, struck a deal with Syria in 1958 to create the United Arab Republic, an eye-catching leap into an ephemeral pan-Arab nationalism. Britain's Anthony Eden and America's John Foster Dulles hated Nasser but could find no way to outflank his tricky diplomatic and military maneuvers. Theologian Reinhold Niebuhr, reflecting a broad Western judgment, described the Egyptian leader not as a "revolutionary" but as a pro-Soviet "dictator imagining himself as a second Saladin." U.S. Marines were preparing to land in Lebanon, an unmistakable sign the United States was not about to bend to Arab guile, nor to Khrushchev's gamble aimed at elbowing the United States out of the Middle East. Diplomats found themselves in constant motion, propagandists incited passions, riots deepened social instability, ships and soldiers were moving into fighting position, and the danger of war hovered on the near horizon.

On April 28, 1958, Nasser arrived in Moscow, and I got a call from Murrow's secretary, Kay Campbell. "Ed would like to see you," she said.

"When?" I asked.

"Now," she responded. It was 3 p.m. I would usually be arriving in the office at 4 p.m., the start of my shift, but lately I'd been arriving earlier to do research and writing for the *Saturday Review* and other periodicals—what the academics would call "extra-curricular activity."

The walk from the newsroom to Murrow's office, a journey of no more than fifty feet, took less than a minute. Campbell's welcome was a smile and a nod toward Murrow's open door. "He's waiting," she said.

Murrow was pacing from one end of the room to the other.

On his large desk were piles of newspapers and ripped-off wire copy. On the wall behind his desk was a placard with Cicero's words: "If I had more time, I'd write you a shorter letter." The moment he saw me, Murrow asked, "What do you make of Nasser in Moscow? What do you make of Khrushchev's welcome? The AP says it's the grandest ever accorded a foreign leader." The wires were in fact reporting that Nasser was being treated like a conquering king—Khrushchev and the Kremlin elite waiting on both sides of a red carpet at the foot of the plane's ramp, scores of school children carrying flowers and singing joyous songs about "peace and friendship," 200 elite Soviet troops forming an impressive guard of honor, and crisscrossing Soviet and Egyptian flags lashed to every pole at the airport.

Murrow, with a straight face, asked, "If you were to write my commentary for tonight's broadcast, what would you say?

I gulped.

He continued, "Blair thinks your stuff for his show has been . . . quite good. I've heard a few of them, and agree."

The renowned journalist sat down behind his desk. "So what would you say?" he again asked. I thought I saw a glimmer of a smile around his eyes.

"Do you mean for tonight's show?"

"Of course." Now I could see the smile. "Nasser arrived today, right?"

I looked at my watch. It was 3:30. Murrow's show aired at 7:45. "When would you want to see the script?" I asked.

"6:30, no later," he answered. "Now what are you going to say?" he asked, this time with obvious impatience. For an instant I did not know what I was going to say. I did know I was suddenly in a new world.

Murrow's fifteen-minute newscast ended with a three-minute commentary, which he often wrote himself. It was his signature statement on the day's news. Only later that evening did I realize that if I'd failed to write an acceptable script, one he would have been happy to voice on his program, he might not have had enough time to write another one. He must have trusted me.

So, what was I going to say? I'd been thinking about a possible approach all day—not for Murrow but for a memo I'd have distributed to producers. For both Khrushchev and Nasser, this love affair was a problematic gamble. By reaching out to Khrushchev, Nasser was abandoning his earlier suspicions about communist expansionism and, in a desperate push for glory, putting his fate, and his country's, in Russian hands. He always feared "active Russian occupation of the Middle East," he once said, leading to a time when "you practically hear the Russian boots clumping down on the hot desert sands." By linking his political fortunes to a restless Arab nationalist, Khrushchev was hoping to secure one or more warm water ports in the Mediterranean, something no tsar had achieved over centuries of effort, and in the process damage Western interests in the Middle East.

"Go to it!" Murrow said, giving me the green light. "I want to know as much about what really drives these men as you know." He had already turned toward his typewriter. He had things to do. "OK?" he asked, almost as an afterthought. Saluting, I replied, "Yes, Sir!" and, as I left Murrow's office, I think, in my euphoria, I blew a kiss at Campbell.

But first things first. I would not have enough time to write the 5 p.m. and 7 p.m. newscasts, my regular responsibilities, and Murrow's commentary. What to do? I explained my problem to the editor, usually a silent, irascible man who had never learned to smile. But now, apprised of my problem, he allowed a small smile to appear on his face. "No problem!" he all but shouted. "If Mr. Murrow wants you to write his commentary," the editor said, with uncommon cheerfulness, "we here in the newsroom are happy to oblige." The editor, pointing to my desk, added, "Great assignment, Marv. Write it. Mr. Murrow is waiting." It had always been "Marvin," but now suddenly it was "Marv."

Nasser had arrived in Moscow in early morning, and by mid-afternoon he and Khrushchev were already in Red Square extolling the wonders of Soviet-Egyptian friendship. I thought I might have trouble writing a Murrow script, my awe for this journalist paralyzing my fingers; but possibly because I had been thinking about the story for much of the day, the words flowed easily.

"A tall Arab visitor joined his short Slavic host atop the Lenin Mausoleum in Red Square today," I began, focusing on the personalities of the two leaders, as Murrow had requested, and what each hoped to achieve during Nasser's long, headline-catching trip to the Soviet Union.

Shortly after 6 p.m., I finished the script. Quietly, I read it, as if I were the broadcaster, and made a few edits. As a courtesy, I also asked the editor to read it. He was pleased I had asked, and, as a sign he accepted this assignment with the utmost seriousness, he actually changed a word here and there, dropped a comma, and asked a question easily answered. "I've never edited a script for Mr. Murrow," he said, a faraway look of pride in his eyes. "Just tell him if there is anything else we can do to help, just ask."

Campbell was next to see my script. It was 6:15 p.m., fifteen minutes ahead of Murrow's deadline. She said Murrow would see it and get back to me before the start of his broadcast.

"But *when* will he see it?" I asked, anxiously hitting the word "when."

"Soon," she replied. "He'll get back to you."

"When?"

"He'll get back to you," she repeated, picking up my script and a few others and heading into Murrow's office, where, through the open door, I could catch a glimpse of the legendary journalist huddled over his typewriter.

I returned to the newsroom, where I pretended to read the afternoon papers and the latest wire copy while I waited for Murrow's reaction. Time passed very slowly. Shortly after 7 p.m.,

Ed Bliss, Murrow's writer of hard news, a kind, highly competent journalist, entered the newsroom, apparently to check the tickers for late-breaking news. He was in a rush, but spotting me, he paused and, holding up his right thumb, like a politician just told his polls had risen, softly mouthed, "He likes it."

For the next half hour or so I walked on air, occasionally pinching myself. Harry Schwartz, move over, I crowed to myself. When, at 7:40 p.m., I spotted Murrow and Bliss heading toward Studio 9, both engaged in hushed conversation, I slipped into Skedgell's office and again called family and friends to tell them that Edward R. Murrow ("That's right, Edward R. Murrow!") was planning to read my commentary at the close of his newscast. Reaction was filled with oohs and aahs. I pressed the radio button on the audio console, sat back, and listened to the program that had been a part of the Kalb household for many years. Now I was to be a part of the program—I still could not quite believe it. Would he really read my commentary?

After a commercial break, Murrow opened his concluding commentary with my words about a "tall Arab" and a "short Slav." It was happening. I leaned forward, elbows on knees, and listened intently. Did he change a word, a thought? No, I did not think so. He must have liked the script. His voice gave my words an authenticity and importance that on their own they would not have possessed. Listening, I suddenly realized that I was crying—the tears were those of pride, pleasure, and professional satisfaction.

Of course, I had been gratified when Clark read my scripts on air, but now I was in a state of unnatural bliss listening to Murrow reading one of my scripts, as he was to read others over the next couple of months. On that evening, I knew I had taken a big step toward a professional goal that, only a few months earlier, I had considered a remote dream.

"Congratulations." It was Clark greeting me the next day. "Good job. I guess Ed's been listening to the *World Tonight*," a humorous reference to the commentaries I'd been writing for his show. Nodding toward his office, he whispered, "When you have a minute?"

I was there in seconds. Wasting little time on pleasantries, Clark said he wanted me to write another piece on Nasser's visit to the Soviet Union, this one focusing on a single theme: the way Nasser was allowing Khrushchev to spread communist propaganda throughout the Arab world. Why was he doing this? And what effect was it having? It was a subject that intrigued me.

"When would you want it?" I asked.

"For tonight," he replied. "A minute-twenty, no more," the normal length of a piece for the *World Tonight*, "and try to get it to me by 7 p.m." Clark usually accepted pieces as late as 7:45. Why the earlier deadline? I didn't ask, and he didn't say.

I had in my overstuffed briefcase, a kind of portable filing cabinet that I carried with me everywhere, several newspaper clips on Soviet propaganda efforts in the Middle East. My thinking was, if you understood the role of Radio Cairo, you would understand a lot about Egyptian and Russian policy. Why would the Russians want to use Radio Cairo? Why would the Egyptians allow it? And how effective was this effort? It was a complicated subject. A Mideast scholar could write a book on the subject. A Harry Schwartz could write 1,500 words for a Sunday spread in the *Times*. But a writer for a minute-twenty radio commentary had to be brief but somehow comprehensive, no easy task but obviously doable. Murrow, citing Cicero, had been writing "shorter letters" since World War II.

Practice did not make perfect, but it helped. The successful writer of radio and television news had to contain the natural impulse to add words when fewer might actually accomplish the same end.

My piece was long, a little over two minutes. I started the painful task of cutting a word here, a word there, a short phrase perhaps. No writer enjoys cutting his own script. I finally got it down to 1:26. Foolishly I thought Clark would accept the extra six seconds. When I submitted my script to him, at exactly 7 p.m., as he had requested, he dropped what he was doing, read it, and unceremoniously cut eleven seconds, meaning five seconds more than I had cut. It was now down to 1:15.

"Good!" he pronounced. "Damned good, in fact. Just what I wanted." He then looked at me, as if he were sizing me up, and asked, "If I'm not mistaken, you're hoping one day to be a CBS correspondent, right?"

"Yes," I replied.

"Meaning, you'll have to do your own broadcasts, right?"

"Yes, one day."

"Well, why not today? Why not right now?"

My heart missed a beat, or two, or three, and I said nothing.

"Why not?" Clark continued, sounding like an adventurous gambler. "Why not? You've got to start sometime." He put his arm on my shoulder and, steering me down the corridor to Studio 9, whispered, "I know this is like throwing someone who can't swim into a pool, and saying, Swim!" Clark squeezed my shoulder. "Only I know you can swim."

"Really?" I asked, a show of timidity masking an inexplicable rush of self-confidence.

"No doubt in my mind," he replied. "We'll tape it tonight, but next time we'll be doing it live."

I sat down in the same studio chair Clark used, and Murrow used, and Trout used, and Townsend used; and when the go-ahead light flashed from the control room, I read my script carefully, made no mistakes and, when finished, looked up at Clark. "No need for another take," he said. "Perfect." At which point he spun around and returned to his office, where he resumed his final preparation for another edition of the *World Tonight*. For him it was another edition; for me it was a breakthrough.

BROADCASTING'S ONE THING, WRITING'S ANOTHER

The following day I got an unexpected call from another relative newcomer to CBS News, an executive producer named Burton Benjamin. "I heard your *World Tonight* piece," he said, "and loved it, and I'm wondering, do you have any time today to stop by and discuss it?"

"Sure," I replied, puzzled but pleased. "When would you like?"

"Well, how about now?"

"I'll be right there."

Benjamin, who also had joined CBS in the summer of 1957, had been a writer and producer of news documentaries for RKO-Pathe since 1946. He was a pro, accomplished, experienced, ready for a new challenge. He left the impression, after only one meeting, of being a very decent man, someone you could trust. Apparently enough of his CBS colleagues came to the same conclusion, because in 1978 he was chosen president of CBS News. All told, Benjamin worked at the network for twenty-nine years.

His deputy was Isaac Kleinerman, another experienced documentarian, who had only recently migrated from NBC, where he'd produced a prize-winning, twenty-six-part series called *Victory at Sea*. Kleinerman's strength was that he made things happen. Tall, his hair graying, a mustache lending an air of dignity to an otherwise dour face, Kleinerman was, for a film maker used to working under tight deadlines, pleasant, pragmatic, and highly organized.

Benjamin's office was in the corner of a large suite, home for a television series called *The 20th Century*. Anchored by Walter Cronkite, a rising star around whom CBS was clearly building a post-Murrow dynasty, the series was relatively new to the Sunday lineup. Successfully launched in October 1957, it was producing a fresh half-hour episode every week. I watched them regularly. I enjoyed their focus on global personalities and problems. The inaugural program, for example, told the exciting story of "Churchill: Man of the Century." The power of the British leader's personality, his electrifying rhetoric, and the drama of World War II attracted almost twenty million viewers, a pleasing statistic for the bookkeepers of the "Prudential Insurance Company of America," the program's sponsor.

The success of "Churchill" set a high standard for the series. Sunday after Sunday, at 6 p.m., *The 20th Century* seemed to follow a fixed pattern: a popular personality, a riveting story, and then a concluding climax, all told crisply against a backdrop of archival and original footage. Though Benjamin was widely credited with coming up with the idea for the series, it was actually the brainchild of Irving Gitlin, CBS's vice president for public affairs. He had read Mark Sullivan's popular book, *Our Times*, and decided, on the spot, that its exciting story of America in the early part of the twentieth century would make an appealing television series. In Benjamin's hands, Gitlin's idea hit the jackpot, an early rendition of *60 Minutes*. It was, the producer noted, with only a trace of embarrassment, "as much a show biz show as any dramatic half-hour." There was no need for embarrassment. Benjamin had a genius for infusing even a simple tale with drama, energy, and a touch of mystery.

As I headed to Benjamin's office, still wondering what he had in mind, I remembered a number of the programs I'd recently seen. Near the top of my list were "D-Day," "Trial at Nuremberg," and, most gripping, "Riot in East Berlin," the story of frightened communist leaders mercilessly machine-gunning their people for the sole purpose of protecting their power and privileges. It was no different from the way Soviet authorities crushed anti-Russian riots in the Georgian capital of Tbilisi shortly after Khrushchev's denunciation of Stalin, a local hero, in February 1956.

My meeting with Benjamin, in one striking respect, was very similar to my first meeting with Murrow. Just as Campbell had warned me that Murrow was "very busy" and could meet with me for no longer than thirty minutes (the meeting actually lasted three hours, Murrow paying no attention to the clock once we got started), Benjamin's gatekeeper also informed me that her boss was "busy" and had no more than a half hour. We spoke for two hours.

After a few minutes, Kleinerman joined Benjamin. Both insisted that we drop formalities and use our nicknames. Having none, I remained Marvin, but they quickly became Bud and Ike. They were seasoned documentarians. I knew how to watch a documentary but not how to make one. With their help, I would soon be on a steep learning curve in the new and exciting world of TV documentaries. I'd been put on a fast track at CBS—that was obvious. In a brief time, I had been taught how to write an hourly radio newscast, based on hard news, then a radio commentary, often based on one's experience and judgment, and now I was being introduced to the news documentary.

For Bud and Ike, the beginning of their tutorial was not focused on the workings of a 35mm camera but the challenge of the mercurial Soviet leader. Like so many others repelled by the rhetoric and antics of Nikita Khrushchev, they chose to spend much of our first meeting asking me about his personality and his policy. Ever since my return from Moscow, in one conversation after another, I found that Americans wanted to know, more than anything else, whether the Soviet leader was "stable." Was it possible that his antics could push East and West into a war that could easily have been avoided? Was he a clown or a shrewd Russian peasant? Why was he pursuing such a dangerous policy in the Middle East? Did he not know the difference between "national interest" and "suicidal adventures"? I told them that I shared the judgment of almost every Western diplomat I'd met in Moscow—that Khrushchev was a "completely stable" leader, who pursued the "national interest" of the Soviet Union in an admittedly flamboyant but hardly suicidal manner. I told them that I had met and talked with Khrushchev, and he seemed to me to be a classic Russian nationalist, serious about his desire for what he called "peaceful coexistence" with the United States, yet capable of embracing a problematic policy in a troubled part of the world, if he thought he could gain a strategic advantage.

But, if that were the case, Bud wanted to know, how could one explain Khrushchev's reckless embrace of Nasser? "That could quickly lead us to war," he observed. While I acknowledged the Egyptian leader might one day drag Russia into a collision with the United States, I thought Khrushchev's strategic aims in the Middle East were limited—that if he sensed Russia was being sucked into a war with the United States, he would unceremoniously drop his "ally" and withdraw from the battlefield, like the drunken cowboy in a western backing out of a saloon with guns blazing. Khrushchev was no fool, though on occasion he seemed to act like one.

Bud and Ike confessed they were fascinated by Khrushchev as the subject of a possible documentary about the troubled

Middle East. Interestingly, the question on their minds was the subject of my *World Tonight* commentary the night before—how the Soviets used Radio Cairo to propagandize the Arab Middle East.

"We ought to do that as a documentary," Bud said. "It's a hell of a story, and Khrushchev's a hell of a main character."

Acting instinctively, Ike quickly looked through the fat notebook he always carried with him. His staff called it his "Bible," a collection of shooting and program schedules, interview dates, and reporter/cameramen travel. "Agree," he said, "totally agree. Great idea." He stopped at a page crowded with schedules. "Late October, I think late October is the best time." Then, spreading his arms out as far as he could, looking like a giant bird about to lift off, he added, "and how about this for a title?" He looked first at Bud and then at me, and, in a soft, serious voice, proposed, "The Red Sell"?

Ike again looked to Bud. "What do you think?"

Bud had an immediate reaction. "I love it," he said.

And that was that! No more than a few minutes had passed, and Bud and Ike had already agreed on the subject of a documentary, when it would be broadcast, and what it would be called. But, in truth, I still did not know what any of this had to do with me.

"Oh, by the way, we'd like you to be our writer," Bud seemed to be reading my mind. "What do you think?"

Bud's question, innocently posed, reminded me of Murrow's proposal that I write his commentary or Clark's surprise offer that I broadcast the commentary I thought I'd written for him. On both occasions, I'd been flattered and obviously pleased, but not overwhelmed. I guess I had built up enough self-confidence from my studies at Harvard and my experiences in Moscow to believe I could do the job of writing and explaining Russia to a network audience. "Bud, I'm pleased beyond words, truly, but I've never written a documentary." I hoped my candor would not prick the bubble of his enthusiasm.

"No problem," Bud smiled. "We'll teach you. What do you say?"

Here was another challenge; but it was one within my lane, and I thought I could manage it. "You've got a deal," I said, grinning like Lewis Carroll's Cheshire cat. I shook Bud's hand, and then Ike's.

Ever the practical producer, Ike then reminded Bud that he would have to formally request my services from John Day and then, turning to me with a slight grin, added that it would be "nice" if I, in addition, would ask Day's permission to accept Bud's offer. "It's a formality, I know," Ike assured us, "but let's do it anyway." A week later, as Ike had predicted, Day gave his approval. If he had any reservations about my new assignment, he did not express them. Starting on May 1, I would be detached from the newsroom for six months to work as a writer for *The 20th Century.*

Things were beginning to change for CBS News in Moscow. Within a brief period of time, they would have a major effect on me, but as winter slipped into spring in 1958, I knew only what I read in the papers or heard in the newsroom.

Dan Schorr was expected to return to Moscow in January 1958, as CBS's resident correspondent, a position he'd held with great distinction since 1955. We had overlapped in 1956, when I worked at the United States embassy as a translator and press attaché. We had become good friends. At one point, Schorr even offered me a job as his No. 2 man in the CBS News bureau in Moscow, a splendid opportunity for a young journalist; but, after much hesitation, I declined, saying I wanted first to finish my PhD program at Harvard. I had promised my mother that before accepting a job, any job, I would complete my dissertation and get my doctorate. She did not want me to be distracted. Yet, less than a year later, when Murrow offered me a job at CBS, I took it without a moment's hesitation, apparently so thrilled by his offer that I had little difficulty forgetting about Schorr's offer or the promise to my mother. Clearly Murrow's impact on me, and many others, had been powerful and lasting.

As required of all foreign correspondents based in Moscow, Schorr applied for his re-entry visa, expecting no problems. But the press department of the Soviet Foreign Ministry responded first with silence and then with an unofficial hint that Schorr would no longer be welcome in Moscow. He was not labeled persona non grata; he was just not welcome. A spokesman, when pressed for an explanation, refused to elaborate, saying only that the problem was Schorr, not CBS. If CBS wanted to continue to staff its Moscow bureau, the spokesman said, it would be wise for CBS to send another reporter.

Schorr, in my judgment, had always been fair in his coverage of the Soviet Union, but he had also been tough. My guess was that he must have offended a senior Soviet official, perhaps even Khrushchev himself. Other foreign correspondents had been similarly tough in their coverage, yet given re-entry visas on request. It was a serious problem, upsetting and frustrating to both Schorr and CBS News. Maybe the explanation lay in the fact that Russia had always been, in Churchill's words, "a riddle wrapped in a mystery inside an enigma." The Russians never explained their decision, and they did not think they had to.

A month later, CBS gave Schorr another assignment. It was in the form of a defiant poke in Moscow's eye. CBS moved him to nearby Warsaw, Poland, where he was able to apply his considerable knowledge of Soviet strategy to cover Russia's restive East European empire. The Russians might have thought they were getting rid of Schorr. They were mistaken. By moving to Warsaw, he had just changed his angle of vision but not the sharpness of his analysis.

But, like any major news organization with global responsibilities, CBS wanted quickly to reopen its Moscow bureau.

From its rich stable of political reporters in the nation's capital, CBS selected Paul Niven, a large, curious, gregarious, well-traveled reporter. He had served in the U.S. Army during World War II. After the war, he completed his studies at Bowdoin College, located near his hometown of Brunswick, Maine, where his father edited the local newspaper, *The Brunswick Record*. In 1946 Niven enrolled in the London School of Economics while, at the same time, dipping into journalism. He became a stringer for the *Manchester Guardian* and, a few years later, joined the London staff of CBS News. Wherever he worked, Niven was an immediate favorite. He was candid, thoughtful, an incredibly decent colleague, which I was to appreciate fully when I met him during the Nixon visit to the Soviet Union in 1959.

But, just as Schorr had run into an unexplained, unexpected roadblock on his way back to Moscow, Niven ran into a totally different kind of roadblock several months after his arrival in the Soviet capital. Whether it was one roadblock or another, the net effect was that the CBS bureau in Moscow was left unstaffed from the fall of 1958 to the spring of 1960. During his relatively brief tour in Moscow, Niven faced a large number of bureaucratic obstacles, many normal for any foreign correspondent in a communist capital, several linked to residual bad feelings left by Schorr, and one he had absolutely nothing to do with, yet proved to be his undoing as the CBS bureau chief in Moscow.

On September 25, 1958, CBS ran a *Playhouse 90* production of a play called "The Plot to Kill Stalin." Using real names, characters, and circumstances, the TV drama was made to resemble the actual drama and betrayal surrounding Stalin's death on March 5, 1953. *Playhouse 90* was Hollywood's version of reality. CBS News was an innocent bystander. Its only connection to *Playhouse 90* was that both functioned under the CBS logo, and Moscow was either genuinely ignorant of the distinction between the two, or chose to be ignorant of the distinction. Either way, Moscow had an excuse to again take action against CBS. A few weeks later, on October 12, 1958, the Russians dramatically closed the CBS bureau in Moscow and expelled Niven, who returned to Washington, a victim of Moscow's real or contrived anger against CBS.

In explaining the CBS/Soviet crisis, Jack Gould, a TV critic of the *New York Times,* seemed surprisingly more sympathetic to the Russians than to CBS. He ripped into the network for even showing the play, arguing that, in the Cold War, CBS "went beyond . . . legitimate theatrical" bounds by leaving the "impression that Nikita S. Khrushchev, Soviet Premier, was morally and perhaps legally responsible for the death of Stalin." This rendering of reality, which more or less conformed to the available evidence, was, in Gould's view, "ill advised," reminding him that in 1949 the Russians foolishly staged a play called "The Mad Haberdasher," showing President Harry S. Truman engaged in wild preparations for a nuclear attack against the Soviet Union. Gould, wrongly in my judgment, equated "The Plot to Kill Stalin" with "The Mad Haberdasher." One was a well-crafted play, based on what was known at the time by reporters and diplomats; the other was heavy-handed propaganda, based on what Kremlin insiders might have imagined Truman was planning.

On June 1, 1958, over the small town of South Orange, New Jersey, the sky was blue, from one end to the other. All day it seemed only to get bluer. The temperature was Camelot in its perfection, never daring to scale 75 degrees. The breeze was gentle, rarely ruffling a hair. It was as if God wanted the day to be perfect for a wedding. It was.

Mady's home on Mayhew Court, where the ceremony was to take place, had been magically transformed into both an impressive chapel and an enticing dining room. Her mother, Rose, the smart, thoughtful magician, had rearranged every room. The kitchen, under her direction, had prepared a cuisine that would have been acceptable at Windsor Castle. Whenever I asked Rose if there was anything I could do to help, she would laugh, "Yes, show up." Mady's father, Bill, a stock analyst with an active green thumb, had willed the roses and rhododendron in the garden to rise to their full height while welcoming the guests. The garden, in the spirit of the day, never looked greener.

It was quite a day, one Mady and I would always consider a blessing. Rose and Bill were exceptional hosts, making everyone feel at home. They were also intelligent, honorable people, who knew right from wrong. They were always accessible to me for counsel, and after a while, the distinction between in-law and family disappeared.

My mother and father, Bella and Max, who had loved Mady from the moment they met her, enjoyed one of the happiest days of their lives, watching their son marry a bright and beautiful woman. They believed it was no mere coincidence that we both shared an interest in Russian studies. *Bashert*, my father had concluded, using the Yiddish word for "destined."

The wedding ceremony was unforgettable. Mady looked enchanting in her long, white gown, a smile never leaving her face. How did I look in my blue suit and striped tie? Acceptable, I guess. But was I nervous? A little bit? Yes. How did I know? After the ceremony, when we all sat down for the splendid feast Rose had prepared, I found that I was not hungry, even though I had not eaten anything since breakfast. The lamb chop was, I'm sure, delicious, but I could not eat it. I watched Mady eat her lamb chop with delicate gusto and then, spying mine untouched, scoop it up and eat it, too. Looking up at me with a mischievous grin, she asked, "Anything wrong? Not hungry?"

After dinner, everyone danced on a floor that moments earlier had been crowded with tables. Mady and I led the way. For hours, we danced, drank, reminisced, gossiped, and giggled. I shall never forget the joyous look on my father's face when he danced with Mady. Even "fake news" would have got the story right: everyone was having a really good time. Also, I was tickled by the fact that my best man, my brother, Bernie, was likely inspired by my marriage to arrange one of his own. He and the woman of his life, Phyllis Bernstein, had considered marriage many times. Apparently, they did once again, because, two months later, on August 1, 1958, they got married and, an hour later, boarded the *Ile de France* for a romantic transatlantic cruise to Europe. They were taking the long route to a *New York Times* assignment in Indonesia.

After a while I noticed that Mady had vanished. I looked around the crowded room and couldn't find . . . my wife. My wife? Rose quickly assured me that she had gone up to her room to change into a more comfortable outfit for our drive to New York. For a wedding gift, Rose and Bill had given us a white 1958 Dodge convertible. Wow! When Mady reappeared, she looked even more radiant. "Everything's ready," she said. I went upstairs, got the bags, put them in the car, and, as everyone was busy throwing rice and flowers at us, Mady, before getting into the car, threw her corsage of flowers over her head toward an assemblage of would-be brides. One of them actually caught it, bringing cheerful hurrahs from the crowd.

For the first time in our lives, Mady and I were now a married couple driving to a hotel near the United Nations in midtown Manhattan. It was one of my favorites. There we spent the night before flying the next morning to the Caneel Bay Resort on St. John in the Virgin Islands for a ten-day honeymoon.

––––––

The summer of 1958 was a busy one.

The manuscript of my first book, a loose collection of notes and impressions of my stay in Russia in 1956, had to be edited, and this proved to be a colossal task. The publisher, Farrar, Strauss and Cudahy, had miscalculated how long it would take for me to convert my notes into an appealing book. Publication was planned for early November, and it was a real question whether I'd be able to finish the edit on time. I was then also absorbed with my new assignment at CBS's *The 20th Century.* Mady came to my rescue, a pattern that was to recur with remarkable predictability over the years. Although she was already saddled with the task of organizing our new apartment on Gramercy Park South and preparing papers and books for her second year of graduate work at Columbia University, she undertook the tedious job of editing the galleys. With help from a patient Phyllis and a restless Bernie, Mady met the publisher's deadline with characteristic class, dedication to fact, and love of style. Because my hours were wildly irregular, I was not much help. On more than one occasion, late at night and tired, I would come home to find my fabulous troika of assistants sitting around a bridge table noshing on tea, cookies, and crackers while marking up a galley in desperate need of help.

"How nice," my brother would exclaim, with feigned exasperation. "Our breadwinner has finally arrived."

Both Mady and Phyllis were superb editors. They performed a minor literary miracle, transforming my notes into prose and my prose into a rather absorbing account of a young American in communist Russia. Their help was crucial to the book's ultimate success, as was the context in which it was written. Had Russia not been our principal adversary in the Cold War, had the American people not been fascinated by Khrushchev, and had I not had the extraordinary opportunity to travel from one end of Russia to the other, talking to ordinary people and communist officials, there would have been no book and therefore no boost to my budding career as a Soviet specialist at CBS News.

Henry Hewes, the talented drama critic of the *Saturday Review*, was the one who came up with the book's bewildering title, *Eastern Exposure.* He had proposed it, and I had foolishly accepted it, largely because none of us could think of a better one. Henry thought it might catch a reader's imagination about the presumed dangers and mysteries behind the Iron Curtain. Mady thought that, at best, it made the book sound like a dull treatise on architecture, more likely to be found in the back corner of a bookstore than upfront on a table reserved for possible bestsellers. Mady proved to be right.

If my late nights were reserved for helping to edit the book, a modest contribution the real editors thought they would have been better off without, my days were nothing less than a crash course in the complicated business of writing a news documentary. I was incredibly fortunate to have Bud and Ike as my professors. They started our tutorial slowly but gradually picked up the pace, and after a few weeks, they were teaching me the delicate interrelationship of word to film.

How does one write for a moving picture? It is a challenge quite different from writing for a newspaper or magazine. The key is to find the words that explain and enrich the film without fighting the film's visual message—what you are actually seeing in the film. For example, if you had film that showed Khrushchev speaking to a Communist Party gathering, no matter what he was actually saying, you could use it to explain his policy in the Middle East. Likewise, if you had film showing worried Arab faces, no matter what they were actually worried about, you could still use it to convey Arab concerns about Soviet policy. Words use film to convey a thought.

But sometimes a sympathetic film editor would arbitrarily flip the order and encourage me to write whatever I considered essential to the story, and he or she would then go on a hunting expedition in archives or libraries to find the film that would strengthen my words. Of course, there were times when no film could be found. What then? If Bud or Ike considered the underlying verbal message to be essential to our story, then there was always the option of the anchorman simply saying it on camera. Bud, better than most producers, seemed to know instinctively the proper mix of word, film, and story. And if he didn't, Ike did.

They were exceptional colleagues, always helpful, friendly, and yet serious. They seemed able to sense when I needed help and be there to provide it. When I needed space to research and write, for example, they unhesitatingly encouraged me to shut my office door, forget about everyone else, including them, and not to emerge until I was satisfied that I had copy I wanted them to see and edit. "You're our man," they'd stress. "Nothing's going to happen until we have a script." I thought for a time that they were just trying to encourage me; but after a while I realized they were telling me the truth: the script was crucial to managing the project. It lay at the heart of all planning. What was to be filmed? Where were reporters to go? Who would be where and when? What was to be promoted? What was to be edited? And, most important, whether at the end of the process there was a documentary worthy of being aired on CBS?

Though Bud and Ike were the key decisionmakers, they often made a point of bringing Cronkite, the anchor of the series, into their deliberations. And their top film and copy editors, too. They even brought me into their deliberations, their way apparently of making sure everyone felt a part of the project. Of course, no one was more important than Cronkite. He was not only the anchor, he was also the rising star at CBS, the reporter who was being groomed to replace Murrow as the brand name of the network.

The transition was not an easy one. Until recently the journalists Murrow had hired to cover World War II—the Sevareids, the Collingwoods, and others—constituted the core of CBS News, those most recognized and heard. Their personal and professional loyalty was to Murrow. In their eyes, he was the network. But, in the late 1950s, as network news expanded dramatically, a new group of reporters, producers, and editors was being hired to carry the CBS banner. Though they all admired Murrow—some even worshipped him—they had no personal loyalty to him, and a number began slowly to rally around the new standard bearer of the network. Bud and Ike, as relative newcomers, were among those who hitched their futures to Cronkite, and they chose well.

Cronkite was an accomplished, experienced journalist who transitioned from print to television with remarkable ease. Like Murrow, he too had covered World War II, working as a correspondent for United Press. When, in February 1943, the United States planned to bomb the German submarine base at Wilhelmshaven, a dangerous undertaking, Cronkite fought successfully to be the pool reporter. "The anti-aircraft fire was intense," he later reported. "Golden bursts of explosives all around us, dissolving into those great puffs of black smoke." His war reporting was outstanding, winning Cronkite the prized assignment after the war of covering the Soviet Union, an ally during the war, the principal adversary after the war. While in Moscow, he learned a lot about communism and diplomacy, which prepared him for yet another major assignment. Cronkite was sent to Washington at the dawning of both television news and the Cold War. It was then that he made his graceful switch from print to television. The term "anchorman" was invented for Cronkite in 1952, when he covered the Democratic and Republican presidential conventions. Five years later, he was named anchor of *The 20th Century* series, and in 1962, he replaced Douglas Edwards as anchor of the *CBS Evening News*, a job he held for nineteen years, covering presidential campaigns and conventions, wars and revolutions, weather and space launches. He did it all with a smooth, easy professionalism that brought kudos to CBS and the affectionate nickname "Uncle Walter" to him.

Bud and Ike used to enjoy boasting that Walter's historic career really began at *The 20th Century*, where week after week Cronkite anchored a news documentary that illuminated an important moment in American and global history. They believed the series helped introduce Cronkite to the American people and to CBS's top management. It also helped introduce me to Cronkite, a friendly professional relationship that lasted more than twenty years. On many occasions, while composing "The Red Sell," Bud, Ike, Walter, and I would work together, a cooperative quartet, to produce a timely and insightful documentary on Russia's exploitation of Radio Cairo to spread communist propaganda throughout the Middle East. Often, taking advantage of Walter's own experience in the Soviet Union, I would run my copy past him before showing it to Bud and Ike. Walter helped in two very practical ways: first, providing his editorial perspective on Khrushchev's motivation and policy shifts, and second, reading my copy to see if its rhythm conformed to his broadcast style. Though I was very much the newcomer to the news business, Walter appreciated my knowledge of Soviet policy—he treated me with respect; and I came to trust his judgment and consider him a valuable colleague. I was still very much a "Murrow man," but I could see how Cronkite could easily slide into the lead role at CBS News, once Murrow, for a variety of reasons, including a growing disillusionment with television news, chose to leave CBS in January 1961 and join the new Kennedy administration.

———

Since 1953 I'd been reviewing Russia-related books for the *Saturday Review*. I started as a graduate student at Harvard and continued during my short career as a diplomat in Moscow, and now, at CBS, I blended book reviewing with my new responsibilities as a journalist—and benefited enormously. By reading and reviewing books written by notable scholars and journalists, I was able not only to keep abreast of the latest developments in the Soviet Union, which was helpful in writing my scripts, but also to develop the reputation and influence of a critic. Writers seeking recognition called not once but two or three times, trying to persuade me to review their books. Then they went one step further, having mutual friends call me. Several of these writers were professors I had met or read; yet unashamedly they too called, pleading for the review that they hoped would enhance their position at a university or their reputation in the field of Soviet studies. I marveled at the lengths writers would go to persuade a critic to review a book—from repeated calls to flowers to personal letters to offers of a steak dinner, almost anything. I tried to explain that I was not the one who selected the books for review, but few of the writers would believe me. "You can do it," they'd plead. "You can do it." I couldn't. Even on a few occasions when I really tried, I couldn't.

Historian Bernard Pares was especially helpful when I tried to explain the roots of Khrushchev's policy in the Middle East. He had spent more than sixty years studying and writing about the history of this fascinating country. He was, according to his son, Richard, "a man with a mission: to interpret Russia to the English-speaking world, and even to bring the two worlds into political partnership with each other." By the time Pares died in 1949, he knew he had failed: the Cold War having already chilled the wartime alliance between the United States and the Soviet Union, but he considered the effort to be worthy of his time. If through his books and speeches he could help head off a nuclear war between the two superpowers, then he felt he had no alternative—he had to try. As well as anyone, he explained the reasons why Russia, and now the Soviet Union, often moved its ambitions south toward Turkey and the Dardanelles and, through them, to the Mediterranean, where, if possible, it would exploit the economic and strategic riches of the region to magnify the glory of Mother Russia. The tsars had persuaded themselves that they were in desperate need of a warm-water port. Bottled up in the north by an aggressive Sweden and a powerful Prussia, whether governed by tsars or commissars, Russia very often moved south, stumbling into one war after another.

Pares was one source; there were others. I wanted my copy for this documentary, my first, to sing, to be appreciated as distinctive, and I hoped the wisdom of historians could help me. Bud and Ike liked my approach. Cronkite loved it. "Marvin," he'd say with a grin, "you're making me look good." I couldn't have been more pleased.

Not just Pares; for the *Saturday Review*, I reviewed many of the classics of Russian history, literature, and government:

- *Ukraine under the Soviets*, by Columbia University's Clarence A. Manning. This was his forty-fifth publication, but it was "hurried . . . and hampered by a Ukrainian bias," I reluctantly concluded.

- *Current Soviet Policies*, by Leo Gruliow, editor of the "Current Digest of the Soviet Press," who for this book collected, edited, and translated major Soviet documents. "With the Iron Curtain still impenetrable," I wrote, "the printed Soviet word is still the best available key for gaining admission into the Soviet system."

- *Soviet Taxation: The Fiscal and Monetary Problems of a Planned Economy*, by Franklyn D. Holzman, a former colleague at Harvard's Russian Research Center, then a professor at the University of Washington. His book was, I said, a "scholarly and exhaustive analysis of Kremlin tax policies," valuable to the expert but no easy read.

- *Soviet Military Law and Administration*, by Harvard's Harold J. Berman and Miroslav Kerner. Though Soviet law was "manipulated opportunistically" by the state, they believed, its "maintenance was nevertheless crucial for the perpetuation of the state." I thought their vision of the

Soviet state was naive, but the book was still an important, if controversial, study.

- *The Origins of the Communist Autocracy*, by Harvard's Leonard Schapiro, another colleague. "Sound scholarship and refreshing writing," I said. It is a "literate and important examination of the political opposition to Lenin and the Bolshevik state from 1917 to 1922."

- *Leninism*, by Harvard's Alfred G. Meyer, another of my professors. His study was an "excellently documented, thoughtfully conceived, beautifully written and keenly stimulating analysis of the ideology that has rocked the world." Meyer deserved the rave review.

- *Gogol: A Life*, by David Magarshack, who wrote the "tragedy" of Gogol's life was that, though born in an Orthodox Ukrainian village and having Polish Catholic roots, he wanted nothing more than "to save Russia, an idea completely divorced from reality but that obsessed him to the exclusion of everything else." While true, Gogol was still a brilliant, incredibly gifted writer.

- *Russian Liberalism*, by George Fischer, a professor at Brandeis University, who "refutes the cliché" that Russia nurtured only "the extremes of political thought" by exploring the important political and economic reforms of the latter half of the nineteenth and early twentieth centuries.

Many of these reviews were published as "shirttails," the term editors used for short reviews, roughly 400 words in length. They would be attached to a much longer review of books that editor Ray Walters considered of greater interest to *Saturday Review* readers. Books on the Russian economy or Soviet law rarely got more than a shirttail.

Question: Would my own book, *Eastern Exposure*, being readied for publication in early November 1958, be worthy in Walters's judgment of a proper review, or of a shorter shirt-tail review, assuming, of course, he considered it worthy of a review at all. Like so many other books, it could be destined for the dusty desks in the back of a bookstore, ignored by everyone except friends and family. Still the optimist in me believed that the subject alone—an American in Soviet Russia during the Cold War—would almost guarantee a review.

Another question: Would I, like so many other writers, ever feel so frustrated by the failure to get a review that I'd call a reviewer and plead for one? I had received such calls from other writers. Would I do what they did? I decided that I would not. I wanted to believe that Walters would assign my book to someone, if for no other reason than to ratify his own judgment that by selecting me to review so many of his Russia books, he had chosen someone who could write his own Russia book and, for his effort, receive a respectful critique. But that was yet to be determined.

——————

For the moment, it was another book about Russia that was exciting the literary world—Boris Pasternak's magnificent *Doctor Zhivago*. It was slated to be published in the Soviet Union in October 1956, but never was.

The Union of Soviet Writers, which censored all Soviet literature, had ruled, with ironic accuracy, that the novel "casts doubt on the validity of the Bolshevik Revolution . . . as if it were the great crime in Russian history." And, as such, the authorities ruled it could and would not be published in the Soviet Union. But an unexpurgated copy of the manuscript made its way to the Italian communist publisher, Giangiacomo Feltrinelli. The Russians angrily demanded its return, but Feltrinelli artfully played for time, refusing to give it up. Apparently more the businessman than the ideologue, he knew Pasternak had written a certain bestseller, and he seized the honor to be its publisher. In the fall of 1957, *Doctor Zhivago* burst into print in Italy, producing a literary whirlwind of admiration and controversy. A year later, over the Labor Day weekend, the good Doctor leaped to the top of the best seller lists in the United States and the rest of the English-speaking world. Overnight *Zhivago* and *Pasternak* became household names for literary genius and ideological resistance.

Harrison Salisbury, who had covered the Soviet Union for the *New York Times*, wrote the major review for the *Saturday Review*. He gave Zhivago a rave. I wrote a long shirttail essay on Pasternak, once praised by Mayakovsky as "the poet's poet." *Doctor Zhivago* was Pasternak's only novel, which is one of those hard-to-believe facts. Spry at age 68, fluent in English, French, and German, a student in Berlin of Western philosophy while still a teenager, Pasternak was a lonely outpost of literary independence on the Soviet landscape. While most writers adjusted to Stalin's cruel rule, he maintained a stubborn aloofness. For decades, he just stopped writing, spending most of his time translating Shakespeare, Shelley, and Goethe into Russian. His father had been a renowned painter and his mother an accomplished musician. Pasternak's upbringing was among pre-revolutionary Russian intelligentsia, many of whom abhorred communism.

Pasternak never fit into Soviet life; he was, till the day he died, a circle in a square world. With his wife, he lived modestly in Peredelkino, a writers' colony in suburban Moscow. Only after Stalin died in 1953 did Pasternak feel comfortable enough to return to his desk and write one of the greatest novels of the twentieth century, the story of a disillusioned doctor struggling to live and love in the bloody aftermath of the Russian Revolution. What so profoundly disturbed the Kremlin was Pasternak's dismissal of the historic importance of the revolution, showing no admiration at all for Marx's hyped utopia, yearning instead for the right of the individual to choose his own path in life. For Pasternak, it was always the individual versus the collective, freedom versus tyranny, a battle he seemed destined to lose but one he felt certain he had to fight. His only weapon was words.

The story of *Doctor Zhivago*'s publication needed no salesmanship in a New York newsroom. It was a compelling story, and both Murrow and Clark quickly accepted my offer to do a commentary for their radio broadcasts—in fact, as it turned out, several commentaries, as the story grew over the next few weeks. Pasternak was hailed throughout the West as a "literary genius," while Soviet propagandists denounced him as a "decadent formalist." Pasternak, under pressure to explain his approach to writing the novel, stressed, "I am not a politician. This is not politics. But every poet, every artist, must somehow grope for the trends of his time." And, as he groped, he became more and more an unwitting symbol of the Cold War.

Then, on October 23, 1958, out of the gray, neutral skies over Stockholm, came an explosive announcement. The Swedish Academy had awarded the Nobel Prize for Literature to Pasternak. It was bulletin news everywhere except in the Soviet Union, where *Doctor Zhivago* still had not been published. The Kremlin, with this announcement, was placed in an awkward, embarrassing position, no more so than Pasternak himself. He would probably have accepted the prize, but he knew, almost instinctively, that the Kremlin would prefer that he reject it. Almost as confirmation, the Central Committee of the Soviet Communist Party dispatched another writer, a neighbor named Konstantin Fedin, to "suggest" to Pasternak that he categorically, in writing, reject the prize, as if it were a dreadful Western disease. An uncertain Pasternak pleaded for time, leaving the inescapable impression that he might actually accept the prize. Shocked, the Kremlin went into overdrive.

First, the Union of Soviet Writers met and officially condemned Pasternak and demanded his expulsion from the country.

Then, on October 26, *Pravda*, the Soviet Communist Party newspaper, ran a blistering editorial entitled, "Reactionary Propaganda Uproar over a Literary Weed." "The snake is wriggling at our feet," it said. "It is irresistibly drawn downward to its native swamps where it enjoys the odors of rot and decay . . . warm and comfortable in the poetical dung waters of lyrical manure." This ugly attack, typical of others hurled at Pasternak, affected his health. For a time, he went into a depression, not eating or sleeping.

The following day, unable because of ill health to attend a critically important meeting of the Union of Soviet Writers, he sent a letter to the Executive Committee, in which he tried to explain his belief that it was acceptable for his main character, Zhivago, to be both a critic of the Soviet system and a loyal citizen. "I have a broader understanding of the rights and possibilities of a Soviet writer," he wrote, "and I don't think I disparage the dignity of Soviet writers in any way."

Pasternak's letter won no friends. Twenty-nine writers, once among his closest friends and admirers, rose as one to denounce his "immeasurable self-conceit." They described the book, a bestseller everywhere, as "the cry of a frightened philistine . . . false and paltry, fished out of a rubbish heap." The writers then switched from what they might have considered literary criticism to accusations of political betrayal, speaking of Pasternak's "political and moral downfall, his betrayal of the Soviet Union, his fanning of the Cold War." Whipping themselves into a fervor of feigned ideological purity, they concluded their meeting with the unanimous decision that Pasternak be stripped of "the title of Soviet writer" and "publicly expelled" from the Writers Union.

Pasternak had not anticipated so sharp and brutal an assault. He went into a deeper depression and actually considered suicide. "I cannot stand this business anymore," he confided to friends. "I think it's time to leave this life. It's too much."

But, on October 29 he chose a more benign course of action. He sent a carefully crafted letter to the Swedish Academy. Only a Kremlinologist could have interpreted its between-the-lines message. "Considering *the meaning this award has been given in the society to which I belong*, I must reject this *undeserved* prize which has been presented to me. Please do not receive my *voluntary* rejection with displeasure." It was signed simply, "Pasternak." (Italics are my own.)

The Swedish Academy, sensitive to Pasternak's position, decided its reply would be brief and understanding. The Academy "has received your refusal with deep regret, sympathy and respect." Clearly, each understood the other.

But Khrushchev was still in an agitated state. Clearly embarrassed by the global uproar over what he derisively referred to as "that book," the Soviet Communist Party leader ordered the trash-talking head of the Komsomol, Vladimir Semichastny, to attack Pasternak before a hastily assembled group of 12,000 young Russians in Moscow's Sports Palace. For many of them, Pasternak had been a cherished poet and translator. Semichastny's task was to belittle Pasternak, to diminish his literary standing, to transform him into a stranger in his own land. His attack was carried "live" on Soviet radio and television.

"Even in a good flock," Semichastny began, "there may be one lousy sheep." Obviously that was Pasternak, "who has decided to spit in the face of our people." He has written a "slanderous so-called novel" that "gladdened our enemies," leading to a Nobel Prize "for slander, for libeling the Soviet system, socialism and Marxism." Semichastny then changed his description of Pasternak from a sheep to a pig, declaring "no pig would do what he did. . . . He has defiled the place where he has eaten; he has defiled those by whose toil he lives and breathes."

Semichastny concluded his attack by expressing "my own opinion" that Pasternak, described as an "internal emigré," become a "real emigré" and "go to his capitalist paradise." The audience, thus prompted, burst into applause. "His departure thus from our midst would make our air fresher."

The next morning, a deeply demoralized Pasternak sent a letter to Khrushchev begging his forgiveness and pleading for his permission to remain in his home. He sent a similar letter of apology to *Pravda*, ensuring its broad distribution.

Pasternak's travails remained an absorbing news story for many months. I heard from friends at *The 20th Century*, where I was finishing a final edit of the documentary script about Khrushchev's propaganda push into the Middle East, that CBS was planning a TV special about Pasternak and his book. It was to be part of a Sunday series anchored by Howard K. Smith, another of Murrow's World War II colleagues. I knew nothing more about it. In those days, Sunday afternoons were not reserved for professional football—that was an era yet to emerge; they were still reserved for public policy programs that won prizes and positive reviews but rarely did they generate the TV ratings that networks craved. Though I had no reason to believe I would be included in the special, perhaps as a writer or analyst, I must acknowledge that in a corner of my mind, I entertained the slim hope that I would be. It would be another confirming marker that I was getting closer to being considered CBS News's specialist on Soviet affairs.

———

One day in late October, as I was transitioning from *The 20th Century* back to the newsroom, my agent, Edith Haggard, called with good news. She had heard from one of her friends at the *New York Times Book Review* that they would be running a review of my new book, *Eastern Exposure,* on Sunday, November 2.

I erupted with joy. "Fantastic!" I shouted. "That's great."

But, after a moment of cautious reflection, I asked, a large question mark in my voice, "Is it a good one?"

Haggard replied coolly that she did not know and brushed aside my concern. In her judgment, any review was better than no review, and she added, "and there may be one in the *Post* too." The click at her end of the line suggested she'd had enough or had to make or take another call.

Still, I could not help but wonder whether the reviews would pan the book or praise it; and if they panned it, would it be a cruel, gleeful critique, or a gentle one? And how would I take it? Still, if Haggard was right, two major newspapers were showing interest in the book, which was a step in the right direction, even if I didn't yet know whether their interest also meant approval.

November 2 was going to be a big day for another reason too. My first big step into TV news—*The 20th Century* documentary I had written, "The Red Sell"—would be shown on CBS. How would it be received?

4

A BOOK, A DOCUMENTARY, AND A NEW IDEA

I had insisted that we be on time. Roger Strauss's invitation to dinner had been quite specific, and I did not want to ruffle my publisher in any way. It stated "7 p.m.," and 7 p.m. it would be. Mady, more knowledgeable than I about the protocol of New York dinner parties, tried to explain that 7 p.m. usually meant any time after that hour, even as late as 8 p.m., always with the excuse about how difficult it was to catch a cab. There really was no need to rush, she assured me. But I was adamant. In Moscow, where I had acquired my thimble-sized experience with dinner party protocol, when an ambassador invited me to dinner at 7 p.m., I would arrive at 7 p.m., and all the other guests would be arriving at roughly the same time too. I assumed that if it was de rigueur to be on time in Moscow's diplomatic community, it would the same in New York's literary community. But no.

In the end, we arrived at Roger's elegant midtown townhouse only a minute or two late. A butler in black tie welcomed us. "The Strausses will be joining you shortly," he said softly, his head dipping in a slight bow. As he led us into a living room with tall windows and an even taller ceiling, he paused, turning first to Mady. "May I get you a drink, Madame?" he asked. Mady declined. I said, before he could ask, "White wine, please." When the butler departed, and we were left alone, Mady whispered, "Told you."

We spent the next fifteen minutes or so wandering from one beautiful painting to another. The living room resembled a museum; all that was missing was a docent. I thought I saw a Renoir, or two, but wasn't certain. After a while, Roger entered, wearing a green smoking jacket and a red striped cravat. His handshake was warm, his face in a welcoming smile. "Did you get a drink?" he asked, looking around for the butler. His wife, Dorothea, exquisitely dressed, followed a few minutes later. "So sorry to be late," she said, not really as an apology but simply as something to say, before adding, "Roger can't even get to his own parties on time." Other guests soon arrived, and introductions followed. Roger had invited a number of his favorite writers, all somehow connected to Russia, but I remember only Max Eastman, the handsome and once radical writer, poet, and translator whose reputation had ranged unashamedly from bedroom exploits to literary and political adventures. He had once been a socialist, editor of *The Masses*, but now shifted his loyalties to a respectable conservatism, writing mostly for William Buckley's *National Review*. He seemed to have little respect for major magazines and newspapers, referring to them dismissively as the "money-making press." In conversation around the dinner table, he casually dropped names such as Einstein and Chaplin. If he was trying to impress me, he succeeded.

Roger had assumed, correctly, that I'd be fascinated by Eastman's stay in the Soviet Union in the early 1920s. He'd gone there filled with sympathy for the communist "experiment" but left after a few years disillusioned with its excesses.

In Moscow, he had met, among others, Leon Trotsky, Stalin's flamboyant adversary, and translated his three-volume *History of the Russian Revolution*. Years later, he would translate Pushkin's poems.

Roger invited me to tell stories about my recent adventures in the Soviet Union, his way of introducing *Eastern Exposure* to the conversation. Whether in 1924 with Eastman or in 1956 with me, Russia was always able to inspire exciting tales. I talked about meeting Khrushchev (how he nicknamed me "Peter the Great"), traveling through Central Asia, the Caucasus and Ukraine, and discussing the admitted failures of communism with Soviet youth. Roger interrupted several times to stress that these stories were the "heart and soul" of a "great new book we're publishing in early November—Marvin's new book, *Eastern Exposure*. Great book." Polite oohs and aahs followed—"Really?" "Oh, my!" "How interesting!"—like a predictable chorus of recognition and approval. Roger had a product, and he was determined to sell it. But first, he realized, he had to create a buzz, that growing awareness, the inescapable chatter and gossip accompanying the rise of a promising new book. *Eastern Exposure*, he kept repeating, "I hear the *Times* and the *Post* will be reviewing it soon. Terrific book." Listening to him, I understood for the first time that a book, no matter how notable, had to be promoted and sold, and Roger was an experienced salesman. In time, I also came to understand that it was not only the publisher's job to sell a book, it was also the author's. I used to believe naïvely that an author's job ended with the writing of a book. No—he, or she, had then to go out and sell it. Everyone, from an American president to a Nobel-prize winning scientist, went through this time-honored test of endurance and salesmanship.

After dinner, topped by a delicious dessert, Roger's guests departed, each promising to spread the word and buy the book. Mady and I were the last to leave. By this time, I was walking on air, believing that in Roger I had met a true friend, a benefactor, a mentor for life. He projected an air of worldly accomplishment with the allure of an endless circle of contacts. With his arm on my shoulder and a twinkle in his eye, Roger predicted a bright future for me and the book. "*Eastern Exposure* is going to do . . . really well," he pronounced, definitively, as if no one could possibly raise an objection. His words, flowing with enthusiasm, suggested I would soon be crowding Harry Golden's *Only in America* for first place on the *New York Times* best seller list. Only later did I realize that I wasn't listening to a small voice in a back corner of my mind cautioning me against believing a salesman's pitch.

Shortly after the famous dinner, still walking on air, I sent a letter to Roger on September 2, recommending that he consider publishing two new books not yet committed to paper: one by A. M. Rosenthal, the highly respected *Times* reporter in India; and the other by me on the soon-to-be-shown report on Khrushchev's aggressive moves in the Middle East to be aired on *The 20th Century.*

On book one: Rosenthal, my brother Bernie's best friend, was just finishing a three-and-a-half-year assignment in India. While there, I wrote to Roger, he reported on "all phases and aspects of Modern India—communism, Nehru, the Congress Party, relation to China, to the United States, the people of India, the religion, the groping toward modernity." I suggested Chester Bowles, the American ambassador to India, could write an introduction, and I'd edit the book. Rosenthal had approved of my idea, I noted in my letter.

On book two: I had talked to Bud Benjamin about a book "growing out" of *The 20th Century* broadcast, and he thought that was a great idea. I told Roger he was "very excited" about it. We were going to discuss it with Gitlin, the CBS vice president. I was certain, I wrote confidently, that he would also be "very excited." Then, hubris driving ambition and beclouding common sense, I penned the line better suited to an already successful writer: "I will try to arrange a lunch or a meeting between the three of us to determine how best this idea could be utilized," as if it were up to me "to arrange a lunch" and "determine how best" to proceed.

I closed my letter with these words: "I was and am deeply pleased . . . and extremely gratified" by your "warm show of confidence in me." I assumed I would get a call from Roger, or a reply by mail, within a week, no longer, the salesman publisher barely able to contain his excitement about the two new book prospects I had recommended, so it seemed to me. I was wrong. I did not get a response from Roger until late November, and it was not the response I'd anticipated. Though cushioned in friendly language, it was an unmistakable rejection of my proposal for two new books. Clearly, I had much to learn about the publishing business, and much else.

Sunday, November 2, was a Kalb doubleheader—a book review in the morning, a documentary in the evening. It proved to be quite a day!

Roger had learned a few days earlier that *Eastern Exposure* would in fact be reviewed by the *New York Times*, delighting him enormously. In the book business, nothing was guaranteed, certainly not a book review in the *Times*. Such a review was the equivalent of a free ad; it also jogged the book world to pay attention—something new, worthy, possibly important, was being published. Edith Haggard had also heard about the upcoming review, and more: she'd heard it was written by Harrison Salisbury, the former *Times* correspondent in Moscow, and that it was "favorable." "How favorable?" I wanted to know. She said she didn't know, and didn't care. A review in the *Times* was the key to the crown jewels.

Needless to say, I didn't sleep much on Saturday night. I was waiting for the distinctive thump of the Sunday *Times*, dropped in front of the door to our apartment.

Whenever I heard something that sounded like the thump of

a newspaper, I jumped from our bed, raced to the door, opened it, but . . . no newspaper. Not until 5:45 a.m. did the thump prove to be authentic. This time when I raced to the door and opened it, there it was—the good, fat, authoritative *New York Times* and, in it, folded neatly, the slender but powerfully influential *Book Review*. I placed the *Review* on the kitchen table, handling it as if it were the original of the Declaration of Independence, opened it carefully, and on page 3, under the headline, "People Who Were Met Along the Way," was Salisbury's review. I read it very slowly, absorbing every word as though each were a nugget of dark chocolate, and then read it again a bit more quickly, until I persuaded myself that it was, in fact, a *rave review.* Harrison Salisbury had loved the book! I exploded with joy. "Mady," I screamed, running into the bedroom with the *Review* flapping from my right hand, like a triumphant flag unfurled. "It's a rave." Mady, already awake, quickly extended her hand. "Let me see it," she demanded, a wide grin from ear to ear. I handed the review to her, and together, side-by-side on the bed, we sat and read the review once, and then twice and then a third time, pausing after every word of the lead paragraph, wondering if any lead could be any better.

Salisbury wrote: "In an age of institutional research, collaborative analysis and organizational men, we need a book like *Eastern Exposure* to remind us that it takes but a single pair of eyes to see the sparrow's fall. *Eastern Exposure* is the diary of Marvin L. Kalb, a young man who spent 1956 and part of 1957 in the Soviet Union. Not since Leslie Stevens's *Russian Assignment* has so perceptive a book about Russia, the Russian people, their way of life, their private aspirations, their secret longings been presented to the American public."

Not just the lead; the entire review radiated praise. Salisbury identified me with Harvard and then with the American Embassy in Moscow, adding that I "spoke Russian and knew a good bit about Russian life, Russian history, and Russian literature as well as Marxist philosophy and contemporary Communist dogma." He described *Eastern Exposure* as a "delightful and rewarding book," stemming in part, he went on, "from the author's warm and engaging personality. His eye is quick. So is his heart. He likes people. His interest is genuine. He likes to talk, and he likes to argue." And therefore "most of us will meet more Russians (and Soviets of other nationalities) on Mr. Kalb's pages and get to know and understand them better than if we spent months of traveling in the Soviet Union."

Salisbury then spoke of a number of the people I had described: a "brash young Russian" who spotted my transistor radio and proclaimed with false pride, "We have got one just like it," only to ponder his words for a moment before asking, "By the way, what is that?" Or a "young intellectual girl," who read only nineteenth-century novels, because, she explained, "We are all—me and my friends—sick and tired of politics in art. We crave art, pure art." Or a "blushing, young Azerbaijani girl whose ideals of love sprang straight from the romantic pages of Byron and Pushkin." Or a Russian graduate student, who said, "Russia was between the old and the new," the old being the "sterile and increasingly unattractive formalistic clichés of communism," and the new being still "vague and undefined."

Concluding his review, Salisbury wrote that as I was wrapping up my Moscow assignment, I felt "confident" of two things: the "Russian people want peace," and "for all their defects the Russian economic and educational systems work."

I could not have been more pleased. Salisbury had caught the spirit of my Russian adventure, and he had written a glowing account of it. And it had appeared in the Bible of book reviews!

Over the next few weeks, *Eastern Exposure* was reviewed in many other newspapers and magazines. I do not remember a single negative review, though there might have been one or two. My favorite was the one in the *Washington Post*. It was written by Chalmers M. Roberts, the foreign affairs reporter who, years later, was to become a close friend and colleague. His lead, focusing on the book's title, was priceless:

> The only thing wrong with this book is its poor title, which entirely misses the point of this first-rate diary-style account of a youthful and intelligent American's year in the Soviet Union. For this is not really the story of Marvin Kalb's "exposure" to Russia. Rather it is the best account yet of what goes on in the minds of all sorts of ordinary Soviet citizens, Communist Party members and not.

Reading the Roberts lead, I remembered Mady's putdown of Henry Hewes's recommendation of the title *Eastern Exposure* and of my hasty, foolhardy acceptance of it.

Roberts, like Salisbury, ran through my qualifications for the Moscow assignment at the American Embassy, and then added that I was "no stay-at-home," traveling through the Soviet Union and arguing my "way into some hitherto unseen nooks and crannies of Soviet intellectual life." Roberts clearly liked the book. "In many ways," he wrote, "this is one of the most heartening books yet written about the Soviet Union. For it gets behind the propaganda façade to show the intellectual restlessness, the nagging doubt, the massive inquisitiveness of so many Soviet citizens, and not only the youth."

I was in Moscow when many Hungarians went into open, bloody revolt against their communist rulers in October 1956. Russians wanted desperately to know what was happening in their restive East European satellite. "Could the rebellion in Hungary spread to Russia?" That was the question I was asked more than any other. Roberts found this conversation in the book:

"Listen, do me a favor?" said the cabbie.

　　"Yes," I replied.

"What's going on in Hungary? At least you have more news than appears in Soviet papers. That's all we've got is the Soviet papers. So please tell me the truth. What's going on there?"

Roberts went on, "And it was Mr. Kalb, then working on his thesis in the Lenin Library in Moscow, who, on October 30, 1956, stood in a room packed with students as they shouted down a party lecturer who tried to explain Hungary and Poland with party slogans. The story has been told before second-hand; now it is told first-hand."

Roberts closed his review with the sad story of a Russian who yearned with every fiber of his being for a close association with the West, but could not have it. "The finale is a fascinating account of Mr. Kalb's encounter in Leningrad with a 45-year-old English teacher, who had never been outside Russia," Roberts noted. "In miniature, this is the clash of East and West, of the Soviet Union and the free world systems. You will not be able to stop until you reach the shattering end of the tale."

His conclusion: "One should be cautious about drawing generalizations, and Kalb has been careful to stick closely to reporting what he heard and saw. This reviewer highly recommends *Eastern Exposure*."

Such reviews filled me with unrealistic expectations. I thought the book would be an instant best seller. Roger must have known from advance sales by national book distributors and bookstores that the book would do well—quite well, in fact—but, short of a miracle, it would not nudge Harry Golden off the best seller lists. Nor, from these initial industry reports, was it a sure bet that it would even make the *Times* best seller list. Roger, the cool, calculating publisher, routinely kept track of such statistical evidence, but Roger, the salesman, kept boasting about the book's potential. He relentlessly encouraged me to make the rounds of radio interviews (in those days it was mostly radio), write newspaper articles about Soviet life and policy based on the book, visit bookstores, and accept as many speaking engagements as I could squeeze into my already busy schedule. Roger did his part, too, running a major ad in the *Times Book Review* on November 9, a week after publication. "The revealing journal of a young American visitor who caught the Russian people 'off guard' during 'The Year of the Thaw,'" read the eye-catching phrase splattered across the top of the ad. At the bottom, in small letters: "$4.50, now at your bookstore." Roger also sent optimistic notes to friendly editors, urging them to feature the book in newspaper stories and pointing to the *Times* posting of *Eastern Exposure* at the top of a listing of books of "particular literary, topical or scholarly interest" as proof that the book was only one short step away from the best seller list. On November 23, *Times* editors recommended it enthusiastically as a "perceptive report on Russia and her people." But it never did make the *Times* best seller list, a big disappointment to me and Roger. The obvious reason—not enough people bought it, but another reason might have been that already on the list were such Russia blockbusters as Pasternak's *Doctor Zhivago* and John Gunther's *Inside Russia Today*, a book I helped Gunther research in early 1956 when he visited Moscow. Still I had my *Times* review. Not bad, I kept telling myself; not bad at all.

The second game of the November 2 doubleheader was "The Red Sell," the documentary about Khrushchev's drive to extend Soviet propaganda and power into the Arab world for *The 20th Century*. For six months, Bud Benjamin and Ike Kleinerman had blended their considerable talents to produce the program. Walter Cronkite was the anchor, as always smooth and professional. I was the writer, for me the first time I'd taken pen to paper to do a television documentary. In the process I'd learned a great deal. "The Red Sell" was broadcast late on Sunday afternoon, when networks set aside time for serious documentaries about world and national events. Like millions of others, Mady and I watched the broadcast on our new black-and-white television set. But, unlike millions of others, we were sitting on the edge of our seats.

On reflection, I should not have been concerned. If Bud had not considered my script acceptable, he would have told me. He'd have sent me back to my typewriter with clear instructions about what had to be rewritten—and how. Ike would have been just as firm, and his message would have been delivered in terse, unsympathetic prose. He was a tough editor. Ultimately, though, if Cronkite had been unhappy with the script, he would have unceremoniously rewritten it himself, the implied message being, "get me another writer."

But none of that happened. The script, as Cronkite read it, carried my message, and my message was that while Khrushchev was audacious, a gambler who seemed to push the boundaries of diplomacy almost to the breaking point, he was also a cautious Russian nationalist, who would not wittingly harm his country. He knew when to pull back, as he did in the Middle East in the late 1950s and later, in the early 1960s, during the Cuban Missile Crisis. His nightmare was a nuclear war, which he sought desperately to avoid. If one were to happen, he warned, "the living would envy the dead."

In my judgment, Khrushchev the man, not Khrushchev the communist firebrand, was the key to understanding Soviet policy. He was born in 1894 in a small Russian village, called Kalinovka, on the Ukrainian border. The son of a peasant, Khrushchev had only four years of formal education. Through much of his youth, he worked in coal mines on the Ukrainian side of the border in a region known as the Donbas, the same Donbas a later Russian ruler, Vladimir Putin, would invade in 2014. Several months after the start of the Russian Revolution, Khrushchev joined the Communist Party. He was always a devoted, committed communist, with a flair for hot rhetoric, though never an extremist, for whom revolution was the answer to all problems. "Whether you like it or not," he told a startled group of Western ambassadors in November 1956, "history is on our side. We will bury you."

Only a few of the ambassadors thought Khrushchev was threatening war; most understood he was mouthing Marxist rhetoric, consistent with his old belief that "if you live among wolves, you have to act like a wolf."

Throughout his long career, Khrushchev played the role of the wolf with a reckless relish, but always mindful of the deadly aftermath of a nuclear war. In his playbook, brinksmanship was one thing; war another. His flirtation with Egypt's Nasser was worth the gamble so long as it advanced Soviet interests in the Middle East. But when it stopped advancing Soviet interests and began to endanger them, it seemed never to be worth the price. If Khrushchev could retreat from a confrontation with a modicum of national dignity, Russian interests still respected on the global stage, then he would pull back, his rhetoric perhaps still inflammatory but his pistol back in its holster.

That was the main point of my script and therefore the main point of "The Red Sell" documentary. As my name as writer quickly rolled past in the closing credits, I felt a rush of professional pride. Mady, bestowing a kiss on each cheek, must have felt a touch of similar pride. "Good job," she said, "really good job." Soon calls from family and friends made me feel even better. This documentary helped viewers better understand the ongoing Middle East crisis and the policy and personal pressures driving one of the most important actors in the Cold War.

I felt I had done my job.

————————

The following morning, when I returned to the newsroom to resume my regular job of writing hourly newscasts, I was struck by the fact that though we all inhabited the same universe, we tended to live in our own worlds. One writer was especially concerned about his son's temperature, which, that morning, had spiked to 102. A producer's mother was fighting a bout of diabetic neuropathy at Mt. Sinai Hospital. Another writer, a Dodger fan, was mumbling angrily about a colleague's support of the Giants, who had just beaten the Dodgers in a doubleheader. Still another writer was grumbling about Secretary of State Dulles's "stupid" Middle East policy that was "sure to get us into a war."

I arrived with my own concern: how would or should I respond to their comments about the *Times* review or *The 20th Century* documentary? Surely, I assumed, some or all would have read the review or seen the documentary. How could they not have? One after another, they would have complimented me, or asked a tricky question, or promised to buy and read the book, or, when they got a chance, would watch a kinescope of the documentary. But, in fact, no one, except my always reliable editor, Hal Terkel, uttered a single word of praise or condemnation about either the review or the documentary. They were, like most people, preoccupied, busy, absorbed with their own personal or professional problems. Hal, on the other hand, rose above the collective silence with praise for the review and admiration for the documentary. "A home run," he shouted above the din of the tickers. "A home run, no question about it, bottom of the ninth, last game of the World Series. Pop! It's gone—home run! Congratulations! I'm proud of you." Hal and I often spoke the language of baseball to describe even the most sensitive global problem. I thanked and hugged him. We chatted for a few minutes about the review before I went to my desk, sat down, and there in a corner tucked conspicuously between my Webster's dictionary and the Pares history of Russia was a handwritten note from anchorman Howard K. Smith, whom I had not yet met, containing an intriguing idea.

Smith was one of the famed Murrow Boys, hired in 1941

when he was in a shrinking pool of Western reporters still covering Hitler's fascist rule in Berlin. In his broadcasts, Smith had frequently criticized Hitler's policies, infuriating the dictator who impetuously one day ordered his arrest. Moments before his capture, Smith slipped through an encircling net of Nazi storm troopers, finding refuge with other reporters on what he later called the "last train from Berlin." That phrase became the title of an exciting book he wrote the next year about his escape. Smith then covered the rest of World War II, mostly from an outpost in Switzerland, before replacing Murrow as CBS's London correspondent, an assignment he truly treasured. It opened his door to fascinating assignments in Europe and the Middle East. But, in 1957, Smith was suddenly ordered to New York. CBS was engaged in a major expansion of its team of television correspondents, and Smith's cool, courtly, scholarly manner caught many an eye. Could he be a potential successor to Murrow? Clearly Cronkite was already on everyone's radar screen for this role, but it was evident CBS's top management was still looking—and Smith appeared to be an increasingly appealing option. Just as Cronkite was being groomed for the top job, his anchoring of *The 20th Century* series cited as an obvious stepping stone, so too was Smith, who kept being selected to anchor one special after another. He was on the rise.

In those days, CBS released a PR photo showing Cronkite and Smith, Cronkite seated behind a large desk, Smith leaning down, looking up, both hands on the desk. Joining them, standing in front of the desk, was the unprepossessing but highly competent Douglas Edwards, anchor at the time of *CBS Television News*, one of the earliest versions of an evening news program. The photo might have been a comical CBS example of Kremlinology, network style—who had the best chance of succeeding Murrow? Was it the reporter who was seated? The one who was standing? Or the one leaning over them both? For more than a year, the question was left unanswered, though often the center of office gossip and speculation. The answer came finally on September 3, 1962, when Cronkite was named the new anchor of the *CBS Evening News*, replacing Edwards. Smith, a wise student of office politics, sensed opportunities at ABC News, where he fled after a bitter battle with CBS management about the coverage of race in America.

Ever since Boris Pasternak's battle with Khrushchev's Kremlin first exploded on the global stage, I had hoped that CBS would one day produce a special report on the story and, maybe, invite me to participate—in some way. Whether as a writer, background analyst or on-air commentator, the specific role was less important to me than an invitation to be part of the Zhivago project. It would have been another sign that management had decided that I was in fact CBS's Russia specialist, now with his name on a book praised by the *Times*. Much to my delight, the invitation, such as it was, came in the Smith note. It was not a formal invitation. Smith stressed that neither John Day nor Sig Mickelson had yet made a final decision. Still, wrote Smith, he favored such a special, and he wanted to be ready. Would I talk to him?

When I met Smith a few days later, he was, in both his manner and interest, a gracious Southern gentleman with a soft Louisiana drawl married to a burning curiosity about one subject in particular: what did the Russian people think of Khrushchev's coarse treatment of Pasternak, a Nobel Prize–winning author? For a few delightful hours over coffee and cookies, we talked about Russian literature, pre- and post-revolutionary, from Pushkin to Pasternak, and the tight, unique bond that existed between the Russian writer and the Russian people. Smith was not new to the subject. At one point in his life, perhaps when he was a graduate student at Oxford, he must have plunged into the endlessly rich oasis of Russian literature and enjoyed the experience. He was familiar with the monumental works of Tolstoy and Dostoevsky but also with such writers as Gorky and Mayakovsky. I was immensely impressed by Smith's knowledge of Russian literature, and I wanted very much to work with him.

Smith must have sensed my enthusiasm. He began to discuss the TV special as if final approval was a mere formality, which indeed it proved to be, and as if I had been part of his planning from the very beginning. He said he had been reading my reviews of Russia-related books in the *Saturday Review* for years; and when he read Salisbury's rave review of *Eastern Exposure* in the weekend *Times*, with its focus on what the average Soviet citizen thought about the government's actions and policies, Smith, the anchor, knew instinctively that he had found a good person to discuss the popular Soviet reaction to the Pasternak book's publication. Besides, the person happened to be a CBS writer.

"I think I know who else I want on this program," Smith went on. "People with individual strengths, people who have seen and heard things, people who know Russia."

He wanted, without any doubt, Salisbury to talk about how the book's central character, Dr. Zhivago, came to represent individual freedom as compared to state communism. He also wanted George Reavey, the former deputy press attaché at the British Embassy in Moscow, to describe the Kremlin's boorish, clumsy response to the book's initial publication in Italy; Jerry Cooke, the photographer, who took pictures of Pasternak during his confusing reaction to the startling news that he had won the Nobel Prize; and finally he wanted a resident Moscow correspondent, such as Whitman Bassow of *Newsweek*, to unmask the Moscow literary elite, those writers who first embraced Pasternak with love and pride and then denounced him with a mindless fury and hate.

"Of course, nothing happens in this crazy world of television news without a producer and a director, and for this program," Smith announced proudly, "we've got the best." He then called producer James Fleming and director Av Westin to his office. They proved to be a formidable pair.

Fleming had the longer history. From 1938, when Fleming was graduated from the University of Chicago, he had been a professional butterfly, flitting from one network to another, while at the same time making meaningful contributions to the entire industry. First, he'd been a writer and then a broadcaster at CBS before becoming one of its foreign correspondents covering the war in the Middle East, the big-power conferences in Cairo and Teheran, and even for a brief time the Soviet Union. Smith recalled a story Fleming loved telling about a verbal sparring match he had with his Soviet censor. Fleming thought he had come upon a great story. He wanted everyone to hear his radio report. The censor agreed—it was a great story, and he wanted no one to hear it. Not surprisingly in wartime Moscow, the censor won. "They ejected me," Fleming joked. "Imagine!" After the war, Fleming was enticed to join NBC's fledgling news staff. His first assignment was "editor" of a new morning TV show called *Today*. Dave Garroway was its first host, and Fleming not only wrote the news, he delivered it, and became a recognizable personality on the show, his dark hair, graying mustache, and thick glasses distinguishing him from everyone else. After NBC, it was back to CBS and then, after a few years, it was ABC's turn, and there he produced a four-hour primetime special on Africa, narrated by actor Gregory Peck and awarded an Emmy.

"I've wanted to do something on Russia for a long time," said Fleming after a quick hello. "Zhivago is perfect except for one thing—we don't have a reporter in Moscow. They kicked out Niven, and the Russians won't let us send in a temp or a crew. We have no interviews with Russians, no new, original footage from Moscow." He frowned before adding, "And, of course, Pasternak won't talk to us, and no one else either."

Director Av Westin, a tall, slender, bespectacled New Yorker, was relatively new to the business, but he had already established an enviable reputation as bright, energetic, and imaginative, a young man on the move. He had directed a number of documentaries for *The 20th Century* and had even done a *CBS Reports*, the most esteemed of the CBS documentaries. "I liked your 'Red Sell,'" he said, as we shook hands. "Really well done. Wish I had worked on it." If he had been searching for the right introduction, he'd definitely found it. Av and I, with that opening handshake, launched a friendship that lasted a lifetime. Throughout the preparations for the Zhivago special, he and I stayed in close touch, calling, meeting, lunching, dining, always with Pasternak at the top of our agenda.

Smith was our guiding light. For this TV special, he had assumed the unusual role of anchor, producer, and inspiration, all rolled into one. He dealt with management, finally securing November 23 as our airdate, a tight deadline for a TV special, since at the time we were only two weeks away. He, more than Fleming, was the one who approached and nailed down our guests. He was often on the phone with me (and, I assume, the others) discussing the latest news from Moscow and elsewhere about the relevant troika of Pasternak, Zhivago, and Khrushchev.

These running discussions were especially important, because, with each passing day, as we approached show time, I grew more anxious about my role on the program. I had never been on television, and I worried that I'd freeze in front of the camera; that everything I knew about the subject would suddenly and mysteriously vanish, like smoke in a sudden rush of air. By this time, I had managed to broadcast about a half dozen radio pieces, and survived. I had a good voice. I sounded authoritative. I knew the subject. On radio, no one could see the perspiration on my upper lip. But, on television, I feared, I'd come through as an unprepared, quivering rookie, and no one would even listen to what I was trying to say. I'd be a flop.

Mady tried to reassure me I'd do well. "You know your stuff—that'll come through," she stressed. "Stop worrying so much." Av reminded me that Murrow perspired during his radio broadcasts, even unzipping his trousers to ease the pressure. And he did brilliantly on television. "People get nervous, but makeup," Av assured me, "can do miracles."

Despite their gallant efforts, I was not persuaded that I could do the job. I decided to confide my concerns to Smith, who could not have been more understanding. "We were all nervous the first time," he said in a voice softer, more mellow than usual. "That's natural." He reached for my hand. "I'm certain you can do it. You know the subject. You and I have talked about it time and again."

"Yes, but that's between the two of us," I said. "Not on television."

"The key," Smith continued, as if he hadn't heard a word I said, "is to ignore the cameras. I'll ask you the same questions I've asked you before, and you answer me the same way. You'll be terrific." He smiled reassuringly, before repeating, "You'll be terrific."

Av echoed the same advice. "Just ignore the cameras. Talk to Howard, to no one else, and you'll be great. Remember, I'm director. I'm in the control room. I'm in charge of the cameras. I'll make you look like a young Edward R. Murrow."

"Absurd!" I thought, but if I was to make it in the world of electronic journalism, I would have to try. My test came on Sunday, November 23. We were to tape the show at 2 p.m. for broadcast at 5 p.m. in the middle of an impressive lineup of CBS documentaries. For example, from 4 to 5 p.m. the science series called *Conquest* would produce a study of the human brain, specifically how much we had learned about it in the past twenty years but, also, sadly how much more we had yet to learn. Commentator Eric Sevareid, the giant among giants of the Murrow Boys, would anchor the "brain" broadcast. Our TV special, called *The Case of Dr. Zhivago*, would follow between 5 to 5:30 p.m. Next, between 5:30 to 6 p.m., would be another edition of the famed Murrow-Friendly series called

Small World, in which the central topic would be the defense of Western Europe. Murrow would moderate an international conversation involving General Alfred M. Gruenther (former commander of the North Atlantic Treaty Organization), Aneurin Bevan (leader of the British Labor Party), and Franz Josef Strauss (minister of defense of West Germany).

In those days of truly substantive programming, CBS could have beamed with professional delight—it was using precious airtime to inform the American people about crucial matters shaping their present and future. But, among top management, there were those who were beginning to think Sunday television ought to do more than inform—it ought also to make money. They raised an obvious question: how many people were watching shows like *Small World*? They concluded, too few, certainly not enough, and they started a search for a Sunday alternative. Sports, football in particular, emerged as the likely moneymaker. In a few years, football rose in the ratings and became the proven moneymaker. Result: *Conquest*, *Small World*, and TV specials such as Zhivago were unceremoniously dropped, and no executive looked back in sorrow.

But, at 5 p.m. on November 23, 1958, those of us explaining *The Case of Dr. Zhivago* felt only pride. Profit was not our concern. For those of us in the news department, the example of Murrow was our inspiration. We wanted to be like him. We wanted to follow in his footsteps. Even after his departure from CBS in 1961 and his death in 1965, he exerted a powerful influence over our work and goals. His values, not those of profit-seeking bureaucrats, governed our daily operations. We constantly measured our product and performance by his standards, even though we realized we often failed to live up to them. We still felt we were all a very special "band of brothers" called to do the job of the ancient scribe—to report what was happening so the people could know what to do. I believed, perhaps naively, that Smith was a "brother," and I a young adherent wanting to be accepted into his "band."

Hollywood might have had its ideas about what a TV studio was supposed to look like, but the brass at CBS had theirs and they won the day. The "studio" I entered shortly before 2 p.m. on November 23 was nothing more than the small corner of a large room on the fifth floor of Grand Central Station. Believe it or not, Smith told me, this was the television headquarters of CBS News, the burgeoning part of an industry still dominated by radio. I could not help but recall how Edwards once described his fifteen-minute evening newscast. It was "primitive," he said, with a playful grin, held together "with spit, bailing wires and high spirits." I was quickly to learn that, for our Zhivago special, Smith had only a little bit more. Fleming had warned that he had no fresh footage of Pasternak or Khrushchev, no new interviews with Russian writers or ideologues, and really "nothing newsworthy," as he put it. But Smith measured the show's value not by whether it produced headlines but whether it provided depth, perspective, and understanding of the day's news—in this case, why would a powerful, nuclear-armed country, such as the Soviet Union, attack one of its best writers? Why would it be so frightened of a beautifully written novel? Why would it not praise Pasternak rather than persecute him?

Smith was busy with last-minute preparations. I watched from the rear of the room. Unlike Edwards, who usually sat behind a wooden desk to deliver the evening news, Smith chose to stand. Behind him, as a visual prop, was a large photo of Pasternak and Khrushchev, a jagged red diagonal separating the writer from the politician. Off to the right was the CBS logo. Fleming, standing near Smith, whispered something in his ear. Smith nodded. The floor manager shouted, "Two minutes, two minutes." Fleming returned to the control room. Smith reread his opening copy, while fixing his tie. My building anxiety was utterly irrelevant to Smith, Fleming, Westin and, it seemed, everyone else. There was a TV show to be done.

After a brief opening, which he had pre-taped, Smith, live on camera, explained the importance of the Pasternak story and then introduced a pre-cut interview with Salisbury, which I thought was brilliant, followed almost immediately with other interviews with Reavey and Cooke, whose photos of Pasternak were riveting backdrops for his comments. After a commercial break, Smith showed film of Soviet writers and interviewed Bassow, who eloquently explained how Pasternak's closest colleagues could one day praise him and the next day denounce him, demanding even that he be expelled from Russia.

During the next commercial break, I was directed to Smith's side. Then, with only seconds to go before he was to resume telling the Zhivago story, Smith turned, looked me in the eye, and said softly, "Ignore the cameras. Talk to me. What's important is the subject, and that you know."

The floor manager at that moment cued Smith, who turned smoothly to the camera, introduced me, mentioning *Eastern Exposure* along the way and asked the question he and I had been talking about for weeks—why would a powerful country be afraid of a writer?

There was no transcript of the broadcast, but I remember answering that there was always a special place of honor in Russian society for any writer, especially a poet. Pasternak was widely known and recognized as Russia's leading poet, and now he had written a novel. That in itself would have produced tidal waves of popular interest. Why a novel? What had he to say? The main character, a doctor named Zhivago, was a modest figure. Yet, during the 1917 revolution, he was portrayed as someone who had the courage to oppose communist rule, even to yearn for the pleasures of the old tsarist regime. In Soviet society, such thought was heresy. Zhivago was to be denounced. But, far from denouncing him, Pasternak described him in sympathetic terms, and his message spread swiftly through the country This infuriated Khrushchev and other Soviet leaders, and they did what was unfathomable in Russian society: they attacked an honored, esteemed poet, even though the poet had just won a Nobel Prize for Literature.

I felt I had only begun to answer Smith's questions when he thanked me, smiled, and launched into his own concluding remarks. On television, time flies. When the broadcast ended, and the studio lights dimmed, Smith playfully slapped me on the back. "Good job," he pronounced. "You did a really good job." Within seconds, Smith was surrounded by Fleming, Westin, and others, all showering compliments on their anchor. I slipped out, searching for a phone. I called Mady. She agreed with Smith; I'd done a "good job." Then, reducing life to basics, she asked if, on the way home, I could stop at the market and pick up a bottle of milk. "You won't have enough for breakfast," she said.

———————

The following morning, I rushed to get our copy of the *New York Times*. What, if anything, did it have to say about our TV special? In those days, the paper often reviewed network documentaries. There was a review, a very short one, by a John P. Shanley, and he clearly did not think much of the broadcast, saying it "consisted unfortunately of a series of statements obviously being read by the participants—and in some instances not being read particularly well." He continued, "The telecast would have been more effective had its panel been more relaxed and informal." By name he mentioned only two of the participants—me and Salisbury: me, for making "the interesting observation that Mr. Pasternak 'looks more like an American Indian than a Russian author,' and Salisbury for noting that the book caused a sensation not just because of its political content but also its deeply spiritual and philosophical elements. Shanley had found "interesting" the one comment I made that, on reflection, I found embarrassingly shallow—I should not have made it. He also described the interviews as a "panel," which was an odd and inaccurate description.

Donald Kirkley, writing in the *Baltimore Sun*, thought the program was "good, as far as it went," but he thought we spent too much time repeating "familiar facts." Kirkley would have been happier if we had spent more time discussing the book rather than the political and diplomatic impact of the book. Though he did not mention Salisbury by name, Kirkley quoted him as describing the book as "a love story about star-crossed lovers, in the great tradition of Shakespeare, Dante and Tolstoy" and Pasternak as "the last of the great Russian humanists who look at life through laughter and tears."

At CBS, the Zhivago special produced quite a few compliments along with pats on the back, all of which pleased me, but I always tried to be realistic about my work. I had now been on radio and television. I had a book, favorably reviewed in many places. I had made decent headway in my hope, one day, to be recognized as CBS's Russia specialist. And Moscow was open, and I thought I had a good chance of being among those considered for this prestigious assignment.

––––––––

The coverage of Russia, or foreign affairs in general, involves a mix of fact, history, and instinct: the accumulation of fact, arranged carefully in a historical context and a gut feeling about people, places, and timing. In late 1958 I began to focus seriously on Russia's relations with China. My reading of Russian and Chinese rhetoric and actions led me to the tentative conclusion that the once seemingly unbreakable Sino-Soviet alliance was moving toward an historic rupture. So unorthodox was this conclusion, so out of step with what the established experts were thinking and writing, that I ran it past Mady before discussing it with anyone else, including Bernie. She was amazed that I could come to such a bizarre conclusion—it fought history, it made no sense. No, she stated flatly, I was dead wrong, and I'd be wise to drop it. When I argued my analysis with her, point by point, she acknowledged it made some sense, she could see the logic, but she still felt very strongly that the recent history of these two communist giants underscored the commonality of their policies and goals. Even if they did have an occasional argument over a point of ideology, it could not shake the foundation of their alliance.

I respected Mady's mind and judgment, I loved her dearly, but on this issue I was convinced she was wrong, and I right. But, even so, how was I to advance my hypothesis when every scholar I admired and respected, every official offering advice to the secretary of state or the president, considered it wrong? First, I would need time; this was a subject demanding sustained research. An old-fashioned all-nighter would not suffice. Second, I would have to do a lot of traveling to be able to interview Russia and China experts all over the world; those in the U.S. government or at universities, able as they were, would clearly not be enough. Third, I would almost certainly be contemplating another book; this could not be explained in a one-minute radio analysis, although over the years I found a lot could be squeezed into a one-minute piece. Finally, all things considered, how could I undertake such a massive project and still do my regular job at CBS?

In short, was I reaching too far? Was I setting myself up for a fall? These were legitimate questions, searching for sensible answers and solutions. At the time I did not have them. But, like my father, a hard-working tailor with a deep faith in the American dream, I knew that somehow I would find them.

"THE RUSSIANS ARE COMING"

That a network would choose to headquarter its television operations in Grand Central Station, where windows rattled and trains rumbled twenty-four hours a day, remained a puzzle to me from the very beginning. But, in truth, I gave the matter little thought. When it arose at all, the only sensible explanation came oddly from a busybody producer who loved to appear to be in the know on all matters. Standing tall, his chin up, he leaned toward me, his nose almost touching mine, and whispered, "Money, Marvin. Money. It's always money." I must have looked interested, for he continued, "This place used to be the Federal Credit Union, part of Grand Central Station. In 1937 CBS worked out a long-term deal, very economical terms, with Grand Central, kicked out the credit union, and in we moved with our lights and cameras. Been here ever since." He paused for only a few seconds. "In 1941 they set up Studio 41—that's probably where they got the name. But it didn't really get started till after the big war, maybe really until the early 1950s."

As a source of both entertainment and news, television

rocketed into national prominence after World War II. For example, in 1946, as America began its postwar economic boom, the number of TV sets in the United States was estimated to be 6,000. By 1951 the number had risen to 12 million, and by 1955 half of American households had a small, black-and-white set, each fixed with shaky antenna reaching to the heavens for electronic signals. From Korea, families would see a bleak, never-ending war; from Paris, the creation of the North Atlantic Treaty Organization; and from Washington, the election of a wartime hero, Dwight D. Eisenhower, and a "red scare" instigated by Joseph McCarthy, the junior senator from Wisconsin. The flickering set quickly became the heartbeat of American politics and culture, Ike sharing a televised stage with CBS's Ed Sullivan, all against a Cold War backdrop of nuclear escalation.

It was in this context in November 1958 that I first arrived at 15 Vanderbilt Avenue, a journalist with only modest practical experience but with a growing expertise in Soviet affairs. It seemed to me that a New York avenue named after the Vanderbilts would have been as bustling as Broadway and as heavily trafficked as Fifth Avenue, but in those days it was a surprisingly narrow street, quiet and short, running only from 42nd to 45th Street. I often wondered why the Vanderbilts would have allowed their name to be used on such an inconsequential thoroughfare. 15 Vanderbilt Avenue was nothing more than a side entrance into Grand Central Station; the main entrance, big and imposing, was on 42nd Street. Besides, opening two large, heavy doors made entry into the Vanderbilt building a forbidding challenge, especially if you were carrying a 35mm camera, which occasionally happened. But, for me, in those early days, the doors did not represent a problem—quite the contrary; they were an "open sesame" to a new world. I was now a reporter, no longer just a writer, and I felt lightheaded with anticipation and excitement.

In those days, reporters were young men, not women, each captivated by the Murrow mystique, most burning with ambition, some slightly terrified but all determined to try to make the world a better place. No one seemed older than thirty, and everyone had at least a baccalaureate. The "assignment desk" was our place of worship. Every morning we gathered there, praying for a good assignment. It would more than likely be a story in New York, but it could also be one in Washington or Chicago. An editor would determine who got what. A handful of reporters seemed always to get the best assignments, but there were a few who rarely got any assignment, and one or two who got nothing—day after day, nothing, prompting doubts, I suspect, about whether they should have gone to law school, as their parents might have advised. After a while, several in my group quit CBS, either for another network, where they might have felt more appreciated, or for an entirely different career.

Only one of us, in my judgment, showed an immediate, almost intuitive, gift for television reporting. He was Charles Kuralt, a native of Wilmington, North Carolina. He joined CBS the same week I did. He too was hired as a radio writer but quickly became a television reporter and then a correspondent. From the start, he was in a league of his own, a future star who was doing stories for the CBS evening newscast before any of us could even summon the courage to say hello to anchor Douglas Edwards. Kuralt struck an appealing figure on television. He was ruggedly handsome, with dark hair, already slightly receding, bushy eyebrows, and a smile that could brighten a rainy day. His voice was extraordinary: a soft southern accent that conveyed authority and authenticity. If anyone sounded like Murrow (and we all tried), it was Kuralt. Though approachable, he seemed often to be by himself. He and I were associates but not really friends.

From others I learned that Kuralt already had an impressive journalistic résumé. While in high school, he wrote an essay about American democracy that won a national award from the American Legion. The award included a White House meeting with President Harry Truman, plus the honor of hearing Edward R. Murrow read his essay at a Washington gathering of journalists. At the University of North Carolina, Kuralt edited the *Daily Tar Heel,* and after graduation, worked as a radio reporter for the *Charlotte News.* Before long he was writing a locally celebrated column called "Charley Kuralt's People," which won prizes and foreshadowed his legendary "On the Road" pieces for Walter Cronkite's *CBS Evening News.*

I wanted to watch and listen to Kuralt—and learn. Once he went to Harlan, Kentucky, to do a story about poor coal miners, locked in a heartbreaking struggle for survival. Never before had I seen such an intimate, creative intermingling of story, film, and voice. On the evening it aired, all of us in the newsroom gathered in front of a large TV screen and watched in wonder. Here indeed was an exceptional talent. Before Kuralt's report, I had never heard of the miners of Harlan, Kentucky, and now I shall never forget them.

After his death in 1997, we all learned that Kuralt had led a duplicitous double life, one wife here, another there, but somehow the news did not significantly detract from the respect he had earned during his remarkable forty-year-long career at CBS. Most of his fans tended to look the other way. From his reporting "On the Road," they remembered his warm, uplifting, compassionate vision of America, which, in his words, could "banish any gloom . . . and fill you instead with wonder." Kuralt's homespun optimism apparently filled a national need. He loved his country. He loved his craft, and he left his mark.

———

Sam Jaffe was another memorable young reporter, but he was no Charles Kuralt. He did not have Kuralt's intuitive feel for television, but he did have a special knack for attracting sources, which was important for any journalist but for Jaffe often seemed wildly indiscriminate and created a set of Cold

War problems he never anticipated. When Jaffe died in 1985, too young, his reputation in tatters, prize-winning author Taylor Branch described him as "the most complete pariah in the history of American journalism." But for a time in the late 1950s, he was a promising prospect at CBS.

An energetic native of San Francisco, Jaffe saw himself as an adventurous Hildy Johnson–type journalist, breaking stories, making headlines, getting scoops, shattering protocol. Soon after graduation from nearby Berkeley, Jaffe joined the International News Service. He had a way of being in the right place at the right time. In late June 1950 he happened to be in Korea when communist forces smashed through the demilitarized zone, starting a hot war that ended in a cold, unsatisfying truce three years later. Jaffe abruptly quit INS to become a United Nations observer of combat operations, allowing him to claim that he had been a combat correspondent. The experience helped him get a job in 1952 as a reporter for *Life* magazine. His first assignment was to help cover UN headquarters in New York. Money apparently was not a problem for Jaffe, because, while there, he bought an elegant apartment overlooking the East River, a perfect place for entertaining many diplomats, including quite a few from Eastern Europe.

In 1955 Jaffe tried freelancing for a while. He left *Life* and flew to Bandung, Indonesia, to cover a conference of third-world leaders. He loved the adventure, an exciting mix of diplomacy and journalism testing his talents for making contacts. At the conference no "get" was more daunting than China's premier, Chou En-lai. Chinese leaders in those days rarely stepped on the world stage. India's Nehru was also there; so too was Burma's U Nu. But Chou was the prize, and every journalist wanted desperately to be the one who would interview the secretive Chinese leader. Though Jaffe as a freelancer enjoyed little journalistic clout (he did not, for example, represent a significant news organization, such as the BBC or the *New York Times*), he got the interview, using an enticing blend of guile, feigned innocence, and luck. Chou was his first big scoop; in time he would get many others.

When Jaffe returned to New York, wearing the laurels of Bandung like a necklace of sparkling gold, and imagining he'd have many news organizations knocking at his apartment door, he ended up, in fact, having to settle for a radio news-writing job at CBS. He managed most of the time to work at the UN, where he resumed cultivating his diplomatic contacts. The big story at the time was the dangerous confrontation between the United States and the Soviet Union. Playing to his strength, Jaffe made friends with Soviet diplomats and correspondents, many of whom were spies. Jaffe might naively have thought that he was doing nothing more than taking the first step to getting a story. He would invite them to lunch at upscale restaurants and, as appealing, to his cocktail parties on the upper east side of Manhattan, and they eagerly accepted, happy to enjoy a good meal with French wine and Scotch whiskey but also undoubtedly intrigued by the possibility of turning an American journalist to their cause.

When the Federal Bureau of Investigation got wind of Jaffe's budding friendships with Soviet diplomats, it quickly contacted him. This was not unusual—it was in keeping with its job of tracking possible Soviet espionage. The FBI had certain questions in mind. Would Jaffe mind telling the FBI what concretely interested these diplomats? Did the Russians ever ask Jaffe to do anything specific? Did they offer to pay him for information? Jaffe, in his rulebook of journalism, saw nothing unusual about meeting and talking with Soviet diplomats, and then telling the FBI what they had discussed. He considered such trilateral exchanges of information to be part of his job. In my judgment, there might have been another reason, having to do with his uncle's earlier collision with communism and McCarthyism.

For all of his cosmopolitan sophistication, Jaffe was at heart an old-fashioned patriot. He wanted desperately to prove his loyalty to the United States. In the early 1950s, during the McCarthy purges, his uncle, the famous actor with the same name, was accused not of being a communist but of associating with them and then refusing to talk about what they said and did. Hollywood was in a nasty mood, and Jaffe ran into a buzz saw of suspicion and controversy. Almost overnight his reputation fizzled; acting roles that were about to be finalized mysteriously vaporized, like puffs of smoke; and his once dazzling career suddenly crashed in ignominy. The lesson that Jaffe the journalist learned from the experience of Jaffe the actor was to cooperate with the U.S. government, no matter how problematic the experience. So, when the FBI asked Jaffe to cooperate, he did not hesitate for a minute to salute and say "Yes, Sir." It was his way of demonstrating his patriotism, which his uncle, for reasons of principle or foolishness, had refused to do; besides, as a journalist, Jaffe did not feel he was doing anything wrong. A source was a source, after all, whether Russian or American.

Stories of Jaffe's lunches with Russians and of his elegant cocktail parties circulated through the newsroom, some disguised as gossip, others as fanciful speculation, all spiked with degrees of envy. "What a life Sam's leading!" was a phrase I often heard, jealousy folded into each word. I approached all of these stories, though, from a slightly different perspective: I kept wondering when Jaffe was going to invite me to one of his now famous cocktail parties? After all, he had to have known that I too shared his interest in meeting Russians and discussing East-West relations.

And then one day he called me.

"I loved your book" were his opening words, his voice filled with excitement. He did not give me his name. "I read it in one night. All I can tell you," he continued breathlessly [by this time, I could recognize his voice], "is [*pause*] I wish I had written it. It's really quite terrific."

From that moment on, Jaffe the competing reporter became

Sam my new friend. "Thank you, Sam," I replied, truly pleased that, at long last, he'd called. "How very, very kind of you." Because Sam spent most of his time at the UN and I most of mine at the assignment desk, we had had little to do with each other. But now finally a bridge was beginning to be built.

"I have another reason for my call," Sam continued. "I'm hosting a cocktail party tomorrow evening. At my apartment. And I was wondering if you would like to join us." Sam paused for only a moment. "There'll be lots of vodka there," he added. I assumed by "vodka" he meant "Russians."

"My pleasure, Sam. Just tell me when and where exactly."

Sam's apartment was in one of the tall, post–World War II buildings overlooking the East River, which on this Friday evening seemed indifferent to the cosmopolitan madness through which it lazily meandered. The East River Drive was, as always, crowded with cars slipping in and out of lanes in a reckless escape to a weekend in the country. Sam was on the fourteenth floor—actually the thirteenth, but the number "13" was missing, as was often the case in modern elevators. The door to his apartment was wide open, and a waiter carrying a large silver tray greeted me. "What will you have, Sir? Vodka? Scotch?" When he saw a question mark in my eyes, he added, "We do have soda and water, too." Over the waiter's shoulder, I could see a crowded room of smokers and drinkers and a door open to a balcony, equally crowded, and just beyond a panorama of blinking lights and passing cars.

"Marvin, Marvin," Sam called, when he spotted me at the door. Sam seemed "dressed" for his party. He had already removed his jacket, loosened his tie, and, as he made his way toward me, raised a glass half filled with a clear liquid, which could not have been water. "Want a drink?" he shouted. Without waiting for an answer, he turned to the waiter. "Paul, give my friend the best." I assumed he had vodka in mind. He pointed to a bottle of Stolichnaya. At the time I did not drink, but I didn't want to dampen Sam's enthusiasm. I accepted the vodka.

While many of the men at the party had also loosened their ties, and some taken off their jackets, one small group stood stiffly to one side, all properly dressed, drinking, smoking, observing everyone else, as if each were on a police line. They were Soviet diplomats, so clearly recognizable, whether in Moscow or New York. They chatted among themselves and looked decidedly uncomfortable. Sam introduced me.

"Meet my friend Marvin. He's also a reporter at CBS, and he speaks Russian," Sam added proudly. "He's also written a really good book about Russia." I greeted each with a cheerful Russian salutation, but they responded with characteristic coolness. They seemed in no rush to make friends. Only one smiled.

"Your Russian is quite good," he said. "I gather you lived in Russia?"

"Yes," I replied. "In 1956, I worked for the 'Joint Press Reading Service' in Moscow, and I had a lot of practice speaking Russian." Actually, I was an attaché at the U.S. Embassy, assigned to the JPRS, where I translated the Soviet press. I thought "Joint Press Reading Service" might have sounded less jarring to him than "U.S. Embassy," especially at a cocktail party in New York.

"I see," the Soviet diplomat said, a knowing grin now forming around his mouth. "Wasn't the U.S. Embassy an official sponsor of the JPRS, as you call it?" a touch of sarcasm dripping from his question.

"Yes, it was, along with the Brits, the Australians, and the Canadians." I tried to sound matter-of-fact.

"So," the diplomat continued, "you were a diplomat in 1956, and now a few years later you call yourself a journalist. Yes?" By now his grin had spread into a broad smile. "I see." In those Cold War days, almost all Soviet journalists were spies, and he assumed therefore that all American journalists were also spies; and that I only posed as an attaché in 1956 and as a journalist now in 1959. I understood his reasoning, warped though it was—he must actually have believed that I was a "spy" using two convenient cover stories.

"I do not 'call' myself a journalist," I answered firmly. "I *am* a journalist, and I *was* a translator in Moscow." I laid special emphasis on both verbs, hoping to draw a clear distinction between the two.

"Of course," he smiled patiently, like an adult to a child. "Of course you are a journalist, and I am a diplomat."

I felt our conversation was edging toward an unpleasant and unnecessary confrontation, and I decided to change subjects but still make a point. "By the way, when will you allow CBS to reopen our Moscow bureau?" I asked.

His response was curt. "I have no responsibility for press relations," he snapped. "Check with the embassy in Washington." He turned back to his colleagues, and I to the balcony, crowded with drinkers. This brief exchange brought back memories of similarly testy, unproductive exchanges with other Soviet officials during my time in Moscow.

But at Sam's parties, Russia was never far away. In a corner of the balcony was a scene reminiscent of one I recalled from a visit to a *pivnye zal*, or beer hall, in Leningrad, the name for St. Petersburg during Soviet times. Then as now, a half dozen Russians were drinking, jousting, cursing, laughing, enjoying themselves, indifferent to the obvious disdain with which the Soviet diplomats observed them from their corner of the festivities. Looking from one group of Russians to the other, I realized yet again that I was seeing two Russias, one authentic, tough, pan-Asian, and deeply religious, the other European, tilting toward Western values and culture—two Russias trapped in an internal conflict between East and West that for centuries they have been unable to resolve.

It was time to leave. I thanked Sam profusely for his invitation. "Did you get anything from Sergey?" he wanted to know. "You know, he's one of their key people."

"No," I replied. "Not really. Let's talk next week. OK?"

It was a story the journalistic gods made for my convenience. I didn't have to go to Moscow. The Russians came to New York.

In late 1957 the United States and the Union of Soviet Socialist Republics signed an agreement widening the scope of cultural relations between the two countries. Now, more Americans could travel to the Soviet Union; more Russians to the United States. The New York Philharmonic Orchestra could— and did—perform in Moscow; the Bolshoi Ballet in Washington. Russians, officially defined as "students," but, as we were soon to learn, were actually spies, could study at American universities; American students (no doubt a few spies among them) at Soviet universities. It all added up to a minor breakthrough; it was called "cultural exchange."

One example in the 1958–1959 academic year was the presence of four Soviet students at Columbia University, where, coincidentally, Mady was pursuing her doctoral studies in international affairs, with a specialty in U.S.-Soviet relations. At the time, fourteen other Soviet students were spending a year at other American universities. All were called "students." Two of the Russians at Columbia were actually trained spies. One was from Soviet military intelligence, and one, at age thirty-three the most senior of the group, represented the Central Committee of the Soviet Communist Party. For an academic year at Columbia, the Russians paid not a cent. Technically they were "Fulbright scholars," meaning the U.S. government gave them a stipend, which they used to pay Columbia for their studies. The Ford Foundation, in its way, also helped the Russian "students." It picked up the tab for their transportation to and from Moscow and, in addition, an enjoyable three-week tour of the United States. After finishing their studies at Columbia, they visited Philadelphia, Chicago, New Orleans, Washington, D.C., and, toward the end, added quick stops in Iowa and Wisconsin. Their visit and travel naturally inspired many news stories. I recommended that CBS do one, and happily the editor on the assignment desk agreed.

"Do it!" he said. "But remember," his eyes narrowing, "they're communists."

"Of course. Yes, sir," I replied, baffled. "I'll certainly keep that in mind." Where, I wondered, had he been?

With a TV crew, I spent the next few days at Columbia following the Russians to class and interviewing two of them. They were good students. They never cut a class. They were always prepared to answer any question put to them, whether by a professor or a student, but rarely volunteered a comment. They never criticized their host country—no denunciations of "capitalism," for example; nor did they boast about the "glories of communism." They were there to learn and set a good example. If as a sideline they managed to charm an American into helping the "Soviet struggle for 'peaceful coexistence,'" then so much the better. If, going one step further, they actually persuaded an American to spy for the Soviet Union, as one of them did, then they were later rewarded with higher rank and salary. On the surface, though, the Russians were simply students, going to classes and writing papers. But their responsibilities were broader, deeper and, in a Cold War context, far more serious.

Was I aware of this additional dimension? Yes. But my job as a reporter complicated matters. My assignment was to do a story about four Russian students at Columbia—what they were doing there, what they thought about the university and America, and what Americans thought of them. It was to be a feature story; it was not intended to be a commentary on the Cold War. I recognized the distinction, but tried at the same time to strike a subtle balance in my copy between a feature story and a commentary. I felt I had to point out that three of the four Russian students were likely spies and the fourth a rising star in the Soviet Communist Party. Also, the Russians had a very unromantic definition of "cultural exchange" (they saw it as a weapon in the Cold War), while the Americans had a much more benign definition (they saw it as a way of gently opening each society to the other's charms and maybe, one day, ending the Cold War). Anyway, no one at CBS objected to my approach.

I especially enjoyed interviewing two of the four Russians. If I had requested such interviews in Russia, the answer would have been a dismissive "nyet"; but, here in the United States, the Russians wanted to tell their story, and they provided (and I quickly accepted) Alexander Yakovlev, the thirty-three-year-old leader of the group, and Oleg Kalugin, the twenty-four-year-old journalism student. They both fascinated me, but for different reasons.

Yakovlev was an intensely serious man, for whom a smile was obviously an effort. As one of the first of the Russian exchange students, selected by the Soviet Communist Party, he clearly wanted to succeed. Taller than most Russians, his hairline receding, his thick glasses slipping playfully to the bottom of his nose, Yakovlev acted as though a Moscow ghost was hovering over his shoulder, observing his every move. He gripped his briefcase so tightly I could not help but imagine that it was stuffed with top-secret Kremlin documents rather than the books, pamphlets, papers, sandwiches, and apples most students carried. His command of English was excellent. He did not want to make a mistake, grammatical or political, and he certainly did not want to make news.

In Moscow, Yakovlev was known as a man on the move, smart, loyal, an expert on Marxist theory. Though comparatively young, he already had a reputation as a reformer, someone who wanted to modernize but not change the sclerotic Soviet bureaucracy. Yakovlev needed allies, and he found one surprisingly in party leader Nikita Khrushchev, who stunned the communist world in February 1956 by denouncing Josef Stalin's cruel dictatorship and introducing Russia to a program of reform. Kremlin windows, shut for decades, were finally being opened. Change was in the air, and, very gingerly, Yakovlev rose through the ranks, where he met, among others, Mikhail Gorbachev, who was later to become president of the collapsing Soviet Union. When the opportunity arose in 1958 for Yakovlev to live and study in the United States for a year, he seized it.

We agreed to do the interview in the History Department, where he spent most of his time. I wanted the interview to be substantive but not confrontational, and I started by asking him why he studied history. "Because," he replied, "only through the stages of history can we appreciate how the world is changing and how one day it will reach communism."

"Really?" I replied, a touch of disbelief in my voice, "What do you mean by 'the stages of history'?"

His answer was disappointing, as if he'd forgotten for a moment that we were at Columbia and not in a Moscow kindergarten. "Well, now here in the United States," he began, "you once had a stage of social development called feudalism. Now you have capitalism. And one day you will have socialism, one stage of history leading to another, and finally you will have communism, the final stage." I decided on the spot to change the subject and my approach. A simplistic lecture on Marxist theory would obviously not do.

"Who's your favorite professor?" I asked.

"Professor Hofstadter, of course."

His choice was understandable. Richard Hofstadter was a student favorite, a wide-ranging intellectual, an appealing lecturer and a brilliant writer. In the 1930s, when depression struck the United States and Hitler's fascists stomped to power in Germany, Hofstadter fell for communism. He joined the American Communist Party in 1938, but a year later quit, fed up with its stultifying ideology but attracted still to its theoretical dedication to social and economic justice. His writings in the 1940s and 1950s reflected a lingering distaste and distrust of capitalism—what he once called "the hegemonic liberal capitalist culture running through the course of American history." One of his most popular books, *The Age of Reform, From Bryan to FDR*, published in 1956, described the power of populist reform to change old, encrusted institutions in turn-of-the-century America. This was a theme that captivated Yakovlev, inspiring him to hope that similar reform could also envelop Russia.

"Why Hofstadter?" I asked, suspecting I knew his answer.

"I am impressed by his attitude toward history," Yakovlev replied, "the way he sees reform as an agent of change, even profound change."

"Do you think reform can change Russia?" I wondered.

"Reform can always lead to change," he said, evasively.

"But even in Russia?"

"Everywhere," he answered.

We spoke for another ten minutes or so, but he began to look so uncomfortable, squirming in his seat, that I decided to end the interview. I felt sorry for him. He then left for a class, and I was left wondering about his future. Would his reform plans for Russia ever be implemented? Or would they die a slow, unhappy death, strangled in the Soviet bureaucracy? I was to learn that every now and then, history would smile on a reform-minded communist. In the late 1980s it smiled on Yakovlev, who at the time had persuaded his friend Gorbachev, then president of a rapidly defunct Soviet Union, to buy into his program of reform, colloquially called "glasnost." Together they introduced a radical loosening up of censorship, travel restrictions, and political expression. For a time they proved that reform could indeed change Russia, but only for a brief time.

Maybe, on reflection, Hofstadter was as much the "godfather of glasnost" as Yakovlev.

Oleg Kalugin, my other Russian interview, did not seem ever to be absorbed with such serious themes as "the stages of history." He was always on stage, playing the role of a budding journalist, a Russian Jaffe eager in his case to befriend Americans and, with his blue-eyed smile, persuade them that all he ever really wanted was a "story." After a few months, the *New York Times* found him, as a subject, to be so appealing it ran a "Man in the News" column about Kalugin called the "Popular Russian," distinguishing him perhaps from the no-nonsense visage of the communist worker one found on Soviet billboards.

Almost every day, Kalugin brought his sunny disposition to Columbia's School of Journalism, located to the right of the university's main entrance at 116 Street and Broadway in Manhattan. Because, like his buddies, he was not there to meet Columbia's strict requirements for a degree, he audited a wide variety of courses, from "Journalism, An Introduction" to the "History of American Journalism"; and when he had the time, he also joined Yakovlev in Hofstadter's course on American populism. He enjoyed all of them. In every class Kalugin was the "popular" Russian, always open to an amusing exchange about baseball or a serious discussion about "freedom of the press." He loved the Yankees, he said, as much as he admired the "investigative" reporting he found in New York newspapers. Though his English was admirable, he did have a strong accent. His American friends seemed not to hear it. He was always in the middle of a conversation, whether in class or in the corner delicatessen, where many students gathered for a quick lunch or a longer dinner. At a school dance he would not have been a blushing wallflower.

It was no surprise then that, even before his first semester at Columbia had ended, the dean would ask him to be the featured speaker at a colloquium devoted to comparing American and Soviet journalism, and he, with feigned modesty but without missing a beat, would agree.

What was memorable about his presentation was his ability

to praise American journalism for its independence of state control and yet at the same time defend a Soviet system of journalism that was very much the stepchild of state authority. This was truly an example of rhetorical jujitsu, KGB style. The differences between the two forms of journalism were so glaring that only by playing with words, ducking and dodging facts, and relying on the inherent good will of his audience, grateful for what they took to be a truthful rendition of a complicated subject, could he have emerged from this talk to a standing ovation. As if he were back in Moscow, he applauded his applauding audience, grinning and waving at friends in the front row. Many in the crowd, Russian and American, clearly saw Kalugin as a gallant warrior for truth and candor. Maybe, they thought, he heralded a break in the Cold War, a glimpse of a broad popular yearning in America for a relaxation of East-West tensions.

Reactions were almost uniformly positive, ranging from admiration to wonder. "He was so candid." "I thought Russian journalists were all communists." "I agree, American reporters have been much too critical of Russia." "See, I told you, the Russian people do want peace. Kalugin made that quite clear." I did not hear a single negative comment.

In my interview with Yakovlev, I must admit to feeling a touch of sympathy for him. He seemed to be in the wrong world, an idealistic Marxist devoted more to the theory than the practice of Communism, different from Kalugin, who seemed more dedicated to the expansion of Communism by any means. Part of me wanted to expose Kalugin for what he was, not for what he projected; but such an approach would have put me in his world of ideological combat and I wanted none of that. I was fortunate to be on a promising trajectory at CBS. I wanted to be recognized as one of "the Murrow boys," maybe one day a Moscow correspondent, and here was a good story about Soviet-American relations—and I was doing it. Besides, if I did a really good, probing interview, maybe I'd be able to get behind his smile, and the KGB-molded Kalugin would yet emerge.

The next day I met Kalugin in the same large room where he'd spoken so impressively. He was, as always, bubbling with enthusiasm. "I watched your evening news last night," he said, as the cameraman, acting as floor director, pointed him to a chair opposite mine. "Really good. I mean, your anchor—is that what you call him? Anchor? He's really good, so accomplished. Ours are like statues by comparison." Again, he was being candid, disarmingly genuine, and open-minded.

"He's one of the best," I agreed. "Douglas Edwards by name. He's been at it for many years."

After a minute or so for sound levels and light adjustments, the cameraman nodded, Kalugin smiled, and the interview began. "Mr. Kalugin," I said, plunging into a key troubling issue, "I'm puzzled. Yesterday you praised both Soviet and American journalism. Yet you and I both know they are profoundly different: one is free, and the other is state-run."

If I thought for a moment that my blunt opening would wipe the smile off his face and put him on the defensive, I was quickly brought back to earth by his response. "Well, of course," he answered, "your journalism represents your society, and ours represents Soviet society." He paused, searching my eyes for signs of understanding, before jumping into a variation of Yakovlev's line of argument. "One day your society will evolve into a higher form, something we call socialism, but you can call it what you like. It's inevitable. It's the way history works. We all go from one form of society to another. Hopefully we all advance to a higher plane."

"No," I objected. "Let's not deal with theory. Let's deal with reality. Your reporters get paid by the government to write and broadcast only what the government wants. They are propagandists."

"Yes, and in this way we can better educate our people," he

responded. "We don't want to confuse them with . . . well, your propaganda." He was drawing me into an ideological debate, and I did not want to go there.

"We believe journalism is the heart of a free society," I argued. "Journalists have to be able to speak truth to power. They have to be able to criticize the president, the whole government, if necessary. And they do. You cannot. And that is the big difference between the two systems of journalism and government. Is that not true?"

Kalugin shook his head, again smiling. When in doubt, he seemed always to smile. "Journalism," he said slowly, "is our way of informing the people. Telling them what the government wants them to do, what it wants them to think about the world. It's not there to hurt the government; it's there to help the government." He sighed, as though he were searching for a concluding thought. "It's just a different kind of journalism. You have yours, and we have ours."

I tried another approach. "Mr. Kalugin," I said, "I think you'd agree that governments are made up of people, and people can make mistakes, even really big ones. Your own leader, Nikita Khrushchev, criticized Stalin's huge miscalculations at the start of World War II. Do you think Russian reporters will ever be free to point out such mistakes and criticize the leaders who make them?"

Kalugin, not missing a beat, replied, "Yes, but that was one leader criticizing another, not a reporter criticizing a leader. A reporter has a different responsibility—at least, in our country." Then he added, "But in your country, you do what you want, and we respect your system of journalism and government. Because, you know, one day your system will change. It will evolve to another level. It is inevitable."

I realized our interview was again running into an ideological wall, and it was time to end it as gracefully as I could. "Tell me, Mr. Kalugin," I asked, "what do you think of your time in the United States?"

"I loved every minute," he smiled. "For me, it has been a dream year, a dream year, and I shall never forget it."

At the time I did not believe him, but decades later, after the Soviet Union collapsed and communism became an unpleasant memory of a failed system of government, I came to believe that Kalugin's year-long stay at Columbia must have left indelibly positive, if concealed, impressions of the American system of government. For in 1995, after a successful but controversial career as a general in the KGB, Kalugin, of all spies, accepted a teaching assignment at Catholic University in Washington, D.C., and then formally defected to the United States where he became a popular authority on the subject he knew best—Soviet espionage. Indeed, Kalugin was, among many other things, an active member of the Advisory Board of the International Spy Museum. Who better to exploit capitalism's endless fear and fascination with communism than a former KGB general, who learned years before that in America a smile could get you a long way?

THE SINO-SOVIET ALLIANCE: MYSTERIES, PUZZLES, AND ENIGMAS

In my study of Russia during the Cold War, China was never far behind. If I read a book about Russia, I'd want to read one about China, almost as if I were trying to balance the ticket. When I prepared for my PhD oral exams, though I majored in Russian history, I also made a point of studying Chinese history, an approach that mystified Harvard professor Benjamin Schwartz. "China is China, and Russia is Russia," this specialist on Chinese history would insist. "The two don't mix." I didn't agree with him then, and still don't. I have always believed that their destinies were intertwined.

In my mind's eye, I often imagined the scene in the sixteenth and seventeenth centuries of thousands of Russians, Orthodox by faith, deeply Slavic by tradition, restless for new adventures, crossing the Ural mountains, finding themselves on the vast plains of Central Asia, and then, for those pushing farther east, coming upon China's ancient civilization along the Mongolian and Manchurian borders and then finally reaching the Pacific, some seven time zones east of Moscow. Everywhere in what was then the emptiness of Siberia, the Russians would build trading and military outposts; in time they would also build churches. Very reluctantly the Chinese would agree to engage with these Slavic "intruders," sometimes signing trade agreements with them but more often fighting them. Eventually an uneasy tension settled along their border.

So it was, and so it has remained—a continuing confrontation and, when appropriate, accommodation, of cultures, beliefs, and national interests. For a reporter, what a fascinating story!

For example, in late February 1956, when Khrushchev boldly attacked Stalin, for almost three decades the fountainhead of global communism, he sent shivers through the leadership of every communist party. When a Soviet leader spoke, everyone listened. What did Khrushchev mean? Since the Russian Revolution in 1917, it had been assumed that Moscow led the global communist movement. It was the first Marxist state. It set the line for every communist party. It deserved—and usually got—unquestioned loyalty. Therefore, it followed that if Stalin could be attacked, then any communist party leader could be attacked. In Peking (now Beijing), the question instantly arose: did this mean that even an ideological giant such as the untouchable Mao Tse-tung could be questioned, even criticized and attacked? So unimaginable was this thought that not a word about the Khrushchev bombshell was published in the official Chinese press for many months. Only around the kitchen table would anyone risk raising the subject, and even then cautiously. In Moscow, the assumption among diplomats and journalists who had been based in Peking or businessmen who had just been to the Chinese capital, people I tried to meet, was that Mao had always been suspicious of Russian policy and decidedly distrustful of Khrushchev. Other communist leaders had tried to persuade Mao that, by attacking Stalin, Khrushchev was only trying to reform the communist system, but Mao did not believe them. He was one for dark conspiracies, and in Khrushchev's unprecedented assault on a renowned communist leader, Mao saw a Kremlin plot to topple him, and more: that Khrushchev also aimed to undermine the Chinese Communist Party and, in this way, severely damage the only other communist party with the potential to challenge the Soviet Communist Party for ideological supremacy of the world communist movement.

My assumption at the time was that Khrushchev acted against Stalin primarily for reasons of Kremlin politics. He wanted to solidify his political position. Mao was not the issue foremost on his mind. However, Khrushchev was a shrewd peasant, who had turned into an even shrewder politician, and he must have realized that his attack on Stalin would have huge implications for communist leaders all over the world. All of them, including Mao, would now be vulnerable to open criticism and even dismissal. Wittingly or not, Khrushchev had thrown an ideological bomb into the global communist movement, at the same time widening the natural cracks then beginning to appear in the Sino-Soviet alliance. At least, that was the way it seemed to me, though I rush to add that most of my colleagues tended to agree with Professor Schwartz— that what was happening in Moscow often had very little to do with what was happening in Peking. After all, they argued, Russia was Russia, and China was China, and each marched to its own drummer, driven more by a devotion to their own political and cultural backgrounds than to their shared commitment to communist ideology.

Two years later, in January 1958, for reasons relating primarily to the rising political and economic chaos in China, Mao launched the historic but tragic Great Leap Forward, his utopian scheme to propel China into the twenty-first century by mobilizing his biggest asset—China's seemingly limitless reserves of manpower. Without regard for either communist ideology or budgetary guidelines, Mao plunged into the un-known. After only a few years, however, when it became clear that his Great Leap Forward had stumbled into an expensive pit, resulting in widespread famine, the death of as many as 40 million people, and a political convulsion in the Chinese Communist Party, Mao was sidelined, suddenly human after decades of worshipful adulation. The argument was then heard in Peking that while he was inspiring as the leader of a revolution, he was pathetically inept at managing a country, certainly one as large and complex as China. Would Mao have been criticized and then sidelined if Stalin's legacy had not earlier been shattered? Though history offered no definitive answer, it had at least now become a legitimate question.

The practical ideologues in Moscow, led by Khrushchev, quickly distanced themselves from Mao's catastrophe, argu-ing that the Great Leap Forward had nothing to do with the proper practice of Marxism-Leninism. If it proved anything, they argued, it was that Moscow, not Peking, was the only re-liable model for communist inspiration and development. The crack in the Sino-Soviet alliance that opened with Khrush-chev's daring denunciation of Stalin had now widened signifi-cantly with Mao's mad dash into the chaos of the Great Leap Forward. Here, once again, a domestic story in one of the two communist giants had an immediate effect on the other, in this case damaging not only their bilateral relationship but also the international communist movement. For me this was the stuff of history; but because it came in the guise of a news story, one few at the time even recognized as such, it raised no more than a passing ripple of interest in the CBS newsroom in New York. Or for that matter at the Russian Research Center at Harvard. Or the State Department in Washington. Or for-eign ministries in Europe and Asia. Everywhere the official line held: the Sino-Soviet alliance was alive and well, powerful and essentially unified in its opposition to the United States. A difference in ideological interpretation might occasionally arise, it was believed, but the alliance was strong, representing an active dynamic threat to the Western world.

With whom could I share my excitement about the early signs of cracks in the Sino-Soviet alliance? Mady, of course. A few of my friends, yes. But in the office, who?

If I had not made the move from 485 Madison Avenue, where CBS radio news was headquartered, to 15 Vanderbilt Avenue, where CBS television news was headquartered, I would have been able to walk down the hall and discuss this story with Blair Clark and perhaps do a piece for the *World To-night*, which was in fact exactly what happened: I did discuss it with Clark, and he requested a piece for his radio program. I also had a chance to brief Murrow, who asked me to write one of his commentaries about the fracturing communist alliance for his evening newscast. Radio had space for such wide-ranging commentary—not so with television, as I was soon to learn.

At 15 Vanderbilt Avenue, my story ran into a stone wall. I could not find a single buyer. In TV news the executive producer of each broadcast made the key decisions about which stories would be aired, and, television being a visual medium, the producer needed pictures. Stories without pictures were generally left on the cutting room floor. The early signs of splits in the Sino-Soviet alliance had no pictures. It was essentially a "tell" story, meaning if there were some extra time in a broadcast, which was rarely the case, the anchorman would "tell" the story, usually in a flicker of fifteen to twenty seconds.

There was another problem, too. No other news organization had the story. It was a lonely CBS exclusive. "Get it first," my brother, Bernie, used to say, always with a smile, "but first get it second." As a rule, producers needed first to enjoy the challenge of competition before allowing themselves to become seriously interested in a story. Of course, sometimes stories could be considered too exclusive. My story about the Sino-Soviet alliance was clearly one of those stories—at least, on television.

Yet, thanks to radio, which was enjoying a golden age of popularity, my reports on the subject, broadcast on Murrow's evening newscast and on Clark's *World Tonight,* must have reached many listeners, for whom possible cracks in the Sino-Soviet alliance would be a matter of considerable interest. In the Cold War, they were curious about this dangerous alliance and, to an extent, frightened by it. They wanted to learn more about this combination of power, ideology, and ambition. Otherwise, why would I have received two invitations to speak about the alliance in Washington, D.C.—the first in November 1958, the second in December 1958?

They were my first from institutions in the nation's capital, and I was delighted. I called my mother (who else?) to boast. "Mom," I said. "I got an invitation to speak in Washington."

"Really?" she replied, with genuine enthusiasm. "From the White House?"

"No, mom," I sighed, after a moment of silent exasperation, "not from the White House." Unintentionally, I had punctured her balloon of maternal pride. "But there are other worthy places in Washington," I added. I could tell she was unimpressed.

The first invitation came from the Brookings Institution, a highly respected think tank that has now been dedicated to public policy research and recommendation for more than 100 years. (Many years later, I was to spend some of the happiest years of my life there, researching and writing books, including this one.) The second invitation came from the American Society for Public Administration (ASPA), which has shared the expertise of resident scholars and former officials with a succession of administrations since 1945 in an effort to improve the quality of government service.

In Washington, where institutional luncheons have become a routine part of the day, there has always been a need for luncheon speakers. An interesting relationship between luncheon and speaker has thus evolved, with policy, ego, and money playing big roles. Some speakers accept invitations in order to propagate or test a policy proposal. That's usually called a "trial balloon." Others accept them with gratitude as a way of promoting and selling their hot-off-the-press books. Still others, already famous as writers, journalists, or politicians, get hefty fees for speaking at luncheons. To be clear, I was not offered a hefty fee—I was not offered any fee. But, as the author of a new book, hungry for publicity, I hastily accepted the terms that were offered: I would speak, and my host would pay for my transportation. I also suspected that Brookings and ASPA were drawn to me because I was a CBS reporter who specialized in Soviet affairs, and we were in the Cold War. In addition, my book, *Eastern Exposure*, had received glowing reviews in the *Washington Post* and the *New York Times,* and the bookers at ASPA and Brookings probably thought I would be a quick and easy catch. They were right.

Brookings wanted me to speak specifically about the Sino-Soviet alliance, and breaking news provided a convenient news peg. In early December, the British news agency Reuters was first to run an eye-opening bulletin from Peking: Mao had been dismissed as Party chairman, and the commune, though still described as "the primary unit of the future Communist society," had been downgraded, no longer to be expanded from rural into urban areas, as had been proclaimed as official policy earlier in the year. Mao, dismissed? This seemed unimaginable, until I remembered the Khrushchev speech. If Stalin could be attacked, why not Mao? And, in addition, the commune, downgraded? Had the Chinese leadership lost its confidence in the concept of the "commune"? What would replace it?

Clearly, China was experiencing a rebirth of Russia's crazy rush to communism in the early 1930s. Stalin had described it as a policy "dizzy with success," desperately in need of adjustment. I tried exploring this emerging upheaval in China from both a Washington and a Moscow perspective: would it have any immediate effect on China's strategic position in East Asia, requiring American action ("probably not" was the quick judgment from Washington), and would it affect China's responsibilities to both the international communist movement and the Sino-Soviet alliance ("yes indeed!" was what I heard from friends in Moscow)? I knew the questions, but did not have the answers, and I decided to tell my Brookings hosts that if, after due consideration, they wanted to withdraw their invitation, I would understand. "No," they declared. The recent news from Peking only made the topic more urgent and appealing.

In the late 1950s, Brookings was located at 722 Jackson Place, an attractive one-block architectural mix of elegant nineteenth-century town houses and two twentieth-century eight-story office buildings in the heart of federal Washington. These later office buildings would soon be demolished, thanks to Jackie Kennedy's taste and clout, making room for other town houses and conveying the impression of colonial times. If Madison Place flanked one side of the seven acres of LaFayette Park, Jackson Place flanked the other. Any tourist strolling through the park would have had no trouble glancing across Pennsylvania Avenue and seeing the single most precious piece of property in the country, namely the White House. This historic setting was especially gratifying, because it allowed me later to tell my mother that even though I had not lectured *in the White House*, I had lectured *in the shadow of the White House*.

My Brookings hosts were two former State Department officials—Robert Hartley and O. Edmund Clubb. Hartley ran the International Studies Group, which sponsored speakers and seminars on issues relating to American foreign policy. He was the one who had issued the invitation. Clubb was a controversial China specialist, who had been consumed in the fires of McCarthyism in the early 1950s. Under a cloud, feeling unjustly humiliated, Clubb decided he had no option but to resign from the State Department. He then taught at Columbia while enjoying the "off-campus" delights of Brookings.

My Brookings appearance resembled seminars I had attended at Harvard. About twenty scholars and their interns gathered around a large oblong table, the same one, it turned out, that today serves a similar purpose in the St. Louis Room at 1775 Massachusetts Avenue, where an expanded Brookings has been located since 1960. Hartley opened the seminar with a brief introduction of the subject and the speaker. He mentioned Khrushchev's speech, Mao's surprising demotion, and the problems it would likely pose for Chinese communism and the Sino-Soviet alliance. He then turned to me, pointing out that I had been an interpreter and press attaché at the U.S. Embassy in Moscow, spoke Russian, had written *Eastern Exposure*, and was now a CBS "specialist on Soviet affairs." It was my turn.

Truth be told, dozens of butterflies were at that moment flittering around in my stomach. I wondered whether I would be up to the task. I had done many seminars at Harvard, but never one at a distinguished think tank in the nation's capital.

I had prepared a short speech. I could have read it as a way of easing my anxiety, but listening to Hartley's introduction, I changed my mind. I decided simply to lay out the evidence drawn from my experience and reporting rather than engage in an academic conversation. I told them about being in Moscow during Khrushchev's historic speech denouncing Stalin, then meeting and actually discussing policy with the Soviet leader and a few of his colleagues, traveling through much of the Soviet Union, sparring with local communist officials and ordinary Soviet citizens, who shared a secret or two about their feelings concerning their Chinese allies, none of them positive or admiring. I spoke with some authority about Russia, having just recently returned from there, but I discussed the political turmoil in China as an outsider. Like many other American reporters, I had tried to get a visa to cover China but time and again I'd been rejected. The Chinese then had no interest in allowing a "foreigner" to observe the chaos caused by the Great Leap Forward. The doors would only be opened much later. "For now," I concluded, "history was not yet ready to disclose its secrets." By implication, how could I? I discussed what I thought I knew, and no more.

Usually at this point the senior fellows, many listening intently, taking notes, some peering skeptically over half-moon glasses, would either praise or pummel the speaker's thesis. That was the modus operandi of the academic seminar, but this time the scholars seemed unusually tolerant. They seemed pleased by my candor and especially my refusal to speculate. I was pleased by their questions, which I found extremely helpful. They carried my analysis to a higher level.

What was the ultimate purpose of the Sino-Soviet alliance? If Russia felt it had to go to war, did that mean that China would also have to go to war?

If it was not a given that each had to fight for the other, what was the point of the alliance?

Was the alliance primarily a union of two like-minded communists? How crucial was national interest in determining one or the other's response to a mortal challenge?

When the current generation of Russian and Chinese leaders passes from the scene, will the need for the alliance survive or pass with them?

If I was ever to do another broadcast on the Sino-Soviet alliance, or write a book about the alliance, I realized, first, how much I had yet to learn about the alliance and, second, whether I could do my day job as a reporter on general assignment and the research that would be necessary for a book. Judging by Hartley's concluding comments, I could tell that he and his colleagues were pleased by my visit. I too was pleased—I felt as though I had just got an "A" on a paper I rushed the night before to complete.

Two weeks later, on December 14, I returned to Washington to speak at an ASPA luncheon at the Occidental Restaurant, still fashionable but not yet globally famous for the role it was to play during the Cuban Missile Crisis when a Soviet diplomat and ABC correspondent John Scali exchanged vital information over lunch. I had heard about the Occidental from reporters who enjoyed the pleasures of an expense account; for me, the restaurant was a new and expensive experience.

I had hoped to meet Charles A. Beard, the prominent, respected historian at Columbia University, who was on ASPA's governing board. But on arriving, I was told that he could not attend—he was teaching. Forty to fifty members and guests did attend. At my luncheon table, U.S.-Soviet relations was, naturally, the topic of interest. I sprinkled the conversation with anecdotes about my time in the Soviet Union, mentioning my book when appropriate. When it was finally time for my lecture, my host, a history professor at a local college, told a story from *Eastern Exposure* about how Khrushchev decided to call me "Peter the Great." It was a story that always produced a good laugh.

During my thirty-minute deconstruction of the Sino-Soviet alliance, I saw and heard very few coughs, sneezes, or yawns, which suggested most people were not only listening but seemed also to be seriously interested in the subject. I was quickly to learn, however, that many of them did not agree with my analysis. This was not to be another Brookings love fest. Most of their questions, though posed in a very friendly way, were decidedly critical. It was as though they had been eavesdropping on my kitchen table exchanges with Mady—their questions echoed her arguments.

"What proof can you offer that there are really splits in the alliance?" Variations of this question were the ones most frequently asked.

"There are always differences here and there; they mean nothing." This too was a frequent reference.

"Russia and China are both communist nations, and they're united against us! That's what's important."

One after another, their questions and comments came hurtling at me, each reflecting the prevailing opinion in official Washington that while there might be an ideological difference or two between Russia and China, that did not mean the alliance was splintering apart. Quite the contrary, they all seemed to be arguing, it was strong, united, and determined to hurt the West. Brookings as a think tank clearly went beyond the official line; ASPA reflected the official line. I tried my best to sound objective, as I imagined a good journalist should sound, using facts and quotes and avoiding sweeping editorial judgments. That I had been in Moscow working at the U.S. Embassy during the time of the Khrushchev speech added to my credibility. That I had then traveled through Asia seeking further insights into the alliance also helped my case. Still, they were not in a buying mood. But who knows? Maybe, after lunch, many rushed to the nearest bookstore to buy a copy of *Eastern Exposure.*

One morning, for no special reason, I arrived early at CBS's television headquarters. Except for a small gaggle of people meeting in what looked like an ad hoc studio in a brightly-lit corner—a producer, a director, a writer, a make-up artist, and a totally unpretentious anchorman—the newsroom was just about empty. Not even the editor of the assignment desk had yet reached his reigning throne of power. Curious, I wandered over to the only place where anything seemed to be happening. It was, as it turned out, a news broadcast in the late stages of creation.

"Who's the anchor? When does it air?" I asked a man passing by with a yellow lined pad in one hand and a pencil in the other.

Looking at me as if I'd just arrived from Mars, ignorant of the ways of Earth, "Richard C. Hottelet," he snapped, "and we go on air in [he glanced at a large stop-watch dangling from his belt] twenty-two minutes." I looked at my watch and, after a quick calculation, mumbled, "7:45?" a question mark in my voice. "Right!" he again snapped, as he dashed off to the control room at the other end of the newsroom. I found a chair close enough to observe and listen to the final preparations for that day's *CBS Morning News with Richard C. Hottelet.*

I had not yet met Hottelet, but I had read a lot about him. (He, I said to myself, would surely be interested in discussing the Sino-Soviet alliance.) Hottelet was one of the original "Murrow boys," hired in London in January 1944, several months before the allied invasion of Nazi-occupied France. At the time, he was twenty-six, a bright, Brooklyn-born reporter, who had joined the United Press in 1938, while a student in Berlin. In 1941 the Gestapo arrested him on "suspicion of espionage." He was held for four months, then released along with another American reporter in a prisoner swap for three Germans held by the United States. Hottelet went to Washington, where, for a brief time, he worked for the Office of War Information.

In 1942, after the United States entered the war, Hottelet, fluent in German, was sent to London. Two years later he met Murrow, and the two reporters—one, already an elder statesman, the other, young and eager for a job at CBS—struck up a lifelong friendship. Murrow was clearly impressed. In a January 1944 letter to his friend, Robert Trout, Murrow wrote, "Think we have found a good man in Dick Hottelet. If you have a moment, let me know what you think of his stuff. He's got a damned good mind, and is, I think, improving as a broadcaster." Trout's response must have been positive, because Murrow then hired Hottelet.

For all reporters, the big story was the approaching Allied invasion of France on June 6, 1944. Hottelet got a key assignment. He was in a B-26 Marauder bomber flying over Utah beach when allied troops landed at dawn. That night, in the first eyewitness account of the invasion by a CBS correspondent, he said, "This is Richard C. Hottelet reporting from London. The Allied forces landed in France early this morning. I watched the first landing barges hit the beach exactly on the minute of H-Hour."

Other important assignments then came his way.

- In October he was in Aachen, Germany, describing a bloody exchange between American and German forces.

- In December he covered the historic Battle of the Bulge. "It's icy cold on the front tonight," he confided to his CBS radio audience.

- In March 1945 he had to bail out of a burning B-17 bomber, rescued in a cow pasture in France by British troops who treated him to liquor and tea.

- Most remarkable, Hottelet was one of the few reporters who actually witnessed the meeting of Russian and American troops at the Elbe River in Germany, effectively ending World War II. "There were no brass bands, no sign of the titanic strength of both armies," he said that night on CBS radio, understating the historic importance of the rendezvous. "Just some men meeting, shaking hands."

During the Cold War, Hottelet enjoyed a further run of key assignments. He was CBS's correspondent in the Soviet Union and then in West Germany, and, as a reward, in the late 1950s he was given the job of anchoring the morning news. By this time, Murrow had become increasingly unhappy with the new rhythms of television news, but his friendship and affection for his old colleagues only deepened. Hottelet, for one, loved Murrow. Years later, he spoke of him in superlatives as a "skilled, tenacious reporter . . . a fine human being, not arrogant or overbearing, with physical bravery matched by moral courage." As Murrow's sun was setting, Hottelet's was rising, but only to a limited extent. For twenty-five news-filled years, Hottelet served as CBS's UN correspondent, where his reporting helped set new standards for fair, objective journalism. But often, when CBS could have turned to Hottelet for a detached analysis of a major news story, CBS went elsewhere, and, in 1975, after forty-one years with the network, an older, wiser Hottelet resigned, his professional dignity still intact. Always, he was modest, informative, and, for students, approachable. Once, when he was honored by the National Press Club, he broke precedent by delivering the shortest acceptance speech on record. After the moderator read his long list of professional accomplishments, instead of then marching to the podium during the applause and reading a prepared speech, Hottelet simply rose to his feet, marched nowhere, and said, with bowed head, "Thank you."

On the many occasions when I'd come to watch him do the *Morning News*, I'd see an anchorman who was never seduced by the glory and adulation normally associated with the job. He did it his way, methodical, old-fashioned, careful about what was fact and what was hype. He would, for example, cut his own copy, write his own script on an old Remington type-writer, rarely if ever raise his voice, always polite—he would even pour his own coffee! He did, however, allow the make-up artist to do her job, because, I was told, his English wife, Ann, whom he'd met in Berlin during the war, thought he needed a professional touch. This was probably an accurate call but these sessions always left Hottelet feeling decidedly uncomfortable. After all, to his way of thinking, what did face powder have to do with telling the news? "Murrow didn't hire me because of how I looked," he'd say.

With only a few minutes to go before 7:45 a.m., Hottelet seemed to retreat into himself, becoming very quiet as he once again reviewed his copy, memorizing a phrase here and there. Then, thirty seconds before air-time, the floor director would break into his reverie, "30 seconds, Dick, 30 seconds." Hottelet put on his jacket, tightened his tie, and slowly made his way to the chair behind a simple wooden desk, framed in back with a cardboard sign that read "CBS MORNING NEWS." Hottelet looked down at his copy once more, then at the one camera facing him, and waited for the floor manager to give him his cue—a right forefinger pointing unmistakably at him. "Good morning," Hottelet would announce, his strong voice booming in the almost empty newsroom, "I'm Richard C. Hottelet, and this is the CBS Morning News."

Though engaged competitively with NBC's *Today* show, CBS's fifteen-minute broadcast was surprisingly Spartan in appearance: it was just Hottelet, the CBS sign, the desk, nothing more. It was as if CBS deliberately wanted to lose the morning news competition. Unlike the evening newscast, anchored by Edwards, the morning show did not have the budget or clout to order up its own news reports, though it could on rare occasions rerun a report that had appeared on the evening news the night before. There were two commercial breaks, the first coming immediately after the lead story and the other seconds before Hottelet concluded his broadcast. "I'm Richard C. Hottelet," he'd say, "and this has been the CBS Morning News."

Many times over the next few months, Hottelet and I, after his broadcast, would review the day's news over a cup of coffee. We also, quite often, treated ourselves to a jelly doughnut or two. "Richard" became "Dick," and the unpretentious anchorman morphed into a warm, intelligent, somewhat shy person, who loved the news business almost as much as his family but who also shared Murrow's deepening concerns about the pursuit of profit in TV news. As Hottelet saw it, this pursuit diluted the raison d'être of news: namely, to fully and accurately inform the public about the major issues of the day. It was doing a moderately good job, he thought, but not good enough.

Hottelet never saw himself as a crusader, never exaggerated his role as a reporter; he was in the business, he explained, simply because he appreciated the need for hard, straight, unembellished news to support the twin concepts of personal freedom and democracy. He held that belief with a burning intensity to the day he died, never forgetting the horrors he had covered during Hitler's unexpected rise to power in the 1930s, and he did not want to see a similar development anywhere else, especially not in the United States.

Perhaps because Hottelet was, like Murrow, Smith, Sevvereid, and other reporters who had covered World War II, a serious student of contemporary history, he seemed only too happy to accommodate my interest in the Sino-Soviet alliance. We must have spent hours discussing different aspects of the problem. How and why was the alliance formed? What were its strengths? And weaknesses? Could Russian and Chinese nationalism overwhelm their ideological commitment to communist internationalism?

We got on so well, in fact, that for a time I thought Hottelet might even accept my thesis that the alliance was in the early phases of ideological disintegration. But that was not the case. Like Mady and most of my friends, Hottelet strongly believed that the Sino-Soviet alliance was powerful, united, and determined, one way or another, to undermine and ultimately defeat the Western world. He listened to my arguments. He even found a number to be moderately persuasive. But he was convinced that even if there were ideological differences, tinged occasionally with nationalistic overtones, Russia and China would at the end of the day remain a unified force.

"I knew the Germans well," Hottelet tried to explain. "My mother and father were born in Germany. They spoke German at home. That's how I learned the language. When I lived in Berlin and met Nazi officials, at first because we both spoke German, I thought we would see the world the same way. But no." Here Hottelet searched for the right words, "An ideology has a way of poisoning the mind. Even imprisoning the mind. In this sense, the communists are no different from the Nazis I met. Their minds are locked into a certain vision of the world, and they won't change."

When I tried to persuade Hottelet that I had met many Russians who I thought might one day change their minds about communism, with a wave of the hand he dismissed my argument. "No," he insisted, "they won't change, and no matter their differences, and here I agree with you, there are some differences, [but] the alliance will hold fast."

After these friendly exchanges about the Sino-Soviet alliance, I was forced to confront an important professional question. If I felt so strongly about the subject, why not take a year off and write a book about it? My first book had done well. Why not a second? Another possible option was abandoning journalism entirely and returning to academe. At a university, I'd be able not only to research and write about the alliance, I'd also be able to teach, which I enjoyed immensely. But, on reflection, that seemed foolhardy. I had already achieved one of my major professional goals, becoming CBS's "specialist on Soviet affairs." Another, becoming CBS's Moscow correspondent, seemed now to be a distinct possibility. I had heard rumors that I was at the time one of those being considered for the job.

As I grappled with these questions, one day the phone rang, and a possible solution peaked over the horizon. The voice at the other end belonged to William Ackerman, a former reporter at the *Cleveland Plain Dealer* now serving as both director of special projects for CBS News and executive director of the CBS Foundation. I had met Ackerman while writing Bud Benjamin's documentary about Khrushchev's aggressive policy in the Middle East. When *Eastern Exposure* was published, he sent me an enthusiastic note of congratulations. Now he wanted to know whether I might be interested in applying for a CBS fellowship for a year's study at Columbia. *Might I be interested in a year's study at Columbia?* Heaven had just come knocking at my door.

"Really?" I tried to sound casually curious. "A year at Columbia? Hmm. Tell me about it."

Ackerman seemed eager to explain the fellowship's history, thinking, I suppose, that he would have to coax me into accepting one. "It was set up a few years ago, in 1957," he began. "It was Sig Mickelson's idea [Mickelson was now head of CBS News and Public Affairs]. He and Jacques Barzun of Columbia thought it would be a good idea for CBS to send eight of its most promising reporters, writers, or producers to spend a year at Columbia."

"Doing what?" I asked innocently.

"The idea was that each would pursue a subject of special interest to them, and that would help, as Sig said in his announcement, 'to meet their growing responsibilities in electronic journalism.' It's a really good deal," he continued. "Each fellowship covers tuition, transportation to New York, a place to live, plus $8,000 for expenses." He sighed. "Not bad. I wish I could apply for one."

Ackerman did not have to be a super salesman. He had an appealing product, and he had come to the right customer. I could barely contain my excitement.

"Bill, I'm grateful that you called," I said. "May I think about it and get back to you tomorrow? I'd like to talk to my wife."

"Of course," Bill replied, and then added, "By the way, a seven-person panel considers all applications, a really impressive group. I thought you'd like to know that your friend, Ed Murrow, is one of them. Sig is another."

Later, on my way home, I thought about my conversation with Bill Ackerman. In fact, I thought about nothing else. I concluded after a while that he was telling me, as candidly as he felt he could, that if I decided to apply for a fellowship, I would get one. Why else had he called? Why else had he made a point of mentioning that "your friend, Ed Murrow" was on the panel. And Mickelson, too. Why else, indeed?

That evening, over a delicious dinner, Mady and I planned an adventure for the ages. I would apply for, and probably get, one of the eight CBS fellowships, and then in June we would go off on a fabulous around-the-world search for expert opinion, informed impressions, and hard data about the Sino-Soviet alliance before returning to Columbia in September, when Mady would resume, and I would start, classes and write a book based on what we'd learned during our journey.

Jules Verne, move over, please.

7

AROUND THE WORLD
IN 100 DAYS—PART ONE

According to Jules Verne, it took the estimable Phineas Fogg, accompanied by his French valet, Passepartout, eighty days to go around the world. They had an adventure fit for the footloose hero of a bestseller. Mady and I needed 100 days, even though we had jet planes but no valet. Our adventure was far more exciting and certainly more memorable—at least, for us.

Fogg could, at a moment's notice, leave London on one of his delightfully capricious adventures. He needed no one's permission, and he had more than ample resources. I could not possibly, on a whim, take a month or two off from my job at CBS. I would need an official leave-of-absence and the support of a generous donor.

Re-enter Bill Ackerman.

The morning after Mady and I decided that a year at Columbia, thanks to a CBS fellowship, would make perfect sense for us, I informed Bill and formally applied for a fellowship. Two weeks later, on March 1, Bill called with the happy but not entirely surprising news that I had been selected to be a CBS Fellow at Columbia for the 1959–1960 academic year. When I informed Mady, she quickly began imagining which courses on Soviet foreign and domestic policy we would be taking together. I went one step further.

"Will you be free for lunch?" I asked, enjoying the idea of having an endless run of lunch dates with my wife.

"Yes, indeed!" she answered.

Next on my informal agenda was funding for our round-the-world research trip. Those were the days when foundations tripped over one another for the tax-saving glory of funding worthy academic endeavors. Nothing apparently seemed more worthy during the Cold War than research about what was often called the "threat of global communism." Our proposed trip fell conveniently under this umbrella.

Who could help us with funding?

Henry Graff, I thought. Henry was a friend and a professor of American history at Columbia. He knew everyone. I called him at home one evening to get his advice and also to test my pitch to a prospective donor or foundation.

On the phone, I stressed the dangers posed by the Sino-Soviet alliance and by the West's basic ignorance about what made this alliance tick. Before I could complete my pitch, Henry interrupted and said, "Ford, the Ford Foundation. It's perfect for what you propose." Henry gave me the name of the officer in charge of communist studies. "He probably knows you or your book. Tell him anyway about the CBS Fellowship." Henry then added, "Tell him also that Mady is a PhD student at Columbia. That should do it."

And it did. I called the officer, made my pitch, and within a few days, was in his office for what he described as a "get-acquainted" session. He suggested, in my formal application for funding, that I emphasize the need for foreign travel, making the point that since Senator Joseph McCarthy's damaging anti-communist crusade in the early 1950s, there were comparatively few experts on communism left in the U.S. government. American universities were also light on this academic discipline, though, ironically, a fresh crop of Russia experts was at the same time being cultivated at Harvard, Columbia, and a few other prominent universities. One effect of this scarcity was that when the United States plunged into the Vietnam War, it knew pitifully little about Peking's policy, history, and attitude toward Hanoi. Once China went communist in 1949, Washington, like a spurned lover, turned its back on China, adopting a policy of nearsighted negligence. It operated on suspicion, guesswork, and ignorance. "Would China intervene, and when?" was the question of the day, and no one seemed to have an informed answer.

But while China experts were in short supply in the U.S. government, they were a rich, expanding resource in foreign ministries and universities in many other parts of the world. My pitch was simple: they ought to be interviewed, as soon as possible, and their knowledge, experience, and wisdom then harvested into a fresh report on the Sino-Soviet alliance that could be of value to policymakers and academics in the United States.

My session with the Ford official must have gone well, because a few weeks later I was informed that my application for financial support had been approved. Though Ford would not provide enough to pay for Mady's plane ticket, it would for mine and for many of the hotels along the way. Undaunted, we dug into our vast Fort Knox reserves and—Bingo!—we had just enough to pay for Mady's ticket. By early June, we would be ready to challenge Phineas Fogg's record for round-the-world travel.

Over the next few months, whenever I got a chance, I prepared for the trip. I read voraciously, starting with the histories of Russia and China, rereading the classics, such as Vasily Klyuchevsky's *A History of Russia* and John Fairbank's *The United States and China*. I re-read China expert Allen Whiting's excellent essays on the subject, Robert C. North's *Moscow and Chinese Communists*, Henry Wei's *China and Soviet Russia*, and a superb collection of studies by Professors Harold Boorman, Alexander Eckstein, Philip E. Mosely, and Benjamin Schwartz entitled *Moscow-Peking Axis*. In addition, I spent many profitable hours at the New York Public Library reading newspaper clips about the alliance from the *New York Times*, the *New York Herald Tribune*, the *Christian Science Monitor*, the *Manchester Guardian*, and the *Observer*. I studied the Soviet and Chinese press in greater detail than usual, searching for insights that might help shed some light on the alliance.

By June I had reached one inescapable conclusion: there was indeed a dangerous shortage of information about the Sino-Soviet alliance in the United States. I couldn't wait to get started on our trip.

There were two central questions: First, where would we go? And second, with whom would we meet?

I contacted many academic, diplomatic, and journalistic colleagues to produce an itinerary and a list of prospective interviewees. We would start in London, an obvious takeoff point, then fly to Paris and Munich, where Radio Free Europe was located, and Vienna, the best listening post for Eastern Europe, I was told, before heading to Warsaw and Moscow and then southeastward around the rim of China, with stops in New Delhi, Bangkok, Jakarta, Singapore, Hong Kong, Taipei, and Tokyo: thirteen stops, thirteen potentially rich opportunities to look, listen, and learn, hoping to lift the lid on the mystery of the communist alliance that at the time represented a serious threat to the Western world, though its true character and essential goals were still relatively unknown.

LONDON proved to be a trove of riches for the visiting researcher. The door to the Russia and China experts at the British Foreign Office was surprisingly ajar, and I was able without much effort to contact and interview a number of top British experts on communism.

Much to my satisfaction, they seemed to share my judgment that Khrushchev's secret speech and Mao's foolish Great Leap Forward had shaken the foundations of the Sino-Soviet alliance, a conclusion Washington was still years away from even acknowledging. How badly shaken was a question yet to be determined.

The *Observer*'s analyst, Richard Lowenthal, a restless bundle of East European brainpower, explained one key to understanding the Sino-Soviet alliance. It was China's sense of self, its belief that it was the center of the universe, whether governed by emperors or communists. Lowenthal reminded his dinner guests (Mady and me among them) that when Lord Macartney of Great Britain arrived in Peking in the 1790s, the emperor insisted that the English negotiator could not speak to him unless he first performed three kowtows and nine prostrations before dropping to his knees to begin the talks. Although Mao abandoned the emperor's humiliating protocol, he imposed one of his own, making it incredibly difficult for foreign dignitaries to get an audience and then even more difficult to negotiate a deal. The process has always been lengthy, problematic, and humiliating, and Russia has been a poor student, never choosing to adjust to the Chinese psyche, and thus leaving their alliance in a shaky, uncertain state from the beginning.

Victor Zorza, the *Manchester Guardian*'s specialist on communist affairs, added that Mao resented Khrushchev, in part because he was a Russian widely recognized as the leader of the communist world. When Mao sensed that Khrushchev's political position was shaky, as it was during an intraparty squabble in 1958, he insisted that the Chinese translation of the communiqué wrapping up their momentous August summit drop the phrase "the leading role of the Soviet Union," which was a form of rhetorical heresy at the time. In its place Mao substituted the words "mutual cooperation." Careful students of communist communiqués, like Zorza, also noticed that when China and Russia were both mentioned in the same sentence, the Chinese translation mentioned China first, nine out of ten times. The Russian translation mentioned Russia first, ten out of ten times. It was as if Khrushchev had insisted on a small measure of ideological superiority, ten out of ten mentions more meaningful to him than nine out of ten.

"In the communist world," Zorza explained, "such things have special meaning."

"Like what?" I asked.

"Like China was on the rise," he said. "No longer the supplicant to Russia."

I appreciated the time Zorza gave me and the wisdom he had accumulated on the subject, but I disagreed with his conclusion. Though China was "on the rise," Russia was still clearly the dominant partner in the alliance, stronger militarily and economically.

The British Foreign Office, which I feared would be less than hospitable to a visiting reporter, was, on the contrary, amazingly helpful, providing interviews with a number of its senior Russia and China experts. Though their comments were generally prefaced with cautionary "ifs," "of course this is on background" and "but, on the other hand," they seemed all to agree on three points:

First, Russia distrusted China, and China distrusted Russia, and though still formidable, their alliance was shaky at its core.

Second, one reason for the shakiness was that Russia feared China's economic potential. Another reason was Khrushchev's concern about Russia's own political instability and economic stagnation.

Third, despite these difficulties, the alliance still represented a dynamic and dangerous challenge to the Western world. One expert said, "The West has lulled itself into a fitful slumber. Faced by a clear danger, it has fallen asleep." "It" meant the United States. A retired British diplomat with Moscow experience added, "Never before has our civilization been so threatened, and never before has there been such complacency." Another British expert, just back from a trip to Washington, added, "I am forced to say that in America I was shocked at how self-defeating your China policy is."

On a trip to Oxford, I checked on whether Sir Isaiah Berlin might be available for an interview. Though not a specialist on China, he knew a great deal about Russia. He was one of the West's outstanding intellects. I wanted so much to talk to Berlin, but he was leaving for Paris. "Could we meet there?" I wondered. His secretary, impressed by my persistence, checked with Berlin, and he agreed.

————————

PARIS was no place to study the Sino-Soviet alliance, not in June, when every flower was in bloom, neighborhood patisseries were rich with their enticing aromas, and tourists were crowding museums and cafés. Paris, as I should have known, was then absorbed not with Russia or China but with Algeria, a colony in fierce and fiery rebellion.

Nevertheless, as planned, I contacted Sir Isaiah Berlin, and we met at the fashionable Café de la Paix, which he described as "so very bourgeois but so very convenient." He spoke very rapidly; occasionally I missed a word or two. That morning there was a news report that a consignment of Chinese weapons had reached Algeria. "Now what does that mean?" I asked, hoping my simple question would trigger an enriching conversation. How could it be otherwise! But, with a shake of his head and a quick gesture of his right hand, he responded, "Oh China. Who really knows anything about China?"

Undeterred, I informed Berlin, whom I had met when he lectured at Harvard, that I was studying the Sino-Soviet alliance, that I was concerned that the Western world might now be threatened by a powerful, but mysterious, coalition of forces, driven by a dangerous ideology, and that the West did not know enough about it. Berlin agreed. "Certainly the threat is mysterious and powerful," he said, "but I think that the mystery is very largely China." He paused, sipped on his wine, a very faraway look in his eyes, as if he was searching for the right formulation of an idea. "Russia's actions can be determined, but China's are complicated by historical and psychological factors.

"Moreover, we are severely restricted in Peking. Our diplomats have difficulty getting about, and we obtain few firsthand impressions, and no source material. It is difficult for us, and, I might add, it is even difficult for the Russians to understand the Chinese.

"Recently," Berlin went on, "I had a chat with the Russian writer, Sholokhov, about the Soviet Writers' Conference that was held in Moscow in May. He told me that a delegation of Chinese writers attended the conference. After long debates about 'socialist realism,' the Russians threw a lavish cocktail party—with vodka, caviar, and *blini*. Everyone, Sholokhov said, had a glorious time—except the Chinese. They huddled together, drinking tea and kept talking about 'socialist realism.' One of the Russians urged the Chinese writers to try caviar, vodka, and possibly a few *blini*. Somberly, the Chinese replied, 'We do not have these luxuries in China, yet, and so we will not have them in Russia either.'"

Berlin said the Russians were dumbfounded and annoyed—dumbfounded at the incorruptibly austere habits of the Chinese communists, and annoyed at the haughty implication that the Russians were getting "soft" and "bourgeois."

Later that day, in conversation with French journalists, I was reminded of a flowery assessment of the alliance offered by none other than President Charles de Gaulle. He stressed the inflammatory issue of race, which had been mentioned but not emphasized in my earlier conversations. "No doubt, Soviet Russia," he orated, as was his style, "in spite of having aided communism to take root in China, recognizes that nothing can change the fact that she is Russia, a white nation of Europe which has conquered part of Asia and is as a result richly endowed with land, mines, factories, and wealth, face to face with the yellow masses of China, numberless and impoverished, indestructible and ambitious, building through trial and error a power that cannot be measured and casting her eyes about her on the open spaces over which she must one day spread."

From his lofty vantage point in history, de Gaulle saw war between China and Russia as virtually inevitable, the result of a "numberless and impoverished" China eyeing the "open spaces," presumably to her north and west, the vast stretches of Siberia, "over which she must one day spread." No doubt, many Russian strategists have felt, like de Gaulle, that they had to plan for a war with China. It was only realistic to do so. In fact, in their long, troubled history, there have been wars; there may yet be others. But during my round-the-world journey in the late 1950s, I came upon few students of the Sino-Soviet alliance who believed that the alliance would one day crumble into open conflict.

———

MUNICH was Ritvo. In the world of Sino-Soviet relations, it was often said that all roads led to Ritvo.

Ritvo was Herbert Ritvo, who, at first glance, looked like an unassuming graduate student, no tie, no jacket, often in a sweater, rather than what one would expect of the highly esteemed chief political adviser to Radio Free Europe, which was funded by the United States and which broadcast news into the East European satellites. When I came knocking at his door, usually wide open, Ritvo had already held the job for six years and become one of the world's leading experts on the alliance. He rarely "speculated," he insisted, warning the West not to indulge in "scholastic alchemy," where one assumed rumor was fact just because facts, a precious commodity in this field, were so difficult to uncover.

To all of my questions, Ritvo had an answer. Most of the time, it was a variation of "I'm not sure," "maybe," "Yes, that's possible," or "God, who knows?" But he was known to be a superb source; and when he was prepared to offer his judgment on an issue, I immediately cleared my mind of extraneous clutter and listened carefully. What he wanted to discuss, more than anything else, was the Mao-Khrushchev summit of August 1958, which he considered an event of "supreme importance." China had recently launched its Great Leap Forward, which emphasized the "commune" as the new catalyst for dramatic social, economic, and ideological change in the communist world, and Russia had already expressed its strong reservations, arguing that the Soviet model, however it be defined, was the proven one, and no other could supplant it. Ideological differences seemed to consume party leaders in Moscow and Peking.

The German journalist, Wolfgang Leonhard, a serious student of communism, believed that ideology drove the communist world, not nationalism. In his book, *The Revolution Betrays Its Children,* Leonhard tried to prove, with specific examples, the preeminence of ideology over nationalism, but Ritvo was not buying his thesis. Though he admired Leonhard, Ritvo placed his money on what he called "facts over ideology." For him, the dominating *facts* in 1958 were Quemoy and Lebanon, not the communes, and Ritvo believed they topped the secret agenda of the August summit between Mao and Khrushchev.

First, Quemoy: The effort to herd half a billion people into communes was so disruptive and costly that Mao found he urgently needed a scapegoat, and none was handier than

Quemoy, an island near Taiwan governed by Mao's enemy, Chiang Kai-shek, and backed by his greater enemy, the United States. In a move as surprising as it was desperate, Mao opened a massive bombardment of Quemoy. Suddenly, headlines around the world spoke frighteningly of another Asian war on the near horizon. An ailing Secretary of State John Foster Dulles flew to Taiwan to reassure Chiang that the Seventh Fleet would continue to protect the island. An anxious Khrushchev flew to Peking to warn Mao that by attacking Quemoy, he was "playing with fire"—that Chiang could use the bombardment as a pretext for invading the Chinese mainland, precipitating a war that could quickly engage the United States and the Soviet Union. Khrushchev promised only limited military support to China—a few planes, nothing more; and he urged Mao to back down. The Chinese leader continued to denounce American "imperialism" and Chiang's "revanchism," but he stopped the bombardment of Quemoy. Under Soviet pressure, Mao felt he had no choice.

Second, Lebanon: The Middle East was in turmoil. Arab nationalism was on the rise, and the Russians were taking full advantage of the changes sweeping through the region. They sought new allies while denouncing American "imperialism." In this mushrooming chaos, the Iraqi monarch was toppled, and American Marines landed in Lebanon to show the flag and restore a degree of stability. While silent in public, Mao privately urged his propaganda apparatus to spread the mischievous view that Khrushchev had been outmaneuvered by the West. A furious Khrushchev, preparing for his Peking summit, realized the situation was getting out of hand. At the summit, he demanded that Mao drop this line of Chinese propaganda and, more important, warned that if Mao hoped to continue to get Russian economic and diplomatic support, which, after the chaos caused by the commune experiment, was more essential than ever, he had better stop challenging Russia's dominant position in the communist world. He would have to play by Russia's rules. Within a few months, in a move few would have imagined possible, Mao was sidelined, and the Great Leap Forward became at best an embarrassing chapter in the history of Chinese communism.

I asked Ritvo if he believed that China was, in fact, a major threat to Russia. "No," he answered bluntly. "China will become Russia's problem in ten, maybe twenty years, but it is not now." He also discounted speculation I had heard in London and Paris that China might soon be forced to expand into the soft Siberian underbelly, driven by demographic and economic needs. "That is one theory we really should not take too seriously," he said with a dismissive wave of his hand. "China still has vast areas for cultivation and irrigation—especially in Sinkiang." Ritvo paused, before adding, "No, Peking is not going to attack Siberia, and Khrushchev is not settling Siberia because of an imminent Chinese thrust."

My final question: I asked Ritvo whether the United States should recognize communist China. I told him the British Foreign Office answered with an emphatic yes. "Yes, for me, too," Ritvo agreed, adding cautiously that he was speaking only for himself, not for Radio Free Europe, which, dependent on U.S. government funding, enjoyed no editorial independence. Ritvo did not want to anger anyone in Washington. "When recognition comes, whenever that be," he said, "it has to have visible punch. It has to satisfy our needs, not China's. It cannot look as if we're catching up with the rest of the world." Only in this way, he summarized, could recognition take advantage of the "frictions" that surely existed in the Sino-Soviet alliance.

———

VIENNA, at first glance, no longer looked like the vibrant capitol of an Austro-Hungarian empire that danced to the diplomatic tunes of a Metternich. Now, on our arrival in early July, it looked tired and shabby, a sad reflection on the recent Soviet occupation of half the city. In 1955 the Soviet Union and Austria signed a long-delayed peace treaty, ending the Soviet occupation. The price was an Austrian pledge to pursue a neutralist policy in East-West relations.

For this reason, among others, Austrian diplomats tried to project an optimistic front, boasting about Vienna's history, architecture, and its exceptional ability, based on its location in the heart of Europe, to read and understand Soviet policy and practice in Eastern Europe. "Indeed," one Austrian diplomat told us, "we are your eyes and ears on the Soviet bloc. What we learn, we pass on to you." An Austrian writer echoed the same thought. "We are Westerners," he explained, "but we know how to deal with the Russians. Don't worry."

One example of Austrian neutrality was Chancellor Julius Raab's decision to allow the Soviet Union to stage the seventh World Youth Festival in Vienna, starting in late July. It was the first in a non-communist capital, and Raab's decision triggered an angry debate. His political opponents argued that he had just given Soviet leader Khrushchev a golden opportunity to promote communist causes, that he had conveniently chosen to forget the Soviet suppression of Hungary in 1956 and to ignore an obscenity closer to every Austrian's soul—the Russian occupation of their own country, which had only recently ended. Raab's counter-argument was that Austria was now a sovereign democratic state and that it had to demonstrate its neutrality with concrete deeds, not slogans. Besides, he said, in any competition between democracy and communism, he was certain, absolutely certain, that democracy would win.

The festival opened triumphantly in Vienna Stadium. Sixty-thousand Austrians filled the stands. More than 17,000 delegates from "friendly" communist countries, from Western countries, and from "underdeveloped Asia, Africa, and Latin America," as it was put, participated in the festival, festooned everywhere with flags and slogans, none more prominently featured than "Peace and Friendship," Khrushchev's favorite saying. Indeed, for Moscow, the festival provided the moment to display communist propaganda, to promote Soviet policies and to convert any number of the delegates to what was called "the correctness of the communist struggle for peace."

Seen through the prism of the Sino-Soviet tussle for influence and power, the festival failed to provide any deep insights. The Russians obviously dominated the proceedings. They had many more delegates. They determined the agenda. They controlled the budget, and they seemed to be making a play for Western sympathy and understanding. The Chinese were a sideshow. They kept to themselves. If they were making a play for anyone, it was the delegate from the "underdeveloped" parts of the world—the writer or student from Asia, Africa, or Latin America. The Chinese proudly projected an austere form of communist governance, different from the Russians, who, they whispered, had grown fat with success. This difference was not ever stated; it was implied.

When it was all over, many Viennese Democrats, Raab included, were decidedly disheartened. Months later, they acknowledged that they had been taken to the cleaners. In the festival's competitive war between communists and democrats, pump-primed by Moscow, the communists won a major skirmish. They were to lose the war eventually, but it took another thirty years.

Though many diplomats and journalists in Vienna were absorbed with the festival, I found a handful still eager to share ideas and impressions about the Sino-Soviet alliance, which they all, not surprisingly, considered a major threat to the Western world. My questions were variations of those I'd been asking since the start of our trip. Did they see cracks in the alliance? How were they manifest, if at all, in Eastern Europe? What effect on the West? No one predicted the alliance would split apart, but everyone saw the cracks, believed they were widening, and, in three areas especially, thought the differences between the Russian and Chinese versions of communism stood in sharp contrast in Eastern Europe.

First, the Chinese were beginning to have an impact on interpretations of communist ideology. When the Chinese in 1958 proclaimed their devotion to the commune as the new basis of society, the communist leaders of East European countries went into rhetorical revolt. No, they shouted, not for us. They looked toward Russia for help and direction. A Hungarian diplomat confided, "A general nervousness swept through this part of the world. We weren't sure what the Russians were going to do." Actually, the commune experiment collapsed before the Russians could publicly express their displeasure.

Second, China's expanding population was a cause of growing concern in Russia and in Eastern Europe, according to diplomats based in Vienna. One of them told me what he described as "the Oscar Lange story" about Russia's new responsibility in Eurasian politics. "Thank God," Polish economist Lange was supposed to have said, "we now have Russia as a buffer state between us and the Chinese." Even if this story was apocryphal, as a few reporters believed, it still conveyed the concern many East Europeans felt about China's demographic growth. The official Soviet position was that there was no reason for anyone to be concerned. The communist world was one big happy family. The unofficial Soviet position was expressed by an uncharacteristically outspoken Soviet ambassador, who pulled aside a British journalist at a cocktail party and murmured, "Can you imagine, there are going to be one billion Chinese in twenty years. . . . Come on now, how is China going to feed a billion people?" The implication was clear: China would not be able to feed its population and would be forced to expand its borders into neighboring countries, one of them being the Soviet Union.

Third, in the past three years, Chinese trade with Eastern Europe had skyrocketed, following the classic pattern of backward countries providing raw materials, such as iron ore, tin, wool, and cotton, and advanced countries providing in exchange industrial equipment, such as locomotives, tractors, and power stations. The first long-term trade agreement between China and Czechoslovakia was signed on April 12, 1959; the first with Hungary on April 22, 1958; and with Albania, Bulgaria, and Poland in 1957. China even struck a large trade deal in 1957 with West Germany, at the time one of Russia's major antagonists. By 1959 China's trade with West Germany had zoomed ahead of its trade with the Soviet Union, a neighbor and an ally.

One of my questions was left unanswered. What was China's mysterious role during the 1956 Polish and Hungarian uprisings? Was China encouraging those countries to hurt Russia? Or was China actually trying to help Russia? No one seemed to know the answer.

A friend at the Austrian Foreign Ministry tried to be helpful. "The answer, if there is one, is not here," he said.

"Then where?" I asked.

"Warsaw," he replied. "The Poles know everything, but I don't know if they'll tell you. They don't even tell us."

My friend's intriguing advice pointed us toward Warsaw, which was where we were going to go anyway.

WARSAW was, for me, a step back into the communist world. I'd lived in Moscow for thirteen months. For Mady, it was her first step into the communist world, her way of bridging a theoretical understanding of communism with the practical realities of communist rule. And, for both of us, Warsaw was a reminder of the devastation left by World War II and the continuing inability of communism to meet the basic needs of the average citizen in the mid-twentieth century.

Like Vienna, Warsaw looked old and weary, even though red-and-white bunting hung from every government building, bright flowers sprouted unevenly from window boxes, and small armies of women scrubbed the streets with brooms of bundled branches. Even Marshalkowska, the still gutted

Broadway of Warsaw, though bedecked with huge portraits of communist leaders, looked shabby. But, in fact, Warsaw was at its Sunday best, as it prepared to welcome an important, if despised, Nikita Khrushchev. "Tomorrow," our hotel concierge mumbled sarcastically, "tomorrow our liberator comes."

Poles made little effort to disguise their displeasure with Russia's gruff leader. He was the personification of Soviet oppression—in their minds, the reason why Poland was locked into the Warsaw Pact, why it could not realize its economic and political potential, why it could not be free. Earlier, in 1956, Poles had staged an uprising, but it was quickly crushed, leaving Poland simmering over the next few years with anger and frustration. A leading poet, Antoni Slonimski, penned what quickly became a popular revolutionary theme:

> *We want the right to gripe,*
> *To joke,*
> *To hold some high-placed dignitaries*
> *Up to ridicule . . .*

But though Poles *wanted* the "right to gripe," they seemed to realize that their freedom was still a revolution away. A. M. (Abe) Rosenthal, the resident *New York Times* correspondent, observed, "There may be freedom of conversation in Poland, but there is not freedom of speech."

With Abe, an old family friend, we went on July 12 to Okecie Airport, where thousands of neatly dressed children carried flowers and a small handful of Polish communists waited fretfully for Khrushchev's arrival. Would it be another October 1956 visit, when Khrushchev threatened to destroy Poland, or would it this time be an attempt at reconciliation? No one really knew.

Poland's place in the communist world was uncertain. Ever since the 1956 uprisings in Poland and Hungary, China had become a player in Eastern Europe's ideological warfare, changing everything. Was China seeking to displace Russia in a region Russia had once dominated—and still did, though to a lesser extent? Or was China simply expanding economically and ideologically, like a maturing adolescent who hadn't yet realized its capacity for mischief but, having made its move, was now ready to exploit the consequences? And, for the West, what effect did China's entry into Eastern Europe have on the Sino-Soviet alliance? Khrushchev's arrival provided an obvious jumping-off point in any of my conversations about China's motivation. It was then only a short hop from Khrushchev to Chou En-lai, who was Mao's master at diplomatic manipulation in 1957. With an easy Confucian charm and a smile radiating self-confidence, Chou represented China's sudden arrival on the scene, which had the effect of gently nudging Russia off center stage in Eastern Europe.

During Khrushchev's 1959 visit, I spoke with many Polish officials and journalists. Bottom line: they all seemed to agree that China did not want to see or contribute to the dissolution of communist rule in Eastern Europe, but did want to be recognized as a rising power in the region, a counterweight to Moscow in the struggle for ideological supremacy. And, in this balancing of caution and ambition, China did manage to plant its flag in the heartland of East European politics.

By early 1957 Eastern Europe was a smoldering mess. The Hungarians were furious and disillusioned: the Russians had smashed their revolution, and the Americans had done nothing. The Poles remained an enigmatic cauldron of continuing discontent. Yugoslavia, the symbol of a communist nation that went its own way, stood defiantly to one side, an appealing magnet for the rest of Eastern Europe. As for Khrushchev, whose anti-Stalin speech in February had inspired this turmoil—was his position in the Kremlin so badly weakened that he could no longer guarantee the continuation of Soviet control over Eastern Europe?

On January 7, 1957, into this dangerous confusion, Chou arrived in Moscow, where the Russians, eager for help, greeted him like a conquering hero. After all, Mao, much to their surprise and delight, had publicly approved of their suppression of the Hungarian rebellion, when much of the rest of the world denounced it. At a gala banquet, Chou followed Mao's line, praising Russia as playing the "leading role" in the communist world.

On January 11, Chou carried this "unity" message to Warsaw, where again he supported Russia but quickly added that Poland "deserved . . . equality and mutual respect." Poles thought they were beginning to hear the sweet music of ideological companionship—that nations, such as Poland, could pursue their own path to communism. That night, at another banquet, Chou juggled his support for both Russia and Poland, saying on the one hand that Russia continued to play its "leading role" in Eastern Europe, but on the other hand that "the Polish nation can always count on the support of the Chinese nation." Its "liberal achievements," he went on, would be "recognized."

On January 15, Chou performed the same juggling act in Hungary. Russia played its "leading role," he asserted, but Hungary, in effect, could also go its own way, sort of.

The following day, Chou returned to Moscow, where he was again saluted as the diplomat who seemed to have again solidified Russia's position in Eastern Europe. He stayed only one day before returning to Peking—mission accomplished, so far as China was concerned. Chou had contained the damage in Eastern Europe that Khrushchev's policies had unleashed, while considerably expanding China's presence in the region.

For Mady and me, it was time to move on to Moscow.

MOSCOW, like Warsaw, was also awaiting the arrival of a foreign leader, Vice President Richard Nixon. He was at the time as unpopular in Russia as Khrushchev was in Poland. Unlike his boss, President Dwight D. Eisenhower, still regarded by Russians as a World War II hero, Nixon was seen as an unrepentant Cold Warrior, dismissive of the East-West thaw Khrushchev was attempting to promote. Yet, there he was, Ike's representative at the opening on July 24 in Sokolniki Park of the American National Exhibition, a glittering display of consumer goods, from color television sets to modern kitchens, mostly unavailable in the Soviet marketplace, capped by an arresting 30,000-square-foot geodesic dome. It was an extraordinary sight! A more somber Soviet exhibition, featuring science and technology, had opened a month earlier in New York City. Both were part of an American-Soviet cultural exchange agreement, signed the year before.

For the United States, the exhibition was a stunning success. For six weeks, more than 3 million Soviet citizens visited this cornucopia of consumerism, each enjoying his or her first taste of Pepsi-Cola, dispensed free of charge in a Dixie cup. It was their first relatively uncensored look at America. For Khrushchev, the U.S. exhibition was a huge gamble. A few of his Politburo colleagues had already made no secret of their disapproval, and the Chinese sneeringly denounced the notion of a real communist making nice to the West when, in dramatic contrast, he should have been following Mao's example of having nothing to do with the West.

During his Moscow visit, Nixon met four times with Khrushchev. American reporters dubbed the encounters the "Nik and Dick" show. They made good copy. Among the Americans was CBS's Paul Niven, a bright, jolly, highly experienced Washington reporter. I informed New York of my coincidental presence in Moscow. Could I be of any help to Niven? I asked. So far as I knew, he did not speak Russian. New York's answer: Yes, indeed! Do whatever he says. I instantly realized that the Nixon visit would be a distraction from my Sino-Soviet research, but, as it turned out, a very welcome distraction. When I introduced myself to Niven, he could not have been nicer. He was the model of collegiality. For the whole time of Nixon's visit to Moscow, I was at his side, learning from an accomplished pro while serving as his interpreter, driver, local sidekick. When Nixon then left Moscow for a five-day visit to other cities in the Soviet Union, where I knew broadcasting directly to the United States was not permitted, Niven and I arranged an unorthodox but effective way of reporting on Nixon's journey. At a pre-arranged time, in whichever city Nixon was visiting, Niven would telephone me in Moscow and dictate his eyewitness report on whatever the vice president had said and done. I took his report to the Central Telegraph in downtown Moscow, where foreign broadcasting was allowed, booked a line to CBS Radio in New York, and then broadcast Niven's report—my voice, so identified, and his words. I was thrilled, Niven was satisfied, CBS was grateful. Nixon was covered wherever he went in the Soviet Union.

Of course, Nixon's one-on-one exchanges with Khrushchev on July 24 at the American exhibition generated the most memorable and exciting coverage. Nixon proudly steered Khrushchev into a model television studio. He wanted to boast about the new American technology. Khrushchev, sensing a trap, went on the offensive. He claimed that the Soviet Union had better technology. (He was to make that claim time and again.) He then denounced a recent U.S. proclamation about "Captive Nations Week," dedicated to praying for "peoples enslaved by the Soviet Union." "Provocation!" Khrushchev shouted. Pointing a finger at Nixon, he snarled, "You have churned the waters yourself. What black cat crossed your path and confused you?" *Times* columnist William Safire later remarked, "The bellicose Soviet leader verbally mauled the American vice president, who was trying to be Mr. Nice Guy." Niven and I were no more than ten feet away. I was able to hear the entire exchange and translate it for Niven, who wrote it all down in shorthand.

The two leaders then sipped a Pepsi, which Khrushchev seemed to enjoy, before wandering over to the "Splitnik," the nickname for what was termed "the average American home." It was there, more than in the television studio, that Nixon and Khrushchev, like two lions unleashed, leaped over the diplomatic guardrails and engaged in what historians identified as the "kitchen debate." Flanked by reporters, security, officials, and exhibition organizers, Nixon and Khrushchev looked around and then stopped at the kitchen. Niven and I were three or four feet away. We heard it all.

Nixon, seeking to regain his rhetorical stride, noted that the house, already derided by the Soviet press as the "Taj Mahal," cost only $14,000, available to most American workers. "It's like those houses in California." Nixon gestured, "See that built-in washing machine?"

"We have such things," Khrushchev deadpanned, with a dismissive wave of his hand. "We have peasants who also can afford to spend $14,000 for a house."

The conversation then turned abruptly from washing machines to weapons, Khrushchev asserting "we are strong, and we can beat you," and Nixon warning, "one side cannot put an ultimatum to another." Nixon gently jabbed his finger into Khrushchev's chest, a photo that was to make its way around the world and reinforce Nixon's image as a tough guy in the Cold War.

Later that afternoon, Khrushchev grudgingly admitted that he felt a "certain envy" of American consumerism, but quickly added that the Soviet Union would soon "overtake" the United States in peaceful economic competition and would wave at the United States as it passed by. His bold promise produced one of the many "anekdoty" that Russians later told about the exhibition.

One Russian to another: "Comrade Khrushchev promised we'd wave at the U.S. as we passed them in production."
The other Russian: "Bad idea."

"Bad idea? Why?"

"Because then the U.S. would see that our behinds were bare."

By the time Nixon left the Soviet Union, his image in the Soviet press as an unrepentant Cold Warrior somewhat softened. Both wanted to ease tensions. One day, while Niven was away with Nixon, I learned, much to my surprise, that Khrushchev would soon be visiting the United States. What? I thought. Khrushchev visiting the U.S.? Could Ike then be visiting Russia? If true, that would be a big story. I checked its accuracy with an American Embassy friend who was in a position to know. He smiled, shook his head admiringly, but did not explicitly confirm it.

"Come on. Can I go with the story?" I asked. "I have to know."

"I can't confirm it," he said. "Sorry."

"But if I go with it, will I get into trouble?"

"That's a question I might be able to answer." He looked around. "Marvin, you're a good reporter," he said. "I like you. I don't know where you got that story. Not from anyone here at the embassy—that's for sure. But, wherever you got it," he paused, "so far as I know, you won't get into any trouble." Then, with a friendly hand on my shoulder, he added, "Not at all." I knew him well enough to know that if he thought I was wrong, he would have said so. He didn't.

I tried unsuccessfully to reach Niven, and when it was clear I couldn't, rushed to the Central Telegraph and broadcast the story to CBS in New York. It was my first exclusive, confirmed the following night in a joint U.S.-U.S.S.R. announcement that Khrushchev would visit the United States in the fall and Eisenhower would visit the Soviet Union the following spring.

Overnight, the Soviet press gushed with stories about the "traditional" friendship between the United States and the Soviet Union, *Pravda* even reminding its readers about large shipments of American aid to Russia during World War II. Interestingly, the Peking press, in reporting the news, mentioned the "peaceful intentions" of the Soviet Union but then stressed "American imperialism" and "Wall Street colonialism" in its continuing denunciation of the United States. China was plainly unenthusiastic about the planned Khrushchev visit to the United States—and clearly wanted the Soviet leader to know it.

The American politician who hoped to succeed Eisenhower was not on my list of favorite politicians—years later he put me on his notorious "enemies list"—but in the summer of 1959 he unwittingly played a positive role in advancing my career. But Nixon was not in Niven's class. Niven was the one who graciously helped me help him cover the Nixon visit, and I was to be forever in his debt.

During my first Moscow tour, spanning thirteen months in 1956–1957, I kept a handwritten diary of events, both major and minor, and reviewing it years later, I noticed that there were only two mentions of China, which seemed odd. Did I miss something? Or, was China not a particularly interesting topic of conversation in Moscow at that time. As I recalled, it sparked little dinner table conversation, and it did not make news, at least not then. But, in 1959, when I returned to Moscow, China had become a hot topic of conversation. Russians made little effort to disguise a strange mix of anxiety, admiration, worry, and fascination with their expanding ally to the southeast. A philologist at Moscow University worried openly about China. Pointing a trembling finger at a map of China, he told me in an urgent tone, "That's why we must be friends . . . . With our aid and support, we Russians lately have been supporting a 'yellow peril.'"

"A 'yellow peril!'" I exclaimed. "But that's a nineteenth-century idea. Surely it makes no sense now."

"It is only now that it does make sense," he shot back. "A

hundred years ago, it was romantic prophecy. Today it is a deadly reality."

On another occasion, I dropped in at the Lenin Library, where in 1956 I had spent a great deal of time. Nothing had changed. The huge reading room was crowded with students. Silence reigned. Portraits of Marx, Engels, Lenin, and Khrushchev (the new apostolic succession) were everywhere. In a corner I spotted a group of Chinese students, about twenty-five of them, each dressed in a blue Mao jacket. I watched them for a while. Not one raised his head. While Russian students often took a break, went to the men's room for a smoke, their Chinese counterparts looked like ideological automatons. This obviously infuriated the Russians, who thought the Chinese were deliberately posturing as more serious students, more dedicated communists.

And early one morning, I visited the offices of the *Soviet Journal of Chinese Studies*, a relatively new quarterly, located a ten-minute walk from the Kremlin. What was to be its editorial focus?, I wanted to know. Pre- or post-revolutionary China? The first three issues featured articles on pre-revolutionary China. The fourth issue was delayed. I asked a young Sinologist, whom I'd just met, whether he thought it was "safer" to write about pre-revolutionary China. "Well," he replied with as much caution as candor, "our relations are so touchy now that we feel it's, yes, safer to write only about the past. We don't get into any trouble writing about the Chinese past. It's the present that presents a problem."

I also had the chance to visit the large and impressive Institute of Chinese Studies, where a meeting with its boastful director was quickly arranged. He was a Russian, who stated with pompous pride that close to a hundred Sinologists worked there and they all spoke Chinese, as though I was to be impressed by the fact that a Sinologist at the Institute of Chinese Studies spoke Chinese. Many of them had been trained at Moscow University, which only the year before had opened a special Chinese language program to train Russia's budding team of China specialists.

I asked the director about "cooperation" between Russian and Chinese scholars. "Excellent," he answered. "Really superb."

"How many Chinese scholars work at the Institute?" Answer: "Only one Chinese scholar has come here. You must realize they are all so busy."

"How many Russian scholars have gone to Peking?" Answer: "Very few of us have gone to China, but don't get the wrong idea. If we want to go as tourists, we can, but it's expensive, you know."

"Have there been any exchanges between Russian and Chinese scholars?" Answer: "No, not yet."

On my way out, I looked briefly at the director's bookcase. Half of the books were written by American scholars, the rest by Russians, none by Chinese.

It was then difficult, if not impossible, for American journalists to get visas to China. I had tried a few times, and failed. There were diplomats in Moscow who had been based in Peking. I thought they were fortunate to have had the experience. They told a different story.

"The Chinese gave us the cold shoulder."

"We had little contact with Chinese officials and none to speak of with the Chinese people."

"Many of us feel that the best thing that can happen to us would be if we were all thrown out."

Finally, a Mongolian diplomat told me, "After a tour of duty in Peking, I can tell you it was wonderful to get back to Ulan Bator—and to the West again."

I did not agree. I would have been thrilled to visit Peking and study and report on China, but on this trip, with no visa, I would have to contain my enthusiasm to visiting the underbelly of this Asian giant for insights and information. We would, for the moment, leave the European angle of vision on the Sino-Soviet alliance and see what we could learn from an Asian perspective. Would it be different, sharper, more focused, or just as hazy, uncertain, and mysterious as it seemed to be in Paris, Warsaw, or even Moscow?

AROUND THE WORLD—PART TWO

NEW DELHI was a blistering 98.7 degrees when we arrived at Palam Airport (now the Indira Gandhi International Airport) after a spectacular flight over the Himalayas from Tashkent, capital of the Uzbek Soviet Socialist Republic, the refueling stop on the twice-a-week Moscow–New Delhi flight. A cheerful flight attendant, waiting at the foot of the plane, chirped, "Welcome to New Delhi. Follow me, please." As she strode briskly toward the terminal building, a young American passenger paused, holding up everyone else, and peeled off his jacket. "Awfully hot," he mumbled, loud enough to be heard.

"Hot?" the stewardess stopped. "Hot? You call this 'hot'? This, Sir, is cool." Slowly shaking her head, she informed the passenger, "Last week, before the rains, Sir, it was 108 degrees every afternoon." Having thus educated her passenger, happily she then led the others, including me and Mady, into the terminal where we collected our bags and headed to a hotel in downtown Delhi. There was much to do, and time was precious. Because of the Nixon visit, we'd had to extend our stay in Moscow. Neither of us complained. Every additional day there was like a gold mine of tips, information, and contacts.

Our tip for New Delhi came from a very helpful Russian scholar. We should make every effort, he urged us, to see and interview Professor S. Chandrasekhar, the director of the Indian Institute for Population Studies. "The professor has just returned from China," he explained, "and he has a lot of fascinating information, we're told." Unfortunately, the institute was located in Madras, and we did not have the time to go there. But, with the help of a friend at the American Embassy, we did manage to get a copy of the report Chandrasekhar had just composed based on his two-month-long trip to China. The report was indeed an eye-opener on China's demography, the result of careful observation and meticulous scholarship. Every diplomat, scholar, businessman, or journalist, anyone who had a serious interest in China or its neighbors, was busily studying its four basic conclusions:

First, China's mainland population in 1956 was an expanding 630 million, and in twenty years it would soar to and beyond an estimated 1 billion, meaning one out of every four people on the planet Earth would be Chinese. (India's population at the time was about 417.5 million.)

Second, China's population, according to Chandrasekhar, was also increasing by 16 million a year; in five years its annual growth rate would rise to an estimated 20 million a year.

Third, on the other side of a nation's population growth was its death rate, and China's was dropping dramatically.

Fourth, China's population was one of the youngest in the world. Almost 50 percent of its people were between the ages of fifteen and forty-nine.

The effect was that China's population for the foreseeable future would continue to expand with no ceiling in sight.

On the night of our arrival, we met with a group of Indian journalists. They knew about Chandrasekhar's projections, and they reacted with a mix of fear and fascination. One journalist, quoting Indian diplomats based in Peking, predicted that when China's population reached 800 million, the Chinese Communist Party would be forced to institute a program of birth control, even though communist purists scorned birth control as a capitalist device for "oppressing" working class women. Another Indian journalist opined that most Asians lived with a deepening fear that China's burgeoning population would simply overflow its existing borders, precipitating a crisis leading to a war that India could not avoid. China's stunning population growth was real and frightening, the journalists agreed, but it was not yet an "immediate" crisis. It was, rather, "one that our children will have to deal with."

Much more immediate, clearly, was their concern about what they saw as a "drastic change" in China's foreign policy, manifest initially by a brutal crackdown in neighboring Tibet and then by aggressive military action along the borders of the Indian protectorates of Sikkim, Bhutan, and Nepal in the Himalayas. Suddenly the possibility of a China-India war was on the near horizon.

An explosion of Indian nationalism swept across the land. Anti-Chinese sentiment erupted everywhere. Overnight, Prime Minister Jawaharlal Nehru's once-praised policy of neutrality, noted for its pro-China tilt, sounded pitifully naïve. His political opponents wickedly reminded him that the world was dominated by East-West tensions and competition. Was it not time, they asked, for India finally to choose between East and West? Can it continue to live above the ideological fray? Wherever we went, with whomever we talked, these were the burning questions of the day, and Indians searched desperately for answers, often with little success. They seemed stuck on the head of a pin, on one side collapsing into war, on the other into a dark pit of strategic uncertainty.

For me, a visiting journalist with a focus on the Sino-Soviet alliance, this was undeniably a hot story. For a while it was even a major distraction. I was in New Delhi. Should I call CBS in New York and, as I did in Moscow, volunteer to help cover what certainly appeared to be the beginning of a war between the world's two most heavily populated nations? What to do? It was not an easy decision, but after much conferring with Mady, I decided to proceed with my original plan to study the historic changes taking place in the Sino-Soviet alliance.

I plunged into a series of meetings with experts at the Indian Foreign Ministry. Their analysis of the Sino-Soviet alliance was understandably framed by the crisis then unfolding at the top of the world. In March 1959, Tibetan monks rebelled against Chinese rule, and a frightened Dalai Lama slipped across the border into India. The Chinese, as though waiting for a pretext, mercilessly smashed the rebellion and launched a fiery propaganda offensive against India, calling Nehru, among other things, "the running dog of American imperialism."

War seemed imminent. Evidence was everywhere. "They've begun to move heavy artillery toward the border," an Indian diplomat told me. "They've started to occupy Indian territory," another diplomat said. Still another leaned forward as he related in whispers a conversation he had had the night before with the Russian ambassador. "We know how you must feel about them," the Russian reportedly said, emphasizing the word "them." "But don't worry," he continued, "you may not be able to get along with them, but you can get along with us. We are two completely different kinds of communists—we and they." In the approach to a possible India-China war, international communism appeared suddenly to break along national lines.

Therefore I found myself surprised by the question continually raised by a number of well-informed Indian diplomats and scholars: was it possible that Russia's smile and China's frown were simply two sides of one communist policy? The image of a powerful Sino-Soviet alliance was apparently so compelling that many Indian leaders clung to the illusion of a well-integrated global communist threat, no matter the evidence to the contrary. In this one respect, the Indian Foreign Ministry, known for its policy of diplomatic neutrality, and the American State Department, known for its staunch anti-communism, were both equally blind to the obvious changes sweeping through the communist world.

From the moment we arrived in Delhi, I'd been trying to get an interview with a leader of the Indian Communist Party. I'd call the main headquarters of the party every morning, and a receptionist would politely tell me that no leader was available and I should call again. On the day before we were to leave Delhi for Bangkok, I called and the receptionist had good news. A party leader had become available. If I could get to party headquarters by noon, I'd have at least a half hour with him. Mady and I had been planning to devote the day to sightseeing and shopping, but we both understood the importance of the interview. I suggested as a fallback that, after the interview, we'd meet at the hotel for a late lunch, and then off we'd go and buy up the town.

On my way to party headquarters, I glanced through my file on Indian communism. Immediately after independence in 1947, the nascent Indian Communist Party had tried but failed to attract popular support. Only in the mid-1950s, during Nehru's misguided love affair with China, did the Indian communists finally acquire a degree of power and support, mostly in the provinces of Kerala, West Bengal, and Andhra. In 1957 they stunned the world of Indian politics by taking power in a free election in Kerala and winning thirty seats in the Lok Sabha (India's lower house of Parliament). The communists felt they had acquired enough political power to be able openly to express their views on key issues of foreign and domestic policy. They were in a dream world, badly misreading the Indian electorate.

Within a few years, Indian president Rajendra Prasad,

claiming the communists had "subverted" the Indian Constitution, stripped them of their power in Kerala. Worse still, when the communists foolishly supported China in the Tibetan crisis, they also lost their seats in the Lok Sabha, and a lot more. Nehru, no longer a fan of Chinese communism, angrily attacked India's communists. They "cease to be Indians," he declared, "having shown a total absence of feelings of decency and nationality." Indian students stoned the Chinese Embassy and denounced Indian communism.

It was in this tense atmosphere that I was escorted, after a brief wait, into the office of the Indian communist leader who had promised me a half-hour of his time. He looked and sounded more like an aristocratic Oxford don than a plebian disciple of Mao Tse-tung. When we shook hands, I gave him my name; he did not give me his—then or later on my departure. Dressed in dhoti, leggings, and a white shirt, he was in dress and manner a Nehru twin, slender, commanding, and yet oddly fidgety, as though at any moment he expected a police raid. Often, he would crack his knuckles and glance nervously at the closed door. Once he even jumped from his chair, approached the door, listened carefully, then slowly opened the door, looked from left to right, and seeing no one, returned with obvious embarrassment to his chair. He rarely smiled but spoke with the ease of an accomplished professor, which he might have been, when he wasn't preaching the glories of communism. With a voice rich in Churchillian rhythm, he ranged easily from Marx to Lenin, from Cromwell to Robespierre and then from the collapse of the old European empires to the rise of communist rule in Eastern Europe.

It was clear to me after only a few moments that this super sophisticated Indian communist was at home with any subject but seemed absorbed with only one—the impact of the Tibetan crisis on Indian communism. The subject obsessed him. No matter where he started, he seemed always to end with Tibet.

Because "we lack popular support," the communist leader tried to explain, "we must follow a program of 'sane opposition.'"

"Sane opposition!" I jumped. "Your support of the Chinese during this Tibetan uprising could hardly be described as 'sane opposition,' could it?"

"That," he exclaimed, his forefinger wagging in all directions, "was probably a mistake. The party has been split on that question ever since." He glanced at a large map of the Indian Himalayas nailed unevenly on the wall behind his desk. "Tibet has broken the discipline of our party, because now we are under two great pressures. Naturally, we want to come to power, preferably through peaceful means. But we also want to remain faithful to the world communist movement. And this presents a grave dilemma. I am beginning to question whether these two desires can be reconciled." He steepled his fingers and looked at me, as though searching for sympathy. I offered none.

Has this dilemma been deepened by China's emergence as a major Marxist alternative to Soviet Russia?, I wanted to know.

"Yes," he nodded. "No doubt."

Was there a conflict in the Indian Communist Party between the Russian and Chinese brands of communism?

"Not really," he said with no conviction. "I think most of us agree that the Russian model is more appropriate for India."

But did he think Peking was beginning to steal Moscow's thunder on the world stage?

"Yes," he answered. "I think so. I was in China in 1956, and I could feel the country alive with ideological excitement."

So, wasn't this a challenge to Moscow?

"Definitely," he conceded. "The challenge these days comes from the East—for Russia as well as for the West. For example, the Indian communists who attended the 21st Congress of the Soviet Communist Party in Moscow were very disappointed by Khrushchev's pep talk. They felt he tried to highlight his advanced Soviet industry and technology—as though this were a substitute for ideology. But it is not, and I think Khrushchev knows this."

"Then why don't you openly side with China rather than Russia?"

"Because," he replied, "we are Indians."

Our brief but interesting interview ended on his affirmation of the primacy of nationalism over ideology. India, his nation, was confronted by a Chinese military threat. He had no option, he felt, but to drop his party's earlier affection for Chinese communism. Not all Indian communists agreed with him. Arguments persisted. But, in the struggle between nationalism and ideology in Indian communism, with the nation edging perilously close to a war with China, nationalism won the day.

But would nationalism triumph over ideology in Southeast Asia? Or would Thailand, our next stop, have its own definition of communism? We were soon to learn that China represented more than just an ideological challenge to Southeast Asia; it also represented an economic challenge, which, depending on the country, proved to be more demanding than any Marxist mandate.

———

BANGKOK looked like a sprightly off-Broadway production of an imaginary play called "Living in China's Shadow."

In India, China was a distinct foreign threat. In Thailand, China was a visible domestic challenge. Thailand was a Buddhist monarchy of 26 million, which dangled like a multicolored pear from the soft underbelly of its massive neighbor to the north. They lived serenely, or so it seemed, a happy people in a fertile corner of Southeast Asia. "Mai pen rai," they'd often say, when confronted with the daily problems of life. "Ah, what the heck!" or "No problem"—either was an acceptable translation. Not even the Cold War challenged Thailand's sense of balance and joy. It threw its security concerns behind American power and refused to recognize communist China. There it was, accepting billions of dollars in American military and economic aid, while it outlawed the local Communist Party.

The Thais opened themselves to communist attacks as "lackeys of American imperialism" but didn't seem to mind. They lived well. In fact, a Thai politician told me, "We would have a paradise on Earth, if it weren't for three things: corruption, communist subversion, and the more than 4 million or so Chinese who live here." He smiled, before turning uncharacteristically grim. "We can't do anything about the corruption—that's our way of life, I guess. But communism and the Chinese—those are our biggest problems."

For this politician, the overseas Chinese, as they were called, might have been one of his big problems, but for his fellow Thais (and this visiting reporter) they were a ubiquitous presence and a commercial necessity. They dominated the economy of Thailand. Whatever anyone needed, the Chinese could and did deliver. They owned about half of the stores on Bangkok's busy boulevards. They controlled much of the country's capital. All of the street corner stands, selling cigarettes, postcards, chewing gum and cheap silk shirts and dresses, were run by teenage Chinese merchants, who drove hard bargains in three languages—Thai, Chinese, and English.

Wat Arun, a spectacular Buddhist shrine, composed of red, blue, green, yellow, and brown mosaics, known to tourists as the Temple of Dawn, was the impressive backdrop for a string of these Chinese entrepreneurs, whose lives seemed measured by the number of postcards they could sell to foreigners. In amazingly proficient English, one of them started hustling us. "Want to buy beautiful postcards?" he asked.

"No, thank you," I replied.

"OK," he continued, undaunted, "How about a straw hat?"

"No, thanks."

"OK," he persisted. "How about some excellent rubbings of Wat Aron?"

We marveled at his salesmanship.

"Cheap," he added, as an inducement, "and excellent quality."

"OK," I relented. "I'll have ten bhat worth of rubbings." What would he do with that not quite serious proposal?

He laughed and handed me three postcards.

"Are you Thai?" I asked, knowing he wasn't.

"No, I am Chinese," he answered, his voice bursting with pride.

Later, I asked a Thai friend, "Aren't you a bit concerned about the economic power the Chinese have?"

"No," he replied with an oddly radiant smile. "You see, whenever we need anything, on Sundays or holidays, any hour of the day or night, they have it for us. There is no need to go into competition with the Chinese and open other stores. They do everything for us. It is a wonderful system."

"Yes," I thought, from the standpoint of immediate personal comfort, but "No" from the standpoint of longterm strategic interest. It made sense for Thailand to recognize China, I thought, but one of Thailand's most distinguished diplomats explained why, at this stage of international relations in the late 1950s, it made no sense at all. "First," he said, "we are dependent on American power and support. America does not recognize China, so we don't either. And then," he continued, "there's the problem of our Chinese. Non-recognition gives us the illusion we can control our Chinese. But if we recognized China, we'd quickly lose all control of them." The diplomat paused for a moment. "The Chinese live here," he said, putting meaningful space between each word, "but they are Chinese and always will be. They are not Thais."

I learned from a Thai journalist that of another way to measure Chinese influence on Thai politics. "There are four communist parties in Thailand," he told me, "and they are all illegal, but they are quietly functioning anyway, as though in business."

All of them were loyal to China. Russia had fallen into the

shadows. Thailand fell within China's sphere of influence within the Sino-Soviet alliance. In 1959 no one argued the point. Shortly after the Russian Revolution in 1917, Russia played the key role in organizing local communist parties throughout Southeast Asia, but lost considerable influence in the region when Mao Tse-tung swung China into the communist camp in 1949. From that point on, China began to infiltrate and ultimately control many of the local communist parties.

A few days before leaving Bangkok, I remembered that my brother, Bernie, had strongly recommended that I call Jim Thompson. "He's a special guy," Bernie said. "You've got to meet him." Bernie was at the time the *New York Times*'s correspondent in Southeast Asia. He was based in Jakarta, our next stop. As a proud kid brother, I was always of the view that Bernie was the most famous American living in Asia. I was wrong. Jim Thompson was the most famous American living in Asia. He was also among the most hospitable. As soon as I called and identified myself, he invited me and Mady to his home for dinner. He also said he would send a guide to escort us.

Only as we made our way from one *klong*, or canal, to another did I realize that Bangkok was indeed the Venice of Asia, a beautiful city built atop an irregular series of intersecting waterways always crowded with small boats rushing in different directions. Without the guide, we could never have found our way to Thompson's home, tucked away on a small island. An American spy during and immediately after World War II, Thompson was now the highly successful businessman who almost singlehandedly revitalized the Thai silk industry in the 1950s. Graciously, he awaited our arrival at the small hump-backed bridge linking his home to the island.

"Hi, I'm Jim Thompson," he said with a friendly wave of his hand. "How's Bernie?"

Jim's remarkable home, which he had started building the year before, was an amazing assemblage of six small Thai houses transported by klong to Bangkok from the northern reaches of the country. The result was so authentically Thai, though cluttered with Chinese porcelain, that it was converted into a state museum after Jim's mysterious disappearance and presumed death in 1967. At that time, not feeling well, Jim had gone for a brief rest in the Cameron Highlands in Pahang, Malaya. On March 26, after lunch, when everyone else took a nap, Jim went for a walk and never returned.

At his home in 1959, though, Jim was an extraordinary host, telling fascinating stories about Thailand, his adopted home, his booming silk business, and his hunger for art, which was never satisfied. Mady and I felt honored to be his guests. He was a special person, and his home was an unforgettable tribute to his taste and talent.

When we flew the next morning to Jakarta, our memories of Bangkok were still fresh with teenage Chinese selling postcards and Jim Thompson's unbelievable home. Mady and I would never forget our visit to Bangkok. Bernie and his wife, Phyllis, lived in Jakarta, and though we would have added Jakarta to our list of Southeast Asian stops anyway, their presence in the Indonesian capital made a stop there a special attraction. At 22,000 feet, a question kept wandering through my mind: how would Indonesia differ from Thailand in its connection to the Sino-Soviet competition for supremacy in the communist world? Or would it differ at all?

———

"JAKARTA is not Indonesia." So observed Bernie, and the morning after our arrival, we were already out of Jakarta and on our way to Bandung, the lovely resort that wise Indonesians once thought about making their capital. Now this comparatively cool jewel thrived in the green mountains of West Java, a roughly five-hour car ride through gorgeous terraced rice fields from the stultifying heat and humidity of the official capital. What we left, scarring the capital's heart, was a wide *kali*, or canal, that served simultaneously as a washing machine, swimming pool, and toilet. Next to a woman on her knees washing her laundry, I saw a young boy peeing into the *kali*. Foul odors wafted through nearby open-air restaurants. If there were complaints from fussy tourists, they were generally ignored. *Betjaks*, or cycled rickshaws, nicknamed *Paris, Sin-Sin*, and even *Morris*, sliced their way through hot, narrow streets. Most rides cost five rupiahs, bargained down from a starting price of ten. The bargaining was an assumed part of every negotiation. Many people wore straw hats, protection against the brutal tropical sun. Killer mosquitos buzzed incessantly. Jakarta seemed busy and yet listless, a place for slow transactions in business and diplomacy but also a place to leave, if one could, and we did.

What I sensed in Jakarta but learned in Bandung was that the roughly 3 million overseas Chinese who had been living in Indonesia for hundreds of years, even during the 300-year-long era of Dutch colonialism, controlled the economy of Indonesia in much the same way as the Chinese controlled the economy of Thailand. They were the cooks, the librarians, the businessmen, and the bankers. No matter how long they had lived in Indonesia, they remained clannish, at home speaking Chinese, the language of the motherland, but on the streets speaking Bahasa Indonesia, the native language of the people of Indonesia.

The Chinese were everywhere, and they did everything, as in Thailand. If I wanted to buy a shirt, I'd go to a Chinese haberdasher. If I wanted to buy a book, I'd go to a Chinese bookstore, one of the many showing Peking's propaganda. If I wanted to buy an aspirin, I'd go to a Chinese drugstore. If I wanted to enjoy an ice cream, I'd go to a Chinese ice cream parlor. In other words, I was completely dependent on the Chinese businessman, the middleman of the Indonesian economy.

And so too were the 87 million Indonesians, who had begun by the late 1950s to resent their dependence on the Chinese but had not yet been able to come up with an alternative economy. They were frustrated. They demanded anti-Chinese action. The authorities in Jakarta momentarily shook off their customary lethargy and took a series of awkward, ineffective actions designed to undercut the omnipresent power of the ethnic Chinese community. At times feelings rose to such passionate levels that it was easy to imagine a collision between the new nationalism of the average Indonesian and the continuing clout of the ethnic Chinese, who more and more seemed to tie their future to mainland China rather than to the government under which they lived.

"Look in their homes," an Indonesian politician told me, "and you'll find pictures of Mao Tse-tung, or you'll see the Chinese communist flag pinned to a map of Indonesia. No, this is not right."

Another politician said, "They are a fifth column, and the Chinese communists have begun to push their weight around as if they owned Southeast Asia. Our Indonesian Chinese will do their bidding right here."

Still another added, "Put it any way you like. The problem is very simple. Peking can use the overseas Chinese for their own national ends."

On July 1, 1957, Jakarta put out the word that all "aliens" would henceforth have to pay an annual tax of 3,000 rupiahs per family. "In Indonesia," a veteran newspaperman told me, "an 'alien' is a Chinese." Of course, the Chinese didn't see it that way, and didn't pay.

On September 15, 1958, Jakarta "nationalized" many "alien" clubs, schools, banks, and even homes. Again, who was an alien? The Chinese, of course.

On May 14, 1959, Jakarta banned all aliens from retail trade in rural Indonesia. The ban existed more in name than in fact, but Peking still accused Jakarta of "subjecting" ethnic Chinese "to the most cruel treatment . . . as nationals of a hostile country."

As Indonesian relations with communist China worsened, Russia saw an opportunity, knocked on Jakarta's front door, and offered a helping hand. Russian diplomats, all singing from the same sheet of music, began calling Indonesian diplomats with sweet, whispered messages of friendship and encouragement. First, the Russians claimed that they did not share Peking's powerful opposition to the rural ban on ethnic Chinese. Then the Russians objected to the recent Chinese crackdown in Tibet. Finally, they proposed a "radical restructuring" of Soviet-Indonesian relations, starting with a new trade and cultural agreement and perhaps a Khrushchev visit.

"Clearly," explained one experienced Indonesian diplomat, "Khrushchev wanted to persuade Asia that China was one thing and Russia another." Though they were both communist, Russia and China were guided primarily by their national needs, which led inexorably to differing interpretations of communist ideology. In turn, these differences in ideology, which were becoming increasingly apparent, led to a weakening in the once unified alliance between the two communist giants.

A Balinese prince, who once served in the Indonesian government but now preferred the air-conditioned comfort of his parlor, served tea and wisdom as he examined the future of the Sino-Soviet alliance. "Russia," he explained, "was fast becoming a 'have' nation, while China is still, undeniably, a 'have-not' nation. You Westerners may think of this distinction in economic terms, and that's fine, but Marxists believe this distinction leads inevitably to antagonism and conflict. I believe that a break between Russia and China is inevitable."

I ventured the opinion that a "break" might be too harsh a prediction. "Perhaps 'split'?" I suggested.

The prince smiled tolerantly. "Split? Yes, that is for sure, but remember it will come, this split or break, at any time; and when it does come, it will come suddenly, dramatically, without any warning."

The prince seemed to be speculating that when the split

came, it could lead to a war between Russia and China. I did not share his dark vision. War was always possible, given their long history of suspicion and antagonism, but I suspected that Mao would do his utmost to avoid war, knowing that war would interfere with his plans for modernizing China, and Khrushchev would also try to avoid war, knowing that the Russian people, still remembering the horrors of World War II, would do anything to avoid another major war.

On the evening before our departure for Hong Kong by way of Singapore, Phyllis and Bernie hosted a fabulous farewell party for Mady and me. They invited Indonesian officials and diplomatic friends. Food and drink were plentiful; just as important, insights and debates flowed with an intense intellectual excitement. Everyone had a great time. Bernie had earlier urged me to "hold nothing back. Run your ideas, whatever you've learned here, run it past them." So encouraged, I shared with a number of guests what the retired prince had told me about how the activities of the ethnic Chinese of Indonesia were leading to a weakening of the Sino-Soviet alliance and possibly a war. Not that war was the intent of the ethnic Chinese, the prince had warned, but that might be the result, no matter their intent.

I wondered, would the guests agree?

The Indonesian officials did not agree. They all felt the prince was reaching too far, that his evidence was scanty, and his projection of war too alarmist. The Indonesian journalists expressed fascination with the prince's speculation, but they were clearly hesitant about jumping to conclusions. One or two, I thought, might write a story about it, but the others agreed with the officials. They said the speculation was interesting, even compelling, but it was still speculation, it lacked evidence, and therefore was not, in their judgment, a legitimate news story.

After dinner, over yet another cup of tea, the four of us—Phyllis, Mady, Bernie, and I—continued discussing the prince's thinking about the Sino-Soviet alliance. Not surprisingly, Bernie urged caution. He said the prince's speculation was interesting and might in time even prove to be true, but at the moment it was only speculation, lacking the fiber of hard data. He sensed that was the direction of my thinking, and he was right. "Well," I acknowledged, "I was thinking about a possible broadcast—that's true, but for now I'll hold off. No rush." I did not want to end our evening or our visit on a sour note. I'd never disagreed with my brother on anything. "Anyway I promise. I won't do anything until we get to Hong Kong."

"Good," Bernie sighed. "Phyll and I will also be in Hong Kong next week, and we can talk about it then. Right?"

"Right."

I adored my brother. He'd been my guiding light in so many ways. He was also a foreign correspondent for the *New York Times*, and I was still trying to become one for *CBS News*. Thinking about it more, I concluded, reluctantly, that he was probably right about the prince's speculation, and I was wrong. Still, I could not shake the feeling that on this story I might be the one who was right.

So, what to do?

I punted.

I thought I had an important story, but I would wait until we reached Hong Kong, where CBS had a bureau. There, I'd give it another thought, maybe even change my mind; anyway, nothing until then.

At the airport the next morning, when we were preparing to leave Jakarta for Singapore, clearly Bernie was still uneasy about whether I'd do a broadcast. "We'll talk again in Hong Kong, right?" he said, his arm protectively around my shoulder. "Nothing till then."

"Right," I replied, giving him a fraternal peck on the cheek. "I won't do anything till then."

———

SINGAPORE, often called the "Jewel of the South Seas," was a small, sparkling island-nation of 1.5 million connected by causeway to Malaya and by political and cultural sympathies to communist China, even though its rapid economic heartbeat was decidedly capitalist. Most of the inhabitants were Chinese, half under the age of twenty-one. Its prime minister, Lee Kuan Yew, a bright thirty-six-year-old, Cambridge-educated lawyer, was as anti-communist as he was anti-colonialist. "I come from a country," he joked, "where 90 percent of the people don't speak English but where all the traffic signs say 'HALT.'"

Singapore, though part of the British Commonwealth of Nations, was a completely Chinese city, inspired by the words and actions of Mao Tse-tung. When we arrived and checked into the Raffles Hotel (where else?), a local journalist told us that the communists were getting to be so "powerful" he would "not be surprised" if they staged a coup, seized power, and established a communist system of government, possibly within the next few years. I was astonished by the boldness of his judgment.

He thought the quarter of a million students would be in the forefront of the revolution. They attended Chinese schools. Their courses were conducted in the Chinese language. They cherished Chinese culture. "As far as they're concerned," a visiting American teacher observed, "all of Southeast Asia will soon be 'liberated' by the Chinese communists. They await Mao as though he were a god, or some kind of infallible social genius."

Singapore's newspapers were distinctive in only one respect—they never criticized China. No matter what China did in Tibet or anywhere else, not a single word of criticism appeared. There was only, as one journalist put it, "praise, praise and then some more praise," as though China were a dear, proven friend. On the other hand, Russia was seen as foreign, distant, increasingly "bourgeois" and unmistakably Caucasian. China was the future, Russia the past.

A British diplomat, expressing what he called "the opinion of Asian communists," said that Maoism had become the relevant blueprint for social and economic revolution in Southeast Asia; Stalinism, by contrast, an outdated, almost discarded Russian blueprint. "Khrushchev runs around and boasts about his rockets, his consumer goods, as though these were accepted measures of social progress," the Englishman continued, "but Mao is much more realistic. He knows he has a revolution on his hands. This was no time for nonsense, just hard work, and this is what's impressed the Asian communists."

"What's the role of the overseas Chinese?" I asked.

"They're the key," snapped my English interlocutor. "Think of them as an advance scouting party. They land, they set up party headquarters, they propagandize, they gain control of the economy, they wait for their orders, knowing the orders will come one day from Peking, and then they'll act."

On an earlier visit to Southeast Asia three years before, many experts told me that Moscow and Peking were running neck and neck for the allegiance of the region's communists. Now, on this visit, I was being told that the race was effectively over—Peking had won. An uncomfortable expectation seemed to have settled on the resident diplomats and journalists that one day soon the whole region would turn communist. That was not what happened, but that was what they expected in the late 1950s. How could they have been so wrong?

————————

HONG KONG was the second best place to study China—that is, if you could not get into China. Like dozens of other Western reporters denied entry visas, I had to see China through a looking glass, and the image was often fuzzy, even distorted, but sometimes, from a place like Hong Kong, I thought I was seeing it with remarkable clarity. This beautiful Chinese island, run by the British since 1842, offered the visiting reporter an intriguing and informative collection of insights and history, color and style, unavailable anywhere else.

On any given day, a delightful scene could be caught on most of Hong Kong's arcaded sidewalks: the shapely, slender Chinese woman in a tight high-necked dress with long side slits sauntering on a shopping spree; not too far behind, another Chinese woman in bell-bottom pants and a pajama jacket, bent under the weight of bamboo shoulder poles carrying the day's food supplies; and, not too far behind both, an Englishwoman, head held high, shoes flat, haughtily surveying what she assumed was hers—in the near distance the granite slopes of Victoria Peak, nearer still the familiar colonial comfort of Repulse Bay, where she probably lived, and directly in front of her, the appealing sight of British destroyers lounging with deceptive nonchalance in Hong Kong's busy bay as scores of Chinese junks rushed among them in frenzied commerce.

We stayed at the Foreign Correspondents Club, a home away from home set in an old, airy colonial mansion on a rolling, green hillside. It played the part of a hospital in a 1955 Hollywood movie, *Love Is a Many Splendored Thing.* On its elegant verandas, over breakfasts, lunches, or late afternoon drinks, the club noted throughout the colony for its superb food and exquisite service, reporters and their guests gathered to exchange stories and secrets, boast about exclusives, and gossip about family and friends. Much was learned, even in a relatively brief stay. I for one learned about the sources "you just have to meet," the diplomats, who have "just returned from Peking," and the tailor who needed no more than twenty-four hours to make and deliver two suits, a sports jacket, and three shirts, all for $50, a Hong Kong bargain considered by some to have more lasting value than an exclusive about the Sino-Soviet alliance.

From them—the sources, the diplomats, even the tailor—I learned that to grasp the underlying reality of the alliance, one had to add a psychological component to the analysis. As one Chinese scholar put it, "Russia and China are not just two nations with different histories and cultures; they are also two psychologies and two races." The scholar sounded like de Gaulle, stressing the importance of racial differences.

Just as I had done in Russia in 1956, translating and analyzing the Soviet press, so too did Tom Tsiang for the Union Research Service. His cluttered Kowloon office resembled mine, only his office was a mess of copies of *People's Daily*, mine a mess of *Pravdas*. Not only because we shared a similar background, I found Tsiang's analysis to be compelling. "The Sino-Soviet alliance? That's what you want to know about?" he asked, playfully stroking his whiskerless chin. "It's never going to last." He grinned at his comment.

"That's a rather rash statement for a scholar," I grinned back at him.

"Not really," he explained, getting serious. "The alliance can't last, because the Chinese and the Russian people are too very different people—in background and in race. Race is very important." He paused for only a moment. "They smile today, but they'll fight tomorrow. Just wait until the Chinese feel they don't have to depend upon the Russians any longer. Just wait. You'll see."

Another expert on China was Father Ladany, a tall, thin, highly respected priest, who had led a Catholic parish in China since the 1949 revolution. He agreed with the thrust of Tsiang's analysis—that once the Chinese felt they did not need the Russians any longer, they would find an excuse to dump them. "The truth is, they really don't like Russians."

Father Ladany continued, "In 1949, when the Russians first started coming to China, bringing aid, the Chinese were grateful. They thought of them as friends. But then the Russians began buying up everything in Chinese stores. This surprised the Chinese. 'These *advanced people* come here, and they buy up everything in *our* stores. Maybe they're not as wonderful as we thought.'" Father Ladany stopped, suddenly broke into a contagious laugh, before continuing, "The Russians isolated themselves, and the Chinese didn't like this. They lived in their own guarded communities. They didn't speak Chinese, very few of them anyway. And they were actually barred from fraternizing with the Chinese. What happened was the Chinese had the deepest feelings of suspicion toward the Russians. Didn't trust them."

It was not until June 24, 1959, a few months before our visit to Hong Kong, that the Russians and the Chinese finally reached a general agreement, after nine years of negotiating, to allow Soviet consulates to be set up in China. There was no agreement on location, number, or function. No agreement either on whether China could open any consulates in the Soviet Union. "Mutual suspicion," Father Ladany commented, "it runs very deep, and only seems to get deeper."

Peggy and Tillman Durdin, who covered China for the *Times* for more than twenty years, carried Father Ladany's analysis one step further. In their view, the Chinese never liked the Russians, not even immediately after the revolution, when they truly needed Soviet aid. "The Russians have always been considered gauche, lacking any civility," Peggy said. "Maybe Till won't agree, but that's what I think." Till added, "I don't disagree, but I would just add that there will be no war between the two so long as China needs Soviet support, and probably there'll be no break between the two either."

An American diplomat who studied Chinese history and spoke Chinese fluently referred to the Sino-Soviet alliance as a "marriage of incompatibles." At my suggestion, we met at the Foreign Correspondents Club, now my office in Hong Kong. The diplomat readily agreed (adding he "always loved" the club and besides, he wanted to save me the "inconvenience" of having to go "all the way to the Consulate"). "The psychological differences between them," the diplomat said, "are deep and consequential. And when 'white Russia' marries 'yellow China,' that raises serious questions and problems in the alliance."

But, the diplomat continued, now echoing the State Department's official line, "that doesn't mean there will be a 'break' in the alliance. Not at all. They share a common worldview. They are both Marxist. They see the world moving in a certain direction, which they approve of. And they think they're both moving in the same direction."

The diplomat stopped for a moment to light a cigarette. "You know I'm not sure I believe what I'm about to tell you. But I think that the Chinese have now taken over the ideological leadership of the communist world. That's a big deal. It might lead to a break in the alliance, with all that could mean in many parts of the world." Again he smiled, thinking perhaps that a smile could also serve as a mask. "I think you know there is a school of thought here in Hong Kong that the Chinese will break from the Russians when they achieve economic self-sufficiency. What I'm adding now is that they may do that even before achieving economic self-sufficiency."

"Let's say for a second that they do make such a break," I wondered. "When do you think that might happen? Soon?"

"That's for you to figure out. And when you do figure it out, let me know." He laughed.

Late that evening, on the same veranda, after a fabulous Cantonese dinner (we could select from hundreds of fish in a huge fish tank the one we wanted for our main course), I told Bernie what I'd been learning about the Sino-Soviet alliance on this trip: what I thought was new and exciting, what was old, and what seemed to confirm what I thought I already knew. I was on a roll. "I'm thinking . . . ," I continued, as though setting up the main point.

Bernie had been listening patiently, occasionally nodding, or, depending on the point I was trying to make, turning especially serious. "I'd still wait," he interjected. He had anticipated where I was going. "Why not? If the story of a possible break is as solid as you think, it'll hold for another day or so, even a week or so. Why not wait until you're back in New York and you can discuss it with Blair Clark or Murrow? Why rush?"

"Bernie, I'm not rushing. I've been sitting on this story for months. I've been reading everything. I've been talking to experts all over the world. I'm not rushing. I just feel I'm right. The time's right. Hong Kong's the right place to break the story. I'll never know more about any other story I do than this one."

Bernie sat in deep thought, elbows on knees, and then, after what seemed like minutes but was probably only a few seconds, he said. "Then do it."

I sent a telegram to New York, suggesting a radio analysis about the growing split in the Sino-Soviet alliance. The idea was accepted. A time was set for a Hong Kong–New York circuit for noon the next day.

I spent half the night writing the piece, which ran a minute-thirty. I'd learned over the last year or two that much could be crammed into a minute-thirty radio analysis, but I'd also learned not to overload the circuit. I decided to emphasize only a few of the things I'd picked up on our trip: The Sino-Soviet alliance was showing signs of splintering apart, despite the judgment of the State Department and other foreign ministries that it still represented a powerful, unified force. On the surface, the problems were ideological: how to manage the legacy of Stalin and how to incorporate communes into the building of communist societies, including the unmistakable rise of China over Russia in Asian communist parties; but, deeper down, the problems, when more closely examined, were rooted in national interests. Russia, for example, siding with India in 1959 and not China, its ideological partner.

Only when I finished writing my piece did I realize I had but one copy of the script. I couldn't find any carbon paper.

We took a cab to the CBS office in downtown Hong Kong. I

was quickly hooked up to New York. Much to my delight, the editor at the other end was my "old friend," Hal Terkel, who not only accepted my piece, he seemed impressed by it. "A really first-class piece, Marvin. Congratulations!" he said happily. "I'll make sure Blair [Clark] and Ed [Murrow] hear about it." I thanked him.

"When are you coming home?" he asked before cutting the circuit.

"In a few weeks."

"We miss you," Hal said.

Later, when I wanted to show the piece to Mady, I realized that I had left my only copy in the CBS studio. Apparently, having finally done the piece, I was enveloped in a profound sense of satisfaction and relief, and I simply forgot to take the script with me. This was to happen many times over the next few decades. But, in this opening round of my career, I knew that I'd done a solid piece from Hong Kong, another to add to my expanding file; and I knew I had the story line for another book. (*Dragon in the Kremlin* was published in 1961.) This was a story I felt I owned, and I'd finally done it.

There were two relevant and important elements to the story that I had deliberately omitted. One was a recent rush of hushed speculation in Hong Kong that the differences between the Chinese and Russian communist parties had become so intense they had led to an open rupture in the top leadership of the Chinese party, and the other was that the Chinese were close to developing their own nuclear bomb. (They did five years later in October 1964.)

I had heard reports of both possibilities but could not confirm either. Nor could Bernie or any other reporter I knew. I wondered: where might one go for clearer insight and understanding of these two possibilities? Taipei for politics, Tokyo for the bomb, I was told.

Mady and I left for Taipei the next morning.

TAIPEI, at first glance, looked like an overgrown Chinese town, bursting at the seams with the best and worst of American largesse. It was also the capital of Taiwan, a lush, semitropical island about 100 miles of rocky waters east of the Chinese coast. Since 1949, when Mao's communists seized power in China and Chiang Kai-shek's defeated Nationalists fled to Taiwan, the American Seventh Fleet had been positioned in these waters between China and Taiwan to protect the island from a possible though unlikely communist assault. With the fleet came the sailors, their support system and American diplomats, businessmen, and students, and Taipei was quickly crowded with juke boxes, Coca Cola, dance halls, and strip joints. The United States pumped billions into the economy. Stores were flush with consumer goods, and restaurants required reservations. Traffic signs on the main thoroughfares were in English. The second language in Chinese schools was English. Education was free and compulsory. Elections were regular but hardly meaningful, since Chiang's Kuomintang party controlled the results. Opposition was allowed so long as it was tame. Chinese women set the fashion style, which naturally reflected Main Street America. They preferred matching skirts and blouses to the high-necked, side slit dresses of Hong Kong.

Doors opened for American visitors. When I told the hotel concierge that I was a reporter interested in Chinese communist politics, he produced a string of interviews with prominent scholars and politicians. To some degree or another, they all mouthed the party line, some more blatantly than others: they were to "return" to positions of power on the mainland; they just did not know when. Still they seemed so knowledgeable about Peking's politics that I thought it was in my interest to listen carefully and then discard what I considered contrived.

The Taiwan judgment of the Russian-Chinese alliance was warped from the start, I thought, by a simplistic view of Mao as a "puppet," a "running dog of Russian imperialism." But, with time, this judgment evolved into a more sophisticated appreciation of Mao and the problems he suddenly faced from other Chinese leaders. As explained by Chen Chien-chung, introduced to me as one of the "younger leaders" of the Kuomintang and an "expert on mainland politics," Mao's position as unquestioned leader was challenged by Liu Shao-chi, a Moscow-trained revolutionary who strongly disapproved of Mao's emphasis on the commune as the focal point of social and economic development. Like Khrushchev, Liu considered it an ideological abomination. The resulting Mao-Liu collision split the Chinese Communist Party into two camps.

By the time Mady and I left Taipei for Tokyo, the last stop on our round-the-world journey, we had also heard variations of the Chen analysis, and we both came to the same conclusion. A communist government could not exist with two leaders. It had to be either Mao or Liu, and we were betting on Mao. Along the way, we had heard of a compromise formula being pieced together in Peking that left the commune in place in the rural areas of China but not in the urban areas. By not eliminating the commune as a key factor in both the rural and urban development of China, Mao left the irritant in the Sino-Soviet alliance that Khrushchev could not accept.

There was also that question about whether China was developing a nuclear weapon, and if it was, when would the rest of the world learn about it? In truth, by this time in our journey, we were both tired and eager to get home and back to the university. It was late September, and we'd been on the road since early June. Marco Polo had nothing on Mady, and I was trying to be at least as vigorously adventurous as Phineas Fogg. Onward to Tokyo!

————————

TOKYO proved to be a nonstop seminar on China's nuclear program, and understandably so. Of all the countries in the world, only Japan had experienced two atomic attacks. When its scientists, in the late summer of 1959, reached the startling conclusion that China was close to developing its own nuclear weapons, the Japanese government realized it faced a crucial strategic decision: should Japan also go nuclear, developing its own atomic bombs, or should it go "neutralist," which would lead to a break in its treaty obligations with the United States? Or, stay where it was.

On September 20, which was also the day of our arrival, a former Japanese prime minister, Tanzan Ishibashi, a liberal who sought better relations with everyone, stunned the political world in Tokyo with word that he had just signed an agreement with China's Chou En-lai, pledging both countries to "normalize" their relations and to "promote mutual friendship, strengthen mutual trust and improve existing relations." Of course, at the time Ishibashi held no official position, and the government quickly denounced the agreement.

Still, among many Japanese intellectuals, students, and journalists, who favored a "neutral Japan," Ishibashi became an instant hero. For many conservative politicians, he was a Quisling, ready to sell out Japan's national interests to an aggressive communist China. In the evening, protesting students filled the streets, demanding meaningful change in policy. They were not specific. "Anything but the status quo," they seemed to be saying. Only one thing was absolute—they abhorred the thought of war. Called the "orphan generation," the "offspring of Hiroshima," they believed in nothing. One student told us, "There is nothing, nothing in the world, that I would die for."

At the time, the diplomats had a pet expression, "for the time being," which they used with abandon to confuse the U.S. Embassy. "For the time being," they would say, "Japan is tied to the United States." Or, "for the time being, Japan accepts the U.S. policy of 'non-recognition of China.'" Or, "for the time being, Japan has no interest in acquiring nuclear weapons." Or, "for the time being . . . ," and so on. Clearly Japan was an unhappy ally, formally mouthing its devotion to the U.S.-Japan Mutual

Defense Treaty, but at the same time hinting and dreaming of other things.

As I hurried from one interview to another, whether at ministries, universities, or political institutions, I was able quickly to confirm what I had suspected—that nothing was more important to the Japanese specialist than China's rush to develop nuclear weapons; and not just nuclear weapons, I was solemnly reminded, but also the means of delivering them, the short-, medium-, and long-range missiles necessary for an attack. I would often ask for a timetable. Would China have a nuclear weapon in five years, or ten years? And just as often, I was told, two or three years, no longer. In other words, the experts believed Japan would soon have to cope with a nuclear-armed China.

The Japanese did not know exactly when, but they made a determined effort to find out, and they shared this intelligence with the United States.

First, in December 1956, they said, China conducted an underground nuclear test near Lanchow in Kansu Province.

Second, in October 1957, Kuo Mo-jo, president of the Chinese Academy of Sciences, publicly boasted that "soon" China would shoot a satellite into space. It did shortly thereafter.

Third, in 1958, China produced four small atomic reactors and two cyclotrons "on their own," suggesting that China had made "astonishing" scientific progress.

While the Japanese continued to dig for more scientific data on China's rapid advance toward nuclear weapons, they kept bumping into intriguing Chinese definitions of "limited" and "general" warfare. A limited war was usually fought between two nations, limited in geographic scope, not involving the use of nuclear weapons; a general war was usually regional, involving the interests of several nations, and possibly resulting in the use of nuclear weapons. To Japan, given its unique perspective on this prospect, a nuclear war was much more than a frightening prospect, a lot more horrific than a "war game" absorbing to military strategists; it instantly evoked hideous images of burning bodies in two totally devastated cities, Hiroshima and Nagasaki—images that were unlikely ever to be forgotten.

The Japanese strategist wondered: would Russia's attitude toward war be meaningfully different from China's? Japan had long ago back-benched the notion of a unified Sino-Soviet alliance, believing, especially after the recent India-China crisis over Tibet, that both communist giants saw the world through the prism of their own national interests rather than a commitment to global communism. Khrushchev and Mao had two radically different visions of war in the theoretical advance of global communism. To the Japanese strategist, Khrushchev, though a potential enemy, was considered a sensible, rational opponent of nuclear war. "The living," he had said more than once, would "envy the dead." His favorite slogan was "peaceful coexistence" between East and West.

Mao's vision of war was "weird," to use one scholar's description, tied to China's massive population. Foreign Minister Chen Yi, reflecting his master's vision, once told an Indian minister: "We are not afraid of a nuclear war. We do not share your moral compunction about the sacredness of life. If the United States were foolishly to attack the Chinese People's Republic, then atomic weapons would be used; Russia would be dragged into the war, whether she likes it or not; and do you know what would happen? The United States and Russia would both be destroyed. We might even lose 300 million people. But so what? We would still be left with over 300 million people—and we would be the strongest power on earth." Mao was also heard making the same point, but could he possibly mean what he said? Could a leader really be so casual about the loss of half of his population? Or, by projecting this image of casual indifference, was he just trying to frighten the United States and Russia? And Japan? Of course, no one really knew, but at the same time no one wanted to test the possibility that he meant what he said.

It was not only the Japanese who worried about China, nuclear weapons, and war, "limited" or "general"; at the U.S. Embassy, which looked like a fortress, American diplomats seemed equally absorbed with understanding Mao's vision of nuclear war and at the same time China's progress toward developing nuclear weapons. The Americans were reluctant to share any information or intelligence about China's nuclear progress, but, as sometimes happens, a friend or fan might see no harm in helping a reporter, and one such friend quietly gave me two classified reports, neither one of which deserved the designation. Both did, however, offer some insight into official American thinking about China and the bomb.

According to one report, China was on the edge of joining the ranks of eleven other nations that already had the scientific and technological capacity to produce nuclear weapons. In five years, an additional twelve nations would have this capacity.

According to the other report, it cost a lot of money to make an atomic bomb, but China had the money and the desire. A "small atomic bomb" would cost about $50 million—"maybe less, if she really does have three or four, or more, atomic reactors producing plutonium as a by-product." Quoting one American scientist, "Once you know it can be done, there are all kinds of shortcuts you can take—and get to the same end. I should think the Chinese could have their bomb in 1961—at the latest." It took the Chinese three additional years to explode a nuclear bomb, probably because the Russians refused to help them; but when we visited Japan in September 1959, it was already clear from the evidence Japan had accumulated that China was on its final approach to having a nuclear bomb it could justifiably call its own. And with the bomb, China could and would change the strategic balance of power in Asia.

For Mady and me, it was room service the night before our departure for New York. We had too much to do, too much to pack, too many people to call to say thanks once again for all the meals, contacts, insight, and information so generously provided during our time in Tokyo, the last of the thirteen places we had visited on this extraordinary trip around the world. I needed an extra suitcase for the papers, notes, and magazines I had picked up along the way, making the usual uncertainties of packing even more problematic. For dinner, we ordered hamburgers, thinking we ought to prepare for our return to America. We both knew we were concluding an exceptional trip. Maybe there'd be another, but we doubted that. We were grateful for this one, and we decided we'd take life one step at a time. The next step for us was Columbia University and then maybe Moscow. Maybe.

A DREAM COME TRUE

"And where the hell have you been?"

Ralph Paskman, CBS's foreign editor, was a force of nature. On any given day he could be gruff, impatient, even, on occasion, cruel; but, when the need was obvious, he could also be splendidly efficient, determined, and devoted to solving the problems of daily journalism. And, as I was later to learn, there was within him (well hidden, of course) a flicker of a generous soul that would on rare occasions sparkle with an unexpected, glorious act of kindness.

But, on this particular morning in late September 1959, when I re-entered the CBS newsroom after an absence of almost four months, Paskman was in one of his foul moods.

"Khrushchev's in the United States, making big news," he exploded, "and our famous Khrushchev expert isn't anywhere to be found." Sarcasm dripped from every word.

"Ralph," I started to explain, "I thought . . . "

He interrupted, "We were looking all over for you. All over. This is supposed to be your story—right?—and we couldn't find you." He looked genuinely angry. "Where the hell have you been?" Not waiting for an answer, he spun around and walked briskly toward his office, one of a small number flanking the newsroom. I followed him.

For a moment, I was tongue-tied, utterly baffled. Was he really saying that CBS wanted *me* to cover the Khrushchev visit, and I couldn't be found? I was flummoxed. I knew about the Khrushchev visit, of course. During our stop in Moscow, I even had a hand in breaking the story. But, as it happened, while I was hopscotching around Southeast Asia studying rifts in the Sino-Soviet alliance, Khrushchev was hopscotching around the United States—and, bad luck, I knew nothing about CBS wanting me to help cover his visit. I'd received no telephone call, no cable, no nothing. For such an assignment, I'd have instantly broken off my Asia trip and returned to New York.

Awkwardly, I stood in front of Ralph's desk and didn't know what to say. My trip around the world was no secret, certainly not at CBS. My CBS Fellowship was no secret. (CBS had even issued a public announcement about it.) John Day knew about the trip—I'd told him. Ackerman knew about it. Murrow knew. Clark knew. I thought everyone knew. But, obviously, on this particular matter, Paskman knew nothing.

I tried to explain, hoping he'd listen. "Last spring, I got one of these CBS Fellowships," I began, "and left in early June for a trip around the world. I've been researching a book on the Sino-Soviet alliance. Mady and I only got back yesterday, and I just wanted to stop by today to say hello. Classes have already started at Columbia."

Paskman looked puzzled, and I quickly apologized. "I should have given you an itinerary. I should have shared our plans. I should have told you. It's my fault."

"No, not your fault at all," Ralph said, slowly searching the floor for invisible scraps. "Maybe one day the top management here at CBS," he pointed to the offices on the rim of the news-room, "maybe one day those of us who run a newsroom will actually talk to one another." He then started reading one of the many memos on his cluttered desk. After a while, he glanced up. "Enjoy Columbia," he said, dismissing me. I noticed a faint smile forming on his otherwise frowning face.

Our year at Columbia started normally but ended in a whirlwind of dramatic change. By mid-May 1960 we were suddenly dropped into Moscow breathless, thrilled, and soon to be challenged as never before in our lives.

According to our original plans, we were to be attending classes, enjoying lunches, sharing insights and impressions, living the life of privileged graduate students in New York: Mady beginning her final ascent toward a PhD (she had already received her master's degree, plus a certificate from the Russian Institute), me delving more deeply into Russian history and politics and writing my book on the Sino-Soviet alliance. And, for a time, that was indeed the life we led.

We had a lovely apartment, conveniently located on Gramercy Park South. We had a car. We had each other. Often we would attend the same classes, read and discuss the same books on Soviet policy, enjoy the company of our friends; we even made time on weekends for miniature golf, our favorite movies, and more than a few cocktail parties, many of which Mady hosted in our apartment with the same skills and enthusiasm her mother displayed at her legendary South Orange parties. We invited students and even faculty, and many accepted. Perhaps because I had a budding reputation as a "specialist on Soviet affairs" at CBS News and my first book, *Eastern Exposure*, had been well received, perhaps because our round-the-world journey had raised more than a few eyebrows at the Russian Institute, perhaps because Mady was such an exceptional student there, perhaps because we were all absorbed with the pressures of the Cold War and shared many of the same anxieties—for whatever reason, Mady and I were able to establish lasting friendships with a few of the impressive professors at the Russian Institute.

Early on, we met a great teacher and mentor in Alexander Dallin, who taught Soviet foreign policy. We also met Ernest Simmons, whose courses on Russian literature were delightful excursions into the worlds of Tolstoy, Dostoevsky, Chekhov, and many other Russian writers. John Hazard opened our eyes to the functioning chaos of the Soviet government. Abram Bergson helped us try to make sense of the Soviet economy, though that was a subject that defied even superhuman efforts at comprehension. Geroid T. Robinson was the esteemed professor of Russian history, who founded the Russian Institute in 1946. His love of history was matched only by his devotion to the institute. With funding from the Rockefeller Foundation, he created the first academic institute specifically designed to study all aspects of Soviet power, from military to economic, from historic to literary, and to develop a fresh cadre of specially trained American scholars of the Soviet Union, recognized at the time as America's major strategic adversary in the Cold War. Harvard's Russian Research Center, where I studied, started two years later but shared the same goal. In both places, graduates generally ended up teaching about Soviet policy or working for the U.S. government. "Know Your Enemy" was more than a slogan; it was also a pathway to a good job.

In addition to meeting the institute's professors and deepening her knowledge of the Soviet Union, Mady also, on a parallel track, sharpened her interest in international law. She met professors Philip Jessup and Richard Gardner and seriously considered a career in international law. But she changed her mind and swung more decisively into Soviet studies when she was advised that a woman would have trouble breaking into the field, especially if the woman happened to be Jewish.

In late November the Soviet Embassy in Washington unwittingly broke into the sweet hum of our academic routine. It informed CBS that it could reopen its Moscow bureau. All the network had to do was request a visa for the new Moscow correspondent. The embassy left the impression the request would be granted. A year before, CBS had broadcast a controversial drama, called "The Plot to Kill Stalin," which infuriated the Russians and prompted the expulsion of correspondent Paul Niven and the shuttering of the bureau. Then, as Khrushchev sought to improve relations with the United States following his successful American tour, the Russians decided that they needed CBS as much as CBS needed them. NBC was already in Moscow, and the Kremlin hoped that another major American network there would amplify coverage of Khrushchev's message of "peaceful coexistence."

For CBS, which, during this period of active East-West diplomacy, had suffered from the absence of a Moscow correspondent, the Soviet decision was a welcome one. Now the big question for the New York brass: who would be the new Moscow correspondent?

I learned about the Soviet decision one morning while casually reading the *New York Times*, and I wondered: could this be my moment? Did John Day think enough of me, my work, and my potential to name me Moscow correspondent?

I recognized this would not be an easy call for him and others in the CBS management. But could I help them make the right call? I had two choices, really. I could drop in on CBS, say hello to Hal Terkel and a few others, knock on John Day's door and remind him of my background in Soviet studies, my weekly "Soviet Digest," which he had fully supported, my help to Niven in Moscow during the Nixon visit, and my just concluded round-the-world fact-finding survey, hoping in this way that the idea might then just pop into his—or someone's—mind that I would be the right choice for Moscow. Or, I could do nothing; I could just wait, striking the totally misleading impression of a confident heir apparent, waiting for his just reward for a course of preparation well considered and well executed.

I waited, not because I had decided to wait but because I could not decide whether to wait—or not. Weeks of indecision passed. I spent my time in course work, in the library, or in writing my book, which I did in our apartment or on long weekends or school breaks at my in-laws' home in South Orange, where I was outrageously spoiled and became a passionate fan of ripe Jersey tomatoes, corn-on-the-cob, and grilled steak, prepared perfectly by the resident grill-master, my father-in-law, Bill Green. I also found the time (truly, I don't know where) to write book reviews and articles about Soviet literature and policy for the *Saturday Review*, the *Times*, and *Gentlemen's Quarterly*. I immensely enjoyed each opportunity.

Then, one day, a surprise invitation to a farewell party arrived from a veteran CBS correspondent, Larry Lesueur. He had been covering the United Nations for CBS for most of the 1950s. I had never met him. Lesueur, it said, would shortly be leaving for Moscow. It was, for me, a stunning, if disappointing, way of learning that CBS had decided, finally, that Lesueur was to be its man in Moscow. From my perch at Columbia, removed from CBS news and gossip, I had not known he was in the running. Only weeks later did I discover that ever since the Soviet decision to reopen the bureau, it had always been a two-man race between Lesueur and me.

Lesueur was apparently Day's choice. To his way of thinking, Lesueur was an experienced, accomplished reporter, a "Murrow boy" from his fearless reporting during World War II (indeed, he'd been the CBS Moscow correspondent early in the war), who was now restless at the UN and desirous of a new adventure. Day saw me as qualified for the job, but essentially inexperienced as a foreign correspondent. It was safer to go with Lesueur. My support came from Murrow, Clark, and few other anchors, who thought I had paid my dues, demonstrated I could live and work in Moscow, knew Russian, and believed CBS needed a fresh voice in the Soviet capital. They all admired Lesueur and ultimately went along with Day's decision, but favored me.

At the party, in a large, elegant New York apartment, Lesueur and his wife, Dorothy, a former newspaperwoman, were gracious, charming, and as happy as teenagers off to a music jamboree. Lesueur made a point of befriending me and discussing, among other things, what he saw in Moscow following the German retreat there in 1941. (Two years later, in a book called *Twelve Months That Changed the World*, he described the scene, "I watched the living soldiers pass by the dead at the roadside without a glance, and the dead scarcely looked human, . . . lying about in grotesque human postures, arms pointing toward the sky, legs frozen as though they were running.") Lesueur was now being given his chance for a second look, and he was very excited, telling me that he had applied for his visa a month before and was expecting it shortly. I could not help but share in his excitement, wishing him God's speed and many exclusives. I was disappointed, of course, but also certain Lesueur would be a very good Moscow correspondent.

Then, on February 25, for reasons that were never, to the best of my knowledge, adequately explained, the Russians abruptly decided that Lesueur was not to their liking. They rejected his visa application. At the same time, they said CBS could submit another name. There was nothing about the Soviet decision in the daily press. I knew nothing about it.

A few days later, Day called and asked if I could join him for lunch the following day. Day inviting *me* to lunch? "Sure," I replied, before he could change his mind. "Where?"

"Best if you come to my office at 1 p.m., and we'll leave from here," he said, and then added, "It's about Moscow, in case you're wondering."

"What about Moscow?" I still had the wit to ask.

"Oh, I thought you knew. The Russians turned down Larry's visa, and I wanted to talk to you about Moscow."

I was momentarily speechless, and Day ended our talk with a simple "See you tomorrow" and hung up.

I was in South Orange, absorbed with trying to explain the coming breakup of the Sino-Soviet alliance, when I realized I was still holding the phone. Then, with a jolt, the reason zoomed into focus. Day wanted to talk to me about Moscow. What about Moscow? Was it the job of Moscow correspondent? Of course, what else? Was he going to ask my advice about whom to send, meaning not me but someone else, which was always possible but unlikely, or was he going to say, in his blunt mid-Western way, "Marvin, the job is yours. Do you want it?" Day, having earlier chosen Lesueur but, for whatever reason, losing on that bet, was now going to offer the job to me. That was the likely scenario.

Mady was thrilled when I told her about Day's call. The two of us promptly shared the news with Rose and Bill, who were equally excited. At dinner we talked about nothing else, raising lots of questions, for which we did not yet have answers. When would we be leaving? Could Mady complete her PhD exams before we left? Could I finish my book? Even if I could, who would edit the manuscript and galleys while I was busy being the CBS correspondent in Moscow? What about our apartment? Our car? Our bills?

"Wait a minute," interrupted Bill, holding up both hands like a traffic cop. "We still don't know what Day's going to say to Marvin. We think we know, but we don't really know. Let's all calm down. We'll know soon enough."

And, of course, Bill was right. It all depended on what Day would tell me the following day.

I arrived early but waited until a few minutes after 1 p.m. before knocking on Day's open door. He was on the phone, but seeing me, waved me in. When finished, he stood up, extending his hand. "Marvin, I've got good news. We want you to be our Moscow correspondent, and we want you to leave as soon as possible. What do you say?" His face, usually etched in a permanent frown, broke into a broad grin.

"So, what do you say?"

The grin on my face was just as broad. After only a moment of reflection, I replied, "John, I'm honored, deeply honored. I'll do the best job I possibly can."

We shook hands. I was now "CBS News Moscow correspondent Marvin Kalb." All I needed was a visa. My professional dream had finally come true. Ever since my time in college, in Army intelligence and certainly when I was in graduate school, the goal of becoming CBS's man in Moscow was a fixed star in my universe, and now I had the opportunity. I was flush with self-confidence—but a realistic self-confidence. Though I had never been a foreign correspondent, and the Russians could always say "No," I knew I was ready for this assignment. I had already lived in Moscow, studied Russian history, spoke the language—I even "knew" Khrushchev. I was determined to be an outstanding Moscow correspondent, one my family would be proud of.

Seventeen stories down from Day's office at 485 Madison Avenue was Colbee's, the restaurant that was a CBS favorite more for its convenient location than for its chef's culinary skills. Whatever I ordered, I barely ate, so excited was I with the news of my appointment, which Day shared with any other CBS colleague we happened to meet on our way in or out. Day ate and drank well, stopping only occasionally to make two points. One was he wanted me at the four-power Paris summit scheduled for mid-May—where representatives from the U.S., the U.S.S.R., Great Britain, and France would convene; the other was his curious concern that the Moscow beat laid too heavy an emphasis on analysis, not enough on hard news.

"When do you think you can finish up at Columbia?" Day asked, impatiently. "If possible, I'd love to have you in Moscow before the May summit." When he paused between bites,

I jumped in with a few important points: first, I had to complete my book, and Mady had to take her PhD exams. Even at breakneck speed, I stressed, neither of us could possibly finish before early May; and, second, I would have to apply for our Moscow visas, and given our sorry experience with Lesueur, we couldn't be sure I'd get them.

For a moment, Day looked concerned and then thoughtful. "Of course," he said. "I was letting my enthusiasm get the better of me." He looked admiringly at his empty plate, crisscrossed his knife and fork, and leaned back in his chair. "You apply for the visas. Fingers crossed, we get them this time, and then we'll decide on a timetable. One thing, though—I want you in Paris for the summit."

"Absolutely," I agreed. "We'll be ready by then, for sure," making a commitment I hoped we could meet. "By the way, what did you mean by not getting enough hard news out of Moscow? Seems to me there's plenty of hard news out of Moscow, always has been."

"Yes," Day smiled, backing away from a question he had raised only a few minutes before. "Of course, you're right." Day clearly wanted our lunch to end on a note of optimism and excitement. And it did.

I walked Day back to his office. "If you have any problems," he said, shaking my hand vigorously, "just let me know."

"I shall, John. And again, thank you for this chance. I won't let CBS down, or you."

I immediately informed Murrow, Clark, and Terkel (they were delighted) and rushed, by subway to Columbia, where I gave Mady the good news. "I knew you'd get it," she exclaimed with pleasure and pride. "Let's start packing."

"Wait a minute," I cautioned, "still got to apply for a visa and then get one."

"Oh, you'll get one," Mady smiled, with a casual wave of her hand.

While waiting at Penn Station for the train to Newark and

then South Orange, I called my parents, who were also excited and proud but in very different ways. My instinctively cautious mother, born in Kiev and sadly experienced in pogroms, balanced her personal pride with a deep skepticism about anything Russian. Her reaction was one of subdued joy. My father, on the other hand, was unabashedly delighted. "I'm so proud of you," he said again and again. "I can't wait to hear your broadcasts from Moscow." He and my mother then asked the usual questions about when we'd leave, where we'd live; then, adding one only parents would think of asking: could they then really *see* and *hear* me from *Moscow*?

Listening to them, I felt a warm, indescribable glow of love and respect for my parents. They had given so much to me— often against odds that seemed insurmountable; now it was my turn to give something of meaning and value back to them.

Rose and Bill, like my parents, were incredibly pleased with the news, but with one unspoken reservation: their only true love, Mady, would soon be going off to Moscow, which in those days of East-West tension and nuclear threat carried a much more forbidding sound than it does today, and she could be in danger. Still, they understood Mady had to live her own life and follow her own intellectual passions. Her field was Soviet studies, and her time in Moscow, if properly used, could be immeasurably valuable in fashioning her career.

Bill uncorked a bottle of champagne (French, of course) and Rose prepared a sumptuous feast, and we later got down to the serious business of dividing up the many challenges involved in sending Mady and Marvin to Moscow in early May. Mady had to accelerate her PhD schedule, which, as a superb student, she felt she could do. I had to complete my book on the Sino-Soviet alliance without in any way compromising the quality of its research and writing. Rose volunteered to edit the manuscript, undertaking a responsibility that, for different reasons, proved to be frustrating and difficult but in her very capable hands meticulously performed. It was the best-edited book I have ever written. And together, Rose and Bill accepted the formidable task of closing down our New York apartment, which meant, among other things, moving our furniture from Gramercy Park to South Orange—no easy job.

But first the visa. The following day, the last day in February, with the help of the CBS Washington bureau, I formally applied for my Soviet visa. I did so, believing I'd get it, but remembering that Lesueur had also been optimistic about getting his visa. I routinely informed Day. He told me CBS was preparing to release a public announcement about my new assignment. "You'll like it," he said.

On March 7 the radio-and-TV-news reporter for the *Times*, Richard F. Shepard, wrote, "Marvin Kalb has been assigned to reopen the Columbia Broadcasting System's Moscow bureau. Mr. Kalb, a network news specialist in Russian affairs, will take up his new post as soon as he obtains his visa." Shepard then explained that Lesueur had earlier requested a visa and been denied one. "The Soviet Embassy gave no reason but invited the network to submit another name." He closed his report, saying "Mr. Kalb has been on leave at Columbia University on a CBS Foundation news and public affairs fellowship. He joined the network as a writer in the summer of 1957."

In mid-March, two weeks later, the Russians delivered. A press officer informed the CBS Washington bureau that my visa application had been approved and was available at the Soviet Consulate in New York or the Soviet Embassy in Washington. The bureau chief called Day, he called me, I called Mady and my parents and in-laws, and together we all entered a new, exciting and unpredictable phase of our lives.

Mady and I had essentially six weeks to finish our work—Mady her PhD exam, me my book. What would ideally take a year, Mady completed in a month. Dallin and a few other professors, enthusiastic about my new assignment, helped expedite the process by sidestepping some of the usual academic red tape, allowing Mady to concentrate on the substance. She passed with flying colors. I tried to follow her example by devoting myself fulltime to writing, emerging to eat and sleep when necessary. Dutton was my publisher (Roger Strauss saw no future in a book on the Sino-Soviet alliance), Curtis Brown was again my agent and Rose was my resident guardian angel, fact-checking, editing, and overseeing the sometimes tricky, frustrating transition from manuscript to galley to book.

Mady and I, by early May, were ready to move on to Paris and Moscow. At least, that was our plan.

10

THE PARIS SUMMIT: IKE VS. NIKITA

Nikita Khrushchev admired and respected Dwight Eisenhower as a World War II general and as president. "I do not doubt President Eisenhower's sincere desire for peace," Khrushchev told his Supreme Soviet on May 5, 1960, but "certain imperialist, monopolist circles" block his path. Even after an American U-2 spy plane was shot down over Sverdlovsk five days earlier, sending U.S.-Soviet relations into a dangerous tailspin, he still wanted to meet the president at the Paris summit. It was there—together, he thought—that he and Ike could settle the vexatious, deadly problem of West Berlin—"a bone in my throat," he called it. Khrushchev knew that Kremlin Stalinists and Mao himself were attempting to scuttle the summit, using the U-2 incident as a pretext, but he was determined, if at all possible, to proceed with the summit, his diminishing dream of a Berlin deal clinging by a thread.

But, from Washington came little reason to believe that his dream would be realized. The U-2 incident caught the United

States with its hand in the cookie jar. Trapped into admitting the obvious—that America spied on Russia, just as Russia had been spying on the United States—the White House tried unsuccessfully to cover its embarrassment. First, there were unpersuasive "Who? Me?" denials, which, with each day, lost every inkling of credibility when the Russians displayed the U-2 wreckage at a public exhibition. Then there were confusing statements by senior officials, which either awkwardly absolved the president of responsibility, placing it solely on the Central Intelligence Agency, or pinned the responsibility directly on the president. The administration looked pathetically inept; worse, it looked headless. Who was in charge? On May 11 Ike felt the need to act. He took full responsibility, saying the U-2 mission was a "vital necessity," though "distasteful," reminding Americans that "no one wants another Pearl Harbor." His meaning was clear—the spying would continue, but in other ways.

In this disjointed manner, the United States and the Soviet Union stumbled toward the Paris summit, neither superpower certain it would even happen.

––––––––––––

Through it all, I was burning with a desire to add to CBS's coverage of the building crisis. I thought I could have done radio analyses for Murrow or Blair Clark, but that was not to be. From morning to night, in the limited time I had between finishing my book and leaving for Moscow, I was huddled away with CBS technicians learning how to use a professional tape recorder and a 16mm camera. Moscow had the distinction of being a one-man bureau, meaning I would be playing the role of correspondent, bureau chief, cameraman, soundman, and driver, depending on the need of the moment. Tape recorders, I learned, had their own peculiarities (the one assigned to me certainly did), and 16mm cameras had an artistic temperament of their own, functionally acceptable for TV news but stuck unhappily between the amateur 8mm and the super professional 35mm. Some reporters, using the 16mm, could perform as a young Orson Welles, but others were what might charitably be described as "technologically impaired." I was in the latter category, but, after several days of patient tutoring, my tech colleagues promoted me. I was no Orson Welles, but I could manage a camera and a tape recorder with just enough skill to produce a piece for radio and TV, though that was yet to be proven.

Finally, on May 13, ready or not, I said my goodbyes to friends and colleagues at CBS, and Mady and I left New York on an overnight flight to Paris. In the early morning hours of May 14, as we drove from the airport to the Hotel Crillon, the French capital looked enchanting, the beauty of the city awakening to an uncertain summit scheduled to begin on Monday, May 16. CBS in those days of fat budgets booked its visiting correspondents at the Crillon, a luxurious five-star hotel fronting on the Place de la Concorde at the foot of the breathtaking Champs Élysées. Our room looked out at the American Embassy.

I immediately called the CBS office, eager to show off my high school French to the hotel operator. "*S'il vous plait,*" I pronounced each word as if it were a jewel, "*donnez-moi Élysée dix-huit quarante-sept.*"

"*Comment?*" asked the operator after a moment of hesitation.

I repeated, this time pausing after each word, "*Donnez-moi, s'il vous plait, Élysée dix-huit quarante-sept.*"

"*Comment?*" Her voice cracked and ached under the weight of French hauteur. "*Comment, monsieur?*"

Exasperated, I retreated into English, "Élysée 1847," I said grumpily.

"*Oui, monsieur,*" she snapped cheerfully, content in the knowledge that another American had bit the dust in his dismal effort to speak French acceptably.

When I finally got through to the CBS office, it sounded like a bustling marketplace of noise, news, and confusion. I asked for Ralph Paskman, the foreign editor, technically in charge of summit coverage, though Bureau Chief David Schoenbrun considered Paris to be his personal fiefdom.

"Who's this?" Paskman barked.

"Kalb," I replied, "I just got in."

"About time!" Paskman shouted, assuming the louder he shouted, the more power he projected. "There's a meeting here at 5. Be here." He then added, "I assume you know Khrushchev's arriving today. Macmillan's already here, de Gaulle of course, and Ike gets in tomorrow." Before I could say anything, Paskman hung up.

After a nap and a light, delicious lunch in the hotel restaurant, we set off on a leisurely stroll up the Champs Élysées, noticing along the way that many Parisians were enjoying their lunch in fashionable outdoor cafes, seemingly oblivious to the pre-summit tumult in nearby embassies. Diplomatic limousines zoomed up and down the magnificent boulevard, escorted by French police cars with wailing sirens. Worldly Parisians, accustomed to hosting major international events, seemed indifferent to the surrounding madness. We continued our stroll, absorbing the appealing sights and rarely pausing to catch our breath. It was as though we were still on our first date. Up the historic boulevard, at the very top, we could see the impressive Arc de Triomphe, a Napoleonic monument to French national honor. By the time we reached the arch, amazed by the number of avenues running into it, we realized we had passed the CBS office on the Rue Marbeuf, a small street off the avenue.

"Oh, my God." I slapped my forehead. "It's ten to 5. I don't want to be late."

We quickly doubled back to the Rue Marbeuf, arriving at the office just in time for Paskman's meeting, which didn't actually start until a half-hour later. I used the time to meet and greet a few of CBS's fabled foreign correspondents—

Schoenbrun from Paris, Alexander Kendrick from London, and Daniel Schorr from Bonn. We knew Dan best. He'd been my friend when we overlapped in Moscow, he for CBS, me for the American Embassy. He'd also attended our wedding. Dan kissed Mady, hugged me, and made a special point of introducing us to Schoenbrun, who acted as the genial, yet firm, host to the visiting CBS family.

I'd never been to a Paskman planning session, especially one planning network coverage of a four-power summit. I tried to look casual, but think I fooled no one. I was a newcomer to an exalted cast of experienced foreign correspondents. I knew it, and everyone else did too. We sat in a loose semicircle around Paskman's desk, listening and taking notes, as he outlined our responsibilities: Schoenbrun obviously was to cover Charles de Gaulle; Kendrick was to keep tabs on Harold Macmillan; Schorr had a broader mandate—what might be called the European angle; White House reporters George Herman and Robert Pierpoint would cover Eisenhower, when he arrived; and I was to look after Khrushchev. The idea was that if anyone came up with new information or insight, it was to be quickly transmitted to Paskman, who would then find a place for it in CBS's overall coverage on radio and television. Crucially important to each correspondent was who among them would be selected to do the lead story and who would do the others. Cooperation among the reporters was explicitly encouraged, but it was the competition among them that drove the day's agenda. Who could produce the best story? Who could come up with the big CBS exclusive that would send shivers of envy and anxiety through every other news organization?

A correspondent's contacts and sources were essential tools of the craft, especially when covering a summit. Schoenbrun had some of the best in Paris. He told us he'd been invited to a "deep background" session with the French foreign minister at 8 p.m. "Anyone interested? I'll try to get you in." He was being boastful but also helpful. Kendrick, not to seem outdone, said he had just been to a "deep backgrounder" with the British foreign secretary. "Happy to fill you in," he added. Schorr spoke of important "background" briefings he'd attended in Bonn. Apparently a "senior German official" had just returned from Moscow and thought he knew Khrushchev's Paris strategy. I listened and learned but was otherwise silent.

Terminology was critically important in the coverage of diplomacy. "Deep background" meant the reporter could use the information but never ascribe it to any source. It was as if he was writing on his own. "Background" meant the information could be sourced to "officials" or to a "senior official" but no names, please. Reporters understood the distinction, but, over the years, I was often surprised by the number of "officials" who would proclaim, as though knowledgeable, that they were speaking on "deep background," not "background," but did not really know the difference.

Paskman asked the big question before he ended the meeting: would there be a summit, or were we spinning our wheels? The consensus among the CBS reporters was that Khrushchev held the key to the success, failure, or collapse of the summit.

"Kalb," Paskman asked, "you have any ideas?"

I sat still, but my heart jumped. I had not expected the question. I told him I had not been briefed by anyone, not by the Russians, nor by any of the American officials who specialized in Soviet affairs. I could offer only my own opinion. I suspected Khrushchev was so eager for a Berlin agreement "of any kind" that he was probably prepared to swallow the U-2 humiliation, let Eisenhower off the hook, and proceed with the summit. Else, I asked, why would he be willing to come here?

"To blast the United States," Kendrick interjected. "A big stage for a major propaganda show." Schoenbrun and Schorr seemed to agree.

An idea popped into my mind. "Why don't I ask him?" I said to everyone's surprise. I remembered that Khrushchev often went on early morning walks when he was in a foreign capital. "Give me a TV crew, and tomorrow morning I'll go to the Soviet ambassador's residence, where Khrushchev's staying, and see first if he'll go for his usual walk and second if he'll talk to me." I was going out on a limb, and knew it.

"I'm short of crews," Paskman said, shaking his head, "and this could be a waste."

"Yes, it could be a waste," I agreed, "but I'd be happy to give it a try."

Schoenbrun came to my rescue. "Ralph, this is a damned good idea. I say, if possible, if you have an extra crew, go for it."

Paskman's head wandered lazily from side to side. "I still think it's a waste, but okay, let's do it," he mumbled, reluctance written all over his face. "What time?" he asked, "and where?"

"6 a.m. at 79 Rue de Grenelle," I quickly replied. "I'll meet the crew there."

As the meeting broke up, Schorr approached and patted me on the back. "Good idea, Marvin. Hope it works out for you."

"I do, too."

The next morning, my cab sped from the Crillon over the Seine into the Left Bank. Paris was dark, and the streets virtually empty. It was only a few minutes past 6 a.m., when I reached the Soviet residence on the Rue de Grenelle. The three-man CBS crew was already there, unpacking its gear across the street. They wanted to be ready if the large iron doors of the residence were suddenly to open and Khrushchev appear.

Philippe, the cameraman, was crew chief. He spoke English reasonably well, better than I spoke French, and we communicated easily. He worked with swift efficiency, and by 6:15 a.m., he and his crew stood like soldiers ready for action. Philippe held his precious 16mm camera on his right shoulder ("my bread and butter," he called it), checking the lens frequently. The soundman clutched a long extension pole, to which he had attached a microphone. The lightman held a small battery of lights, which he seemed to be testing every five minutes or so. The crew was obviously getting ready for a walk-along interview.

"When do you think he'll come out?" asked Philippe, anxious but also curious.

"I don't know," I said, shrugging my shoulders. "6:30, maybe?"

We stood in the middle of the street, waiting. Occasionally a car would pass. I looked at the elegant, three-story residence, which dated back to the early eighteenth century. For a succession of Russian ambassadors (Moscow bought it from French aristocrats in the mid-nineteenth century), it served as both residence and embassy. Only the large iron doors seemed out of place, the needs for security obviously taking precedence over the natural beauty of the embassy itself.

Philippe checked his watch, and again his lens. The darkness was beginning to fade into a pale light. It was almost 6:30 a.m. Would he now appear? Had I wasted Paskman's time and tolerance? The time passed, and the iron doors slept on.

A young Agence France-Presse (AFP) reporter joined us. He and Philippe engaged in a brief conversation. "What did he want?" I asked Philippe.

"He said he'd heard there was a crew here and thought maybe we had an interview all set. So he came over."

"What did you tell him?"

"Nothing, really."

Then Philippe asked, "Do you think he'll come out at 7?"

"Yes, if he comes out at all."

And he did. At exactly 7 a.m., the sun now peeking over the roof of the residence, the iron doors clanked and opened, and there he was—Khrushchev and two bodyguards. At first Khrushchev looked one way down the street and then the other, deciding which way to turn, before focusing on me, the CBS crew, and the AFP reporter.

"Well," he exclaimed, with what sounded like genuine surprise, "it's Peter the Great!"— remembering the nickname he had given me at the 1956 July Fourth embassy party in Moscow. Smiling broadly, I started walking toward him, but both bodyguards instantly blocked my path while reaching into their jackets. "No, he's a friend," Khrushchev laughed. "He's Peter the Great. He's good."

We started our interview as we walked along the still empty Rue de Grenelle. We made an odd-looking couple. I stood a slender 6'3", and Khrushchev was a round 5'6", if that. The cameraman, walking backward, filmed our conversation.

"Did you have a good flight?" I asked, getting started.

"Yes," he replied, "on an excellent four-engine jet aircraft, Russia's best." (The year before, he had flown to a Geneva summit in a two-engine jet, and he resented comparisons to the four-engine jet aircraft Western leaders had used.)

Keeping it light, I remarked, "You were here only two months ago on a state visit, and people may be thinking that maybe you wish to become a French citizen."

Khrushchev grinned. "No, no, no," he said. "I am a proud Russian, and always will be."

We were speaking in Russian. In those days, my Russian was quite good, though not fluent, but Khrushchev did not seem to mind. Unlike the Crillon Hotel operator, he appreciated the fact that I was making a sincere effort to speak his language.

We were approaching a boulangerie, rich with a captivating aroma. Instinctively, we both paused, sniffed, and smiled. "Mr. Chairman," I asked, "have you ever tasted a freshly baked croissant?"

"No. Is it really good, tasty?" he asked.

"Irresistibly so," I answered.

"OK then, let's have one."

I rushed into the store, Khrushchev only a few steps behind me, Philippe filming the scene. I purchased eight croissants, three for Khrushchev and his bodyguards, one for the AFP reporter, and the remaining four for the CBS crew and me. Bustling with barely contained excitement, Khrushchev bit into his croissant, like a youngster into a chocolate bar, and the widest grin spread across his face. "*Vkusno,*" he said, "*ochen vkusno.*" ("Delicious, really delicious.") The boulanger could not have been happier. He came out from behind his counter, extending a friendly hand. He asked a question that went right to the heart of the Paris summit. "Will we have peace, Mr. Khrushchev? Will we have peace at the summit?" Khrushchev held the boulanger's hand for an extra second. "I shall do my best," he replied solemnly. "But it's not only up to me."

It was now clearly my turn to question Khrushchev. The preliminaries behind us (the polite greetings, the croissant, the baker), I mentioned to Khrushchev, "You seemed especially angry the other day about the U-2 episode. I wondered whether you would even show up for the summit."

"Wouldn't you be angry?" Khrushchev shot an angry look at me. "The U.S. violated our sovereignty, after all, clearly violated our sovereignty. They offended our national honor, our pride, our dignity. We are the injured party, mind you, and you will have to apologize."

"But, you know, there has been no apology, and you're still here. Does that mean there will be a summit, even if there is no apology for the U-2?"

By this time we were walking back to the residence, slowly at first until Khrushchev picked up the pace. "We'll see," he said, lowering his head.

"You mean whether there will actually be a summit?"

Khrushchev kept walking.

I continued, "So there is still a big question mark in your mind about whether there will be a summit?"

We were approaching the iron gates in front of the residence. Khrushchev stopped. "Listen, and listen carefully," he said in a low growl, more in frustration, I thought, than anger. "I am here because the Soviet Union wants a peaceful solution to the Berlin crisis. We also want a disarmament treaty. We want peace, but I cannot do this alone. You violated our borders. You humiliated us. Is that what you want? Is that the way to peace? No, you must apologize." Khrushchev let a few seconds pass in silence. "You must apologize. How else can we achieve anything?"

"So, without an apology, no summit?" I persisted.

"We'll see," he repeated. "The summit doesn't open till tomorrow." We shook hands, and Khrushchev walked slowly back into the Soviet residence. I told Philippe to keep shooting until the iron doors closed behind him. Then I quickly did a brief on-camera close, my first as a CBS correspondent covering a foreign story. I did it in one take. Philippe, with a smile, pinned a new nickname on me—"One-take Kalb," he said in admiration. The nickname stuck for a long time.

By 8 a.m., dozens of other reporters began arriving at the residence. "Where's Khrushchev?" they wanted to know. "Has he already done an interview?" The crew and I made ourselves scarce. We retreated to Philippe's car, parked a half block away. We had an exclusive, a big one. Nothing was "live" then, and exposed footage had to be developed; so the key was to get the film to New York as expeditiously as possible. There was no 6:30 evening newscast on Sundays, but Eric Sevareid did anchor an 11 p.m. network news program. If we hurried and shipped the film to New York, it would arrive in plenty of time for it to be developed, and, I thought, I could then lay in a soundtrack from Paris. I'd have a scoop, and CBS would have a major exclusive on the eve of the summit.

Philippe called for a courier to pick up the film and ship it to New York on a late morning flight. From a nearby public phone, I called Paskman, who, as usual, was busy. I left a message for him. I said we had a really good story, Khrushchev demanding an apology before the summit could proceed. We had it alone. We're shipping the film to New York, and I would soon be heading into the office.

Dan arrived shortly before 9 a.m. I was delighted to see him. "I heard you got the interview," he said. "Tell me about it." He seemed as excited as I.

We got into the back seat of Philippe's car, and there, away from the other reporters, I told Dan the whole story, happy and thrilled to share it with him. He had helped me in so many different ways, mentoring me on what it meant to be a network correspondent. In Moscow, in 1956, he'd even offered me a job as his deputy in the CBS bureau. I described the boulangerie episode, my questions, and of course Khrushchev's demand for an apology before the summit could proceed.

"But he didn't say specifically that he wouldn't attend the summit without an apology," Dan emphasized, pinpointing a loophole Khrushchev could yet exploit.

"Absolutely, I agree. But he strongly implied it. Look," I went on, "he could still show up for the opening of the summit, and then blow it apart. He's angry. I think he's capable of anything."

"Well, we'll see," Dan said, stuffing his ever-handy notebook into his inside jacket pocket. "See you later." He thanked me and left.

I expressed my gratitude to Philippe and his crew. "Let's do this again," Philippe said. "I love exclusives."

"No more than I."

We laughed, and a moment or two later, I left, feeling elated. At first I decided to walk back to the office, literally dancing down the middle of the street, until, like a rocket, it hit me—I had a big exclusive! Enough dancing, get to the office! I took a cab the rest of the way.

Coincidentally, Schoenbrun and I entered the office at the same time. "How did it go?" he asked. "Did you get him?" Schoenbrun was short and bald, a bundle of barely contained energy. Blessed with a beautiful voice and boundless curiosity, he had become a superb broadcaster and a jewel in CBS's crown of European correspondents.

"Got him," I responded, as proud of my accomplishment as

he was of his Poirot mustache. "We got him, just the two of us. He said we had to give him a public apology for the U-2."

"Or else no summit?" Schoenbrun asked.

"That's not clear. Maybe a summit, maybe not."

"Well, congratulations anyway, Marvin. Terrific work. You got us off to a great start."

Schoenbrun went into his office, I in search of Paskman, who was, of course, on the phone. When he finished, he mumbled something like "Hold on for a minute" and raced into another office, screaming about a crew missing an assignment. I fidgeted, sat down, stood up, looked out the window, sat down again, until Paskman returned and started, as always, rearranging papers. But instead of congratulating me, as Schoenbrun had done, he asked where I'd been and why it had taken me so long to tell him what Khrushchev had said about the apology.

"Ralph," I objected, stunned as much by his tone as his questions, "I called you immediately. You were not available. Didn't you get my message? It was all there."

"Yes, I got it, but Dan was already here. He told me the whole story," his tone somehow suggesting not satisfaction with a CBS exclusive but questions about my tardiness in getting to the office. "Dan told me about Khrushchev, about the apology, about the summit. Anyway, Dan's going to do the big story for us tonight. I'm sure he'll include the Khrushchev interview. You can do radio."

In disbelief, I sputtered, "But Ralph, I got the interview, not Dan. It's my story."

"It's CBS's story," Paskman exclaimed with a feigned righteousness perfect for the occasion. "Not yours, not mine." He paused to repeat his decision. "Dan's doing the story tonight."

Angry, fearful I might burst into tears in Paskman's presence, I pivoted and stalked out of his office, left the bureau, found a small café on the busy Rue Marbeuf, ordered a hot chocolate, and watched the passing parade of Parisians for what must have been an hour or more. Many conflicting and troubling emotions raced through my mind. Paskman was an irrational bully, but Dan was my friend, in many ways my network mentor. I wondered, did he object when Paskman told him to do the Khrushchev story? Or did he, as a senior correspondent, a former Moscow bureau chief, feel entitled to the story? At the time, I felt what any good reporter would feel. I got the interview. I should be doing the story. But I learned that day that just as diplomacy follows a certain protocol, network news follows one, too. Senior correspondents get certain privileges, and junior correspondents, if they are lucky, may one day age into senior correspondents who enjoy a certain privilege or two of their own.

It was, in many other respects, a very busy day, leaving little time for moping. I returned briefly to the bureau, wrote and broadcast two radio spots featuring my interview with Khrushchev, and then joined Philippe's crew to cover Khrushchev's meetings with de Gaulle and Macmillan. At both, I later learned, he laid special emphasis on his demand for an American apology for the U-2 spy flight before the summit could proceed to the dangerous issue of Berlin, the same point he had made in my interview with him earlier in the day. With de Gaulle, he put it in the form of an official ultimatum. With Macmillan, he put it in angry words. Sidestepping an earlier ambiguity, he now left little doubt that without such an apology, there would be no summit. He also went two steps further, hardening his demand to include an American pledge to abandon all U-2-type surveillance and to punish those responsible for such aerial espionage. Khrushchev had brazenly upped the ante. He had allowed his anger, his hyped sense of Russian pride, to overwhelm his judgment.

On his approach into Paris, Eisenhower might have wondered which Khrushchev would he meet—the one who advocated "peaceful coexistence" or the one who threatened "class warfare." He was to learn soon enough that Khrushchev was in no mood for a serious, substantive summit. Vituperation was to replace negotiation. Shortly after his arrival, Eisenhower visited de Gaulle and Macmillan, satisfying protocol but also learning of Khrushchev's ultimatum. He realized he had to confer with his senior advisers, which he did until late into the night. One key question loomed before them. Should he apologize for the U-2 flight and in this way save the summit and perhaps advance prospects for a Berlin agreement? Why not? he asked. He had already decided to end the U-2 flights. Why not apologize? He and Khrushchev sat on the cusp of a major improvement in U.S.-Soviet relations. The American president was scheduled to pay a ten-day state visit to the Soviet Union in June, only a month later. Much was anticipated; much could be accomplished.

But Ike's team of senior advisers was adamant in its opposition to an apology, arguing that an American apology would be an unacceptable and unnecessary humiliation for a great power. No, they insisted, no apology. Surprisingly, the five-star general, the World War II hero turned president, shelved his own instinct for accommodation and yielded to their pressure. He would refuse to apologize to Khrushchev. The summit thus hung in the balance, as the four world leaders prepared for the formal opening on Monday, May 16.

On Sunday evening, the lights in the CBS Paris bureau burned late as the correspondents gathered for still another Paskman meeting. We were to get our assignments for Monday. Mine would again be Khrushchev, Schoenbrun's was de Gaulle, Kendrick's Macmillan, and Schorr no one special. In passing, Schoenbrun and Kendrick congratulated me on the Khrushchev interview, which I deeply appreciated.

Mady joined us for a late-night dinner, filled with rich, insightful conversation about Khrushchev, the summit, Ike, the Western alliance, and lots of speculation about the American presidential race, whether the young senator from Massachusetts, John Kennedy, could beat the more experienced vice president from California, Richard Nixon. I listened more than talked, but it was clear the reporters hoped Kennedy would win, and win big. They believed it was time for a change.

Though very late, Mady and I decided to walk back to the Crillon. The others took cabs. Paris was a twenty-four-hour-a-day enterprise; it did not sleep. There were cafés still busy, and the Champs Élysées bustled with a steady drumbeat of excitement and pleasure. Even the American Embassy, usually quiet and dark at a late hour, pulsated with action, bright lights, and a bubbling sense of excitement. On pre-summit nights, diplomats clearly did not sleep.

Along the way, I told Mady the whole story of my first day as a foreign correspondent—my early morning interview with Khrushchev (imagine, eating croissants with a Soviet leader!); my backseat briefing of Dan and Paskman assigning him to do the lead story on television; my disappointment, obviously, but I did do the story for radio, including the interview; then running after Khrushchev when he visited Macmillan and de Gaulle, another radio spot before our evening meeting, and the stimulating late-night dinner. I was exhausted but proud; I'd learned a great deal about covering an East-West summit, including my exclusive interview with Khrushchev, and, perhaps as important, I felt as if I was beginning to be accepted by my colleagues as an equal.

What an opening day!

The following morning, at exactly 11 a.m., at the Élysée Palace in downtown Paris, President de Gaulle as host gaveled the four-power summit to order. Khrushchev asked for the floor. He read, word for word, the ultimatum he had left with de Gaulle the day before, demanding an apology, an end to U-2 flights, and punishment for those responsible. He spoke with emotion, his left eyebrow twitching, his hands trembling. He charged

Ike with "treachery" and a "Cold War intent" to "torpedo" the summit. Then, he unceremoniously pulled his invitation for Ike to visit the Soviet Union in June, and, busting every basic rule of diplomacy, plunged into American domestic politics by suggesting that the Paris summit be "postponed" until after the November presidential election, when Ike would no longer have presidential authority.

Khrushchev closed his rhetorical attack with an appeal for understanding. "If there had been no [U-2] incident," he said, "we would have come here in friendship and in the best possible atmosphere. . . . God is my witness that I come with clean hands and a pure soul."

Eisenhower fumed with anger, later calling Khrushchev a "son of a bitch." Listening to Khrushchev's tirade, Eisenhower's face and neck reddened, but when he spoke, he did so in a subdued manner. With the summit collapsing around him, Ike said that Khrushchev had arrived in Paris with an "ultimatum" he knew would be unacceptable and that he had, from the beginning, clearly intended to "sabotage" the summit. Ike pointedly ignored Khrushchev's demand for an apology and punishment for the offenders, but he did express a willingness to "undertake bilateral conversations between the United States and the USSR," a sign Ike was prepared to turn the other cheek and, in this way, save the summit. Khrushchev had his chance, but blew it. With a wave of the hand, he impetuously rejected Ike's overture, saying an American apology was still required. Disappointed, de Gaulle adjourned the meeting. Khrushchev was left staring angrily at Eisenhower, and Eisenhower at Khrushchev. Neither shook the other's hand.

They would never see each other again.

On his way out of the Élysée Palace, one of Eisenhower's bodyguards overheard the president say, apparently mimicking Khrushchev's appeal to the Almighty, "I don't care. My hands are clean, my soul is pure."

Macmillan's summation of the Paris summit was emotional, short, and sad. "So much attempted," he said, "so little achieved."

The Paris summit, though, was not yet ready for the history books. Summits follow precise protocol. Khrushchev had left a proposal on the table—that the summit be "postponed" until after the American elections. It was now up to Ike, Macmillan, and de Gaulle either to accept or reject it, formally. That was the pretext for the trilateral meeting, which took place on Tuesday, May 17. The outcome was never in doubt—Khrushchev's proposal would be rejected—but the three leaders used the day for a serious review of the status of East-West relations. Not surprisingly, with the state of U.S.-Soviet relations already in sharp decline, likely to get worse before they got better, they saw little chance for improvement, agreeing only to try to keep the pot from boiling over. They then bowed to the requirements of protocol and voted to end the Paris summit. They sent their decision to Khrushchev, assuming he was waiting impatiently at the Soviet residence.

But he was not at the residence; he was secretly visiting Pleurs-sur-Marne, a small French village more than sixty miles from Paris. His sentimental defense minister, Rodion Malinovsky, spent part of World War I there as a machine gunner in the Russian Expeditionary Force sent to defend Paris, and he wanted to revisit it. Khrushchev decided to join him, rejecting the option of again sightseeing in Paris, which he had done only a few months before. A drive through the French countryside, dotted along remarkably straight side roads with blooming Linden trees, was more appealing to the restless Russian leader. It would have been as well to the small army of reporters and cameramen, waiting in front of the Soviet residence, but they were not informed. An official TASS photographer followed Khrushchev and Malinovsky, but I knew of no others who covered their unusual visit to the small French village. It would have been the perfect TV feature story wrapping up a failed summit.

I'd love to have done it, but at that time Paskman summoned me to the CBS bureau. "Now," he insisted. He had just received word from John Day in New York that I was to leave Paris and proceed to Moscow as soon as possible. It made sense. The summit had failed. East-West relations were tense and tumbling toward a colder Cold War. CBS finally had permission to reopen its Moscow bureau, and it had a correspondent with an entry visa. The bureau manager told me, however, there were no Paris-Moscow flights that evening, but there was an early morning Air France flight on Wednesday, May 18. She booked two seats for Mady and me, and we would soon be on our way.

Except for one very interesting dinner, when a lesson on the treasured traditions of CBS News was taught reverentially by a senior to a junior correspondent. Schoenbrun, hearing about our early morning departure, invited us to dinner, suggesting, if we had the time, to stop at his apartment for drinks and the chance to meet his wife, Dorothy. The apartment was breathtakingly beautiful, David and Dorothy were gracious hosts, and the dinner at their favorite restaurant was delicious. The lesson came with the coffee.

David explained that CBS had a very special tradition, stretching back to Murrow's experiences during World War II. At its heart was the belief that CBS correspondents looked out for one another. They composed what he called a "gilded brotherhood." They were what made CBS tick, not the vice presidents, not the executive producers, not even the anchormen. While the others played a role, no doubt, it was the correspondents who carried the CBS banner for honest, dignified, balanced coverage. They were the ones seen and heard. Murrow started the tradition. "It's now up to us to maintain it," Schoenbrun said convincingly, "wherever we are, whatever we're covering."

If one of the correspondents happened also to be a bureau chief, then he had the extra obligation always to protect the visiting correspondent against any possible mistake or misjudgment by management. Paskman could be dispatched by New York to manage summit coverage, he stressed, but it was understood that Schoenbrun ran the Paris bureau. The example he gave was how he supported my idea about interviewing Khrushchev, even when Paskman was reluctant; how he and Kendrick both praised me, even when Paskman was less than enthusiastic. He had an obligation, he said, to help a younger colleague, me in this case, when Paskman lacked "the brains, the sensitivity" to do the right thing. "He was on my turf; and if he made the wrong call, I had a moral responsibility to right the wrong."

He leaned forward to make his final point. "You will be the bureau chief in Moscow," he said. "Moscow will be your turf. New York can send God to Moscow; it's still your turf. You're the boss. You make the call. You're there not just to cover the news for CBS but to protect CBS traditions. You are the key, no one else!"

As we walked back to his apartment, I thanked David for his lesson, telling him what I believed he already knew—that Murrow was the one who hired me, that he had always been my role model, and that maintaining the CBS tradition would always be my goal.

"I hope I can measure up," I told him.

"I'm sure you will," he replied.

I was sure only that I would try very hard.

... AND, FINALLY, MOSCOW

In the early morning hours, the Paris airport was already crowded with passengers. But the Air France flight to Moscow had no more than a half dozen passengers. That was not uncommon. In those days, only a small circle of people flew to Russia: a businessman or two, a tourist, a journalist, an occasional student or scholar, few others. After decades of oppressive Stalinist rule, Russia was finally opening its heavy doors. Though too slowly for many, major changes were underway. Some were obvious; others, less so. Soviet leader Nikita Khrushchev demolished Stalin's legacy in a remarkable 1956 speech. He then began preaching better relations with the West. No longer, in his view, was war the inevitable result of a historic conflict between communism and capitalism.

This was the Russia, caught between the old orthodoxy of Stalinism and the new uncertainties of a Khrushchev-inspired populism, that greeted us on a hazy day in May 1960.

The international section of Sheremetyevo Airport, eighteen miles northwest of the Soviet capital, echoed with emptiness and reeked of an awful odor, probably a Russian form

of lye. Once a military airbase, it had only recently been converted into a civilian airport serving both domestic and international flights. Two small passport control windows were
open for business, but one was not manned and the other had
a squinty-eyed security officer who examined our passports
with suspicion, checking our photographs, looking up at us
and then back at the photographs and then up at us again,
turning each passport over and then over again, until finally,
after what seemed like an hour, but was probably only a few
minutes, he started to hand them back to me and suddenly
changed his mind.

"It says here you're a journalist. Yes?" He held our passports tantalizingly close to my outstretched hand.

"Yes," I replied, with a smile, projecting an aura of calm I
did not actually feel. I was eager to drop our bags off at the
Metropol Hotel and then race to Gorky Park to see the well-
advertised wreck of an American U-2 spy plane.

"Are you going to be an honest journalist?" he asked. "Are
you going to favor Comrade Khrushchev's policy of 'peaceful
coexistence'"?

"I am not going to lie, if that's what you mean. I shall always
tell the truth." I meant what I said without answering his
question.

The security officer looked puzzled for a moment before
casting a critical eye at me, then at Mady, then back to the
photographs in our passports and only then did he, finally,
stamp them both and hand them back to me.

We thanked him and hurried to the cab stand, a young man
behind us pushing a cart with all our bags. And there were
many. We each had two suitcases, Mady carried a purse and
a large carry-on bag, and I lugged my briefcase, a Hermes
"Baby" portable typewriter, a heavy camera case, and a tape
recorder.

At the cab stand, there were no cabs. I should have known—
there never were any in 1956 on my earlier tour in Moscow;

why should there be any now? The young man, seeing my disappointment, suggested we check in with Intourist, the official Soviet travel office. "They can be helpful, sometimes," he said, looking away.

"But we are not tourists," I objected. "I'm a journalist."

"It's still better if you check in with Intourist," he mumbled.

Realizing my options were dwindling to zero, I went to the Intourist desk where two women were reading magazines. Neither seemed eager to help me. My earlier experiences with Intourist reminded me that one of the women would usually be surly and the other only reluctantly willing to listen and help. The question now was which one? I chose the older of the two, and chose well. She was, for Intourist, remarkably efficient. I told her I needed a limo to take us to the Metropol Hotel. "Yes," she said. "Passports, please." I gave her our passports, paid an exorbitant fee, waited a half-hour or so for the paperwork to be completed and then for the limo to appear. Finally, our bags stashed away in the trunk, we were at long last heading toward Moscow, driving through a rough Russian countryside dotted with occasional dachas, giant cranes, and construction trucks.

Suddenly the city seemed to erupt before our eyes, from rural Russia to urban Moscow in a flash. I began excitedly to recognize landmarks, pointing here and there, knowing that in a few minutes, standing in the middle of the Soviet capital, only a few blocks from the Kremlin, across Theater Square from the Bolshoi Ballet, would be the fabled, five-story art nouveau Metropol Hotel, which would become our most uncomfortable home for much longer than we then realized.

By the time we reached the Metropol, it was already approaching 4 p.m., Moscow time, meaning 9 a.m., New York time. Had anyone in New York booked a circuit for me, I was thinking. (A circuit was a specific time for a broadcast, arranged between CBS and the Central Telegraph in Moscow.) The Hotel entrance was large and impressive in its way, remi-

niscent of earlier pre-revolutionary times when the ruling aris-
tocracies of Europe vacationed there. Now cigarette-smoking
cab drivers loitered nearby, and young Russians gathered in
small groups to catch a glimpse of well-dressed foreign guests,
perhaps even to exchange a phrase or two in English. A door-
man with a tall, fake-fur hat helped with our bags. I entered
the lobby, looking for the Intourist office. I wanted very much
to get a room and unload our bags so we could hurry to see
the U-2 wreckage on display at Chess House in Gorky Park and
possibly do a radio broadcast on my first day as a CBS correspondent in Moscow. That was my goal.

Much to my surprise, the Intourist clerk was both pleasant
and cooperative. She had a telegram for me (yes, Hal Terkel
had booked a circuit for 17:30 local time), and she assigned
two rooms to us, one for our office, one for our apartment.
Both were unbelievably small, with just enough room to get
around a double bed while heading to a miniscule bathroom,
which had a small bathtub and no shower. We were at that
time so obsessed with seeing the U-2 spy plane, ultimately the
cause of the failure of the Paris summit, that we didn't focus
on the obvious—the pitifully small size of the rooms. We just
dropped our bags in one of the two rooms, arbitrarily selecting it to be our "apartment," and, picking up my camera case,
my tape recorder, and my typewriter, we rushed to the nearest
cab outside the hotel.

"Gorky Park, please." I began to breath more easily. We
might yet make the 17:30 circuit.

It was a fifteen-minute ride from the hotel, looping us
around the Kremlin, along the Moscow river embankment,
across a massive bridge and to the capital's biggest, busiest
park. "It was no accident," as *Pravda* was often fond of saying,
that the U-2 was exhibited in Gorky Park. Khrushchev wanted
everyone to see it. He was under attack in many parts of the
world for "sabotaging" the Paris summit. He wanted Eisenhower, who had authorized the U-2 flight, to be the one under

attack. Gorky Park had a huge, colorful entryway, worthy of more than the moment of admiration we gave it. We hurried to Chess House, which was not hard to find. Everyone seemed to be walking in the same direction.

Security guards manned the doorways but stopped no one, not even a foreign correspondent, who was conspicuously lugging a camera and a tape recorder. Normally, to film or record anything defined as official, the correspondent would have needed the advance permission of the press department of the Soviet Foreign Ministry, the small but important part of the Soviet government responsible for the actions and rhetoric of all foreign correspondents based in Moscow. That I needed no such permission was proof that Khrushchev wanted the publicity.

After only a few minutes, I could see that in this episode of non-kinetic warfare between East and West, the Russians held the clear advantage. The plane wreckage itself, in the middle of a room usually devoted to the storied history of Russian chess masters, spoke volumes about American sponsorship of U-2 espionage. On surrounding tables were the pilot's helmet, his uniform, his poison pill, American maps and charts— unmistakable proof that an American pilot named Frances Gary Powers had flown the U-2, had been shot down over Soviet territory, and was now being held by the Soviet government. Speaking Russian, I interviewed a few of the people there. Though the exhibition was clearly designed to generate a wave of anti-American sentiment, I sensed none of that in my brief conversations—in fact, just the opposite. The Russians often live in two worlds, one of personal sentiment, expressed only to family and close friends; the other of imposed ideological conformity, safe to discuss with anyone, even a foreigner. Occasionally the two worlds coincide, as they did that day. Though the Russians showed no hostility toward me or Mady, they did hew closely in their comments to what they had read in *Pravda*—that the president of the United States had ordered the U-2 flight, that he was responsible for the collapse of the Paris summit, that Khrushchev tried valiantly to salvage the summit but couldn't, and finally that the Soviet Union, even after the U-2 fiasco, still stood for "peaceful coexistence" with the United States.

I used my tape recorder for the interviews and my camera for footage of the U-2 wreckage. Did I employ them correctly? Was there any audio? Any usable film? I had no idea, but as I checked my watch, I knew I had just enough time to get to the Central Telegraph, two long blocks from Red Square. Because all foreign correspondent copy had to be cleared by Soviet censors before broadcast or publication, the Central Telegraph became every reporter's second home. They often wrote their copy there, submitted it to censors never seen or met, befriended other reporters from Western Europe, Asia, and Africa, and sometimes sat there for hours exchanging gossip or news tips while waiting for the censors to do their nasty work of cutting a word, a phrase, a sentence; occasionally they'd cut a whole piece in a process conducted in total secrecy. Soviet leaders, from Lenin on, had always worried about how their policies and actions would be perceived in the outside world. Therefore, what foreign correspondents wrote and broadcast was of fundamental importance to the state. Hence the Communist Party's need for the mysterious, anonymous foreign-language-reading-and-speaking-censors.

They all worked for a little-known committee, called the Main Administration for Literary Affairs, colloquially referred to as Glavlit, which had been under the jurisdiction of the Foreign Ministry before it was shifted to the Central Committee of the Soviet Communist Party in early 1946. The shift was an indication of the importance the Communist Party placed on controlling and fashioning its image around the world.

The press entrance into the Central Telegraph, on a side street that I remembered well, led to a second-floor newsroom, where foreign correspondents routinely submitted their copy to one of two clerks seated behind a long, dark counter. Small telephone booths and broadcast studios were on the other side of the newsroom. There were also a half dozen or so writing cubicles in an alcove near the entry, plus several round tables and chairs, used both for writing and lounging. The clerk would then write the name of the correspondent and the time of the submission into an old-fashioned ledger before giving the copy to the censor working behind a closed, green-curtained door.

I dropped my camera case and tape recorder on the floor near a table and quickly wrote a short piece about my visit to the U-2 exhibition in Gorky Park and then a longer analysis that I hoped would be used on the *World Tonight*. I began my first report from Moscow as a CBS correspondent:

> It's all there, if you needed the proof—the smashed-up plane, the pilot's helmet, his maps, even the poison pill he never took. All there, in a large, crowded exhibition in downtown Gorky Park. Soviet leader Khrushchev wants the world to see that it was an American spy plane, the U-2, shot down over Soviet territory, that was the culprit, the real reason for the collapse of the Paris summit. But, interesting, Russians I talked to at the exhibition say Khrushchev still wants peaceful relations with the United States.

Here, to emphasize this point, I asked the editor in New York to choose an appropriate quote from one of my interviews. Then, my close, which read,

> Russians normally echo the party line when talking to foreigners, and the party line here is that Khrushchev tried to save the summit but couldn't because so-called "Western imperialists and aggressors" do not want peace. Now back to CBS News in America.

I pulled the copy from my typewriter, checked it for accuracy, submitted it to one of the clerks, who noted name and time on her ledger and gave it to the censor. I was certain the censor would clear every word (Khrushchev urgently wanted the U-2 story to be broadcast and front-paged all over the world) and return it to me in time for my 17:30 circuit. And that was exactly what happened: my script was returned to me, nothing cut or changed, the censor's stamp on the bottom of the page, with two minutes to go before I was told by loudspeaker that CBS in New York was on the line in Booth No. 2.

The first voice I heard from New York in my first Moscow broadcast on May 18, 1960, belonged to my first editor, the incomparable Hal Terkel. "I knew you'd want to do a piece on your first day in Moscow," he said, happily welcoming me to the small editing room next to Studio 9. "So I booked this circuit on spec, but I knew if you got there, you'd want it." Since this was strictly an audio transmission, I couldn't see Hal's face; but I'd have bet it was spread into a broad grin. "And here you are."

I was thrilled.

"Give me a voice check," Hal said, trying to sound crisply professional.

I too tried to sound professional. "One, two, three, four, five," I counted. "Enough? Want more?"

"Enough. Fire away."

When I finished broadcasting both scripts, the shorter and the longer, I fed the taped interviews to New York. "Did you get it all?" I asked.

There was a pause. Hal, emotional, a click in his voice, answered, "Got it all, kid." Another pause. "You were great, Marvin. I'm proud of you. You sounded like you've been there for years."

In response, I said, "I had the best teacher in the business." I meant what I said. Hal demystified broadcast news—for me and probably for others as well. He had earlier taught me about the difference between news writing for the ear, meaning radio, and news writing for the eye, meaning TV news. He had also identified the element of fear that many new broadcasters felt in front of a live microphone, and he showed how it could be contained. Most important, he had insisted that we respect the power and influence of words on radio. "Remember," he'd say, "Ed [Murrow] had only words to paint a picture of World War II. But his words were all his listeners needed."

Hal and I agreed on a circuit time for the next day, 2 p.m. Moscow time, one hour before the *World News Roundup* was broadcast. "You did good," Hal concluded. "Proud of you."

I bounced buoyantly out of the broadcast booth. I'd done my first broadcast as CBS's Moscow correspondent, and I'd done it on my first day in the Soviet capital. Only then was I able to look around the newsroom to see who else was there. A few other reporters were busy writing their stories. One was dictating his copy to London on a telephone hookup. No one I knew. Mady and I sat down for a moment to catch our breath. We'd been on the move since dawn in Paris. "Now," I grinned, trying to soft pedal the bureaucratic problems looming before us, "all we have to do is try to figure out how we can fit into that small room at the Metropol. Fortunately, it won't be for long."

Problem No. 1 was that by the time we got back to the Metropol, the Intourist agents had left for the day, and the concierge showed no interest in doing what concierges do routinely all over the world—help hotel guests. But we had our room keys, the elevator worked, and we headed to our new "apartment," the small room at the back end of a long dim corridor on the fourth floor. It was as we had left it, overstuffed with suitcases and dismally lit by two low-voltage lamps on both sides of the bed and a third lamp on a round table near the only window in the room, tall, narrow, and curtained. It was a disheartening sight, and before Mady could fully absorb the dim meagerness of her surroundings throwing her into a justifiable depression, I suggested with charged though clearly feigned excitement, "Time for a drink and dinner, right?" I could tell Mady was about to groan. I took her by the arm. "We'll worry about all this later," I said.

The main dining room at the Metropol was cavernous, easily two stories high, well-lit with enormous chandeliers, and yet oddly unreal, as though its current Marxist owner had failed to wash away its pre-revolutionary veneer. An orchestra played its version of Western-style music, and we didn't have to wait for a table. The menu listed many dishes that were, when requested, unavailable, but the amiable, resourceful waiter, sensing our dilemma, seized the initiative and recommended *ikra* (caviar) for an appetizer and *kievsky cotlety* (chicken, Kiev style) for our main course. He wanted us to be happy, and with a nod and smile I obliged, while also ordering a tasty Georgian white wine I remembered from my earlier time in Moscow— Tsinandaly, by name. The waiter was short and dark-skinned, probably a product of the Caucasus.

After the waiter left, I asked Mady if she would like to dance. No, it was clear from her countenance, she did not want to dance, and if I had to venture an opinion, I'd say she wanted either to scream or cry. She must have been thinking about her new "apartment," which bore no resemblance whatever to the one we had just vacated on Gramercy Park South less than a week before. "They can't really be serious," she moaned, shaking her head. "Maybe for a night or two, but . . ."

"Mady, first thing in the morning, I promise, I'll talk to Intourist," I tried to sound confident, "and I'll also check in with the press department. Maybe Kharlamov, the guy who runs it, can help get us an apartment. I know the other news bureaus have nice apartments and also an office." I held her hand. "Things will get better. I'm sure of that." I wasn't sure of anything, in fact, but I was desperately trying, on the first night of our new assignment, to be an optimist, an attitude that in Moscow often opened doors to serious disappointment. I didn't want Mady to be unhappy.

The dinner was fine, and the wine as smooth as I remembered it, but, though truly exhausted, we did not sleep well, mostly because we could not fit into the bed. It had a tall, heavy headboard, four very thick pillows, a blanket for a Siberian winter and a footboard that rose forbiddingly only five feet ten inches away from the headboard, making it difficult if not impossible for me, at six feet three inches, to adjust to that cramped space. I tried to sleep diagonally across the bed, from one corner to the other, but that cut into Mady's already limited space. The upshot was that sleep, a precious necessity for anyone, had overnight become the equivalent of an impossible dream, leaving us both in a less than charming mood the next day.

I assaulted my Intourist agent the moment she opened the office door. "We must be moved to a larger room with a larger bed," I all but bellowed. "The room is much too small for us, and there's no room for our luggage. It's simply much too small, and you must help me."

The agent tried to sound accommodating, though she might only have been buying time. "Come back after lunch," she advised, "and we'll see what can be done."

"Why can't we make a change right now?" I asked.

"Because you know, Mr. Kalb, I must check with my director," she said. "Maybe we can do something, maybe not, but I can't do it by myself."

We agreed I'd return at 3 p.m. Meantime I asked if she could help me call Mr. Kharlamov in the press department of the Foreign Ministry. Could he see me asap? I wanted to know. "Yes," was his surprising response. "9:30 a.m." Could I make it?

"Yes, I'll be there."

I sat in the Intourist office for the next hour or so reading the Soviet press, much the way I used to, when I worked for the

U.S. Embassy in Moscow in 1956. I had learned how to "read" the Soviet press, which word or phrase signaled a possible shift in policy, which signaled only a desire to emphasize a certain aspect of policy, and which meant little or nothing. On May 19, 1960, one message jumped from the front page of every Soviet newspaper—the Eisenhower administration was guilty of destroying the Paris summit! Khrushchev was determined to absolve himself of all responsibility for the summit's collapse. That was to be my story for the day.

Before leaving for the Foreign Ministry, I checked on Mady. She was still asleep. I put the "Do Not Disturb" sign on the doorknob and left, pleased she was finally getting some well-deserved rest.

Stalin must have loved ugly architecture. It was apparent everywhere. The Foreign Ministry was among the ugliest—a jagged, bulky, pointed, uneven structure on a broad boulevard that would have been hard, I suspect, even for those who worked there to admire. My cab stopped about fifty yards from the main entrance. The driver claimed he could not drive any closer. I think he was afraid. Fortunately, the weather was mild. Inside I went up to a large information desk where I asked for Mikhail Kharlamov, director of the press department. Told to wait, I meandered off to one side, primarily to watch and wonder about the many young, old, and middle-aged diplomats who crisscrossed the lobby. Who would be an ambassador? Who a deputy foreign minister? Who was really an intelligence agent?

"Mr. Kalb?" one of them asked, breaking into my reverie. "You're here to see Mr. Kharlamov?"

"Yes."

"Please come with me." Nothing else was said. We walked at a brisk pace to an elevator, which slowly ascended to one of the top floors. There another young man escorted me to the director's office, which was large and impressive, not at all like the director, who looked like an undistinguished bureaucrat from a Chekhov play, yearning one day to return to Moscow. His hairline was receding, his voice reedy, and his smile forced.

"Hello, Mr. Kalb," he said, trying to sound friendly. "Did we meet in Geneva?"

The question startled me. "No, Sir, I was not in Geneva. This is my first foreign assignment for CBS."

"Oh yes, you worked for what they used to call the 'Joint Press Reading Service' when you were last here in Moscow. Am I correct?" Kharlamov's game was obvious. He was implying that though the JPRS was known for providing a translation service, it must really have had a more devious purpose, namely, espionage.

"It was indeed the 'Joint Press Reading Service,'" I responded, "and all we did there, day after day, was translate the Soviet press." I tried to tell him in this rather direct way that I knew his game and wanted to move on to the business at hand.

But he still wanted to play. "Of course, you were called a translator then, and now you are called a correspondent."

"Mr. Kharlamov," I replied as firmly and convincingly as possible, "I was a translator in 1956, and I am a correspondent now. Both titles were and are accurate."

"Of course, Mr. Kalb." He did not sound persuaded. "So how can I help you?"

"First, on behalf of CBS News, I want to thank the Soviet government for allowing us to reopen our Moscow bureau and for giving visas to me and my wife." No one had told me to deliver that little speech, but it seemed right for the occasion.

"That is our pleasure. We hope you will use the opportunity to advance the cause of peaceful relations between our countries, to be an objective reporter."

"I'm here to cover the news, Mr. Kharlamov. I'm a reporter, not a diplomat." I didn't want to get into a debate with him about the meaning of objectivity. His definition would be different from mine, as different as socialism was from capitalism.

Kharlamov then delicately raised the subject of the CBS broadcast, "The Plot to Kill Stalin," which prompted the Russians in late 1958 to close the CBS bureau in Moscow and expel correspondent Paul Niven. "Your company," he said, "has done bad things, which must not be repeated." I jumped on his comment to stress that while "I assume full responsibility for my news reporting, I cannot in all fairness accept responsibility for *Playhouse 90*," which produced the controversial account of Stalin's death.

"Please understand, Mr. Kalb," he said in closing the subject, "CBS had to be punished." I chose not to pursue it.

Walking over to a big window with a view of the busy boulevard below, Kharlamov beckoned for me to follow him. Looking down at a group of street cleaners, women carrying bunches of bundled branches used in this case to sweep the overnight debris into the back of a waiting truck, he asked, "How would you cover this scene?"

"In a rather straight forward way," I replied, surprised by his question. "If it was for radio, I'd describe the overall scene, the Foreign Ministry building, this group of women workers, two supervisors, both men, smoking, while the women swept the debris into the truck. If I could, I'd interview one of the women and one of the men. I'd probably also say this was a rather common scene on a Moscow street."

"But when we have reached the final stage of human development—that's communism, Mr. Kalb, you understand these women will be using modern brushes, not branches, and the men will not be standing around smoking. They too will be working. There will be total equality between men and women. And that, not what you were describing, would be an example of objective reporting. You want to be objective, don't you?"

"Mr. Kharlamov," I replied, calmly, "when you have communism, invite me back, and I'll report what I see then. If the women actually have brushes, I'll say that. And if the men are really working, I'll say that too. But now I can only report what I see at this time."

Kharlamov stared at me in despair for a moment, then walked back to his desk, lit a cigarette, and impatiently asked, "Is that all? I'm a busy man, Mr. Kalb."

"No, not at all," I declared. "I was merely responding to your questions about the street cleaners. My questions are these. I would like to know, for example, whether you will allow a CBS television crew to be based here in Moscow? As you know, we do television as well as radio. I would also like to know when we can expect to have our own apartment and a proper office, the same as other American correspondents. What we have now at the Metropol is totally unacceptable. And, finally, when I have a question about the news, which I'm sure I shall have, can I call you for an official comment?"

Kharlamov still seemed impatient, determined apparently to bring this meeting to an end as quickly as possible. Each of my questions got only a brief response. "I'll have to think about a visa for a TV crew, but at this time only on a tempo-rary basis, and only when we think there is a story deserving film coverage."

"Isn't that a decision that I, as a journalist, should be making, not you?"

He continued, ignoring my question, "Now, concerning an apartment, I'll look into that. And, finally, you can, of course, always call me. Whether you'll get an answer is another matter."

Kharlamov started walking toward the door, expecting me to follow. "Mr. Kharlamov," I said, stalling, "the matter of an apartment is of crucial importance to me and my wife. When can we expect one?"

He seemed for a moment sympathetic. "Your wife is here

with you? I didn't know." Of course, he did know—he was the one who issued visas to both of us. "All right, I'll see about an apartment. You will get one."

"When?"

"That I'm not sure about. But I hope as soon as possible, in a month or so."

We shook hands in a formal way. Almost as an afterthought, he handed me an official press pass. "Here you'll need this," he said, returning again to his desk. Our meeting was over. The same escort walked me to the elevator, where another took over the heavy responsibility of seeing me out of the Foreign Ministry without incident. Near the street corner, where I found a cab, the women street cleaners were still at work, sweeping the overnight debris into a waiting truck. The two men, still smoking, stood on the side, laughing, paying no attention whatever to the women, the truck, or to the process they were technically in charge of supervising.

———————

I spent the rest of the morning with Mady, writing my reports for the 2 p.m. circuit at the Central Telegraph. Room service was available, according to Intourist, but when I tried to order a simple breakfast of coffee, toast, and juice for Mady, I was told it was unavailable that day and would probably remain unavailable for the next day or two. I called the main dining room. Could someone please prepare a pot of coffee and four slices of toast, and I'll come and pick up the order and bring it to our room? No, I was told. According to the rules, "strictly observed," I was assured, only a waiter can carry a tray, and besides no tray can leave the dining room. In building frustration, I then called the concierge and asked whether there was any way I could "buy" two cups of coffee.

He seemed stunned by the question. "*Buy* two cups of coffee?" he sputtered. "Buy? We don't sell coffee at the Metropol."

"All right," I replied, "how can I get two cups of coffee?"

"Oh," replied the concierge, "the dining room opens at 11:30. I'm sure you can get two cups of coffee then."

Losing patience, I decided to call my all-purpose "friend" at Intourist. I posed my problem.

"No problem," she said. "The dining room opens at 11:30. They have lots of coffee."

I carried this message of hope to Mady, who was by this time dressed and ready to skip breakfast and plunge directly into a light lunch, which we did at exactly 11:30 a.m. The famous Metropol, we learned, had no juice, but could prepare an omelet, toast, and coffee. At this moment, informed that a meal—with coffee!—might actually be on our near horizon, it seemed as if we'd scaled the Mt. Kilimanjaro of Soviet service and, at the very summit, found a coffee shop. While momentarily enjoying our good fortune, I told Mady about how I'd "read" the Soviet press earlier in the morning, before meeting with Kharlamov, and then written my scripts. "Want to hear them?" I asked.

"Of course," Mady said. (What a good wife!) I read my piece for the *World News Roundup*. It began,

> There's no question about it, here in Moscow, the United States "sabotaged"—and "torpedoed"—the summit conference in Paris, and the world is "up in arms" against the "aggressive" policy and "tragic blundering" of the Eisenhower administration. That is the gist of almost every story in the Soviet press this morning. "Shame on the policy of provocation," says *Izvestia*. "Responsibility lies with Washington," says TASS.

"Should I continue?" I asked. "Or had enough?"

"No, please continue."

"You talked me into it."

I continued,

Supporting the vitriolic assault are mass meetings held all over the Soviet Union, denouncing Washington and President Eisenhower. "The Soviet people," one irate Soviet citizen reportedly said, "had high hopes for the summit conference in Paris." However, the meeting of the heads of government was "torpedoed" by the "reactionary circles" in Washington.

Out of a corner of my eye, I could see the waiter preparing our tray. I went to my close.

Opposing Washington, with "vigor and firmness," was Soviet Premier Khrushchev, who came to Paris, TASS says, as an "apostle of peace." But even he could not turn the tide. The Russian leader's news conference in Paris yesterday is banner-headlined in all Soviet newspapers. Interestingly, there are references to occasional "catcalls." But these, *Izvestia* assures its readers, were drowned out by the "generally stormy applause" greeting Premier Khrushchev. Now back to CBS News in America.

As I finished my reading, the waiter arrived with our brunch, which we both gobbled up. "Good piece," Mady said, sipping her coffee. "How long was it?"

"A minute twenty," I replied.

"You got a lot into a minute twenty."

"That's the beauty of radio. You can get a lot into a little."

We arrived at the Central Telegraph in plenty of time for the censor's review (every word cleared) and the 2 p.m. circuit. Terkel was again the editor. His reaction to my report was similar to Mady's. "You got a lot in there," he said. "Let's book a 2 p.m. circuit every day. That way we'll have a Moscow piece for the *World News Roundup* every morning; and if for whatever reason, if you can't make it, just let us know." That was Hal's way of complimenting me, and I was grateful. With his help, I'd become a regular on CBS's most important radio newscast, measured by listenership. "One other thing," Terkel said before we broke the circuit. "The Edwards show wants a voiceover for the U-2 exhibition footage. I think the producer has a minute-fifteen spot in mind. OK? Is a 7 p.m. local time good for you?" It was indeed. That meant the footage I sent to New York yesterday was getting there in time for a spot on the *CBS Evening News with Douglas Edwards.* That also meant the Russians wanted my U-2 footage to get to New York. That would be my first TV spot from Moscow.

We returned to the Metropol a few minutes before our 3 p.m. meeting with Intourist. We didn't realize as we entered the office that we were also enlisting for a frustrating lesson in the workings, or non-workings, of the Soviet bureaucracy.

Things started poorly, no surprise. First, the director was "busy," we were told. "OK," I said, "we'll wait for her." We waited for about fifteen minutes when I reminded her assistant that we had a 3 p.m. appointment. "Yes, she knows," was her reply. With growing impatience, we waited for another fifteen minutes until finally the director, a short, chunky woman with dark hair and thick eyeglasses, emerged, trailed by my "friend," who had earlier seemed so helpful. The director sat down behind a small desk; we were obliged to stand in front of it. It was an awkward arrangement but one deliberately designed to put us in a position of subservience before this symbol of Soviet power. The director, Borisovna by name, glanced at a piece of paper on her desk and, after a moment, looked up at me and pronounced, "Every correspondent gets two rooms, one for an office and one for rest. We gave you two rooms. So, what is your problem? Why the complaint?"

"Madame Borisovna," I said, "Mrs. Kalb and I are going to live here at the Metropol for only a short time, until the press department of the Foreign Ministry gets an apartment and an office for us. But the rooms you gave us are really too small, even for a short time."

Reasonableness oozed from every one of my words. "For example," I went on, forcing a smile, "as you can see, I am very tall, and I could not fit into the bed and therefore could not sleep. Surely in this magnificent, historic hotel, there is a larger room, a suite possibly, with a larger bed." I tried sounding ever so accommodating and understanding.

Coldly, the director interrupted me. "Mr. Kalb," she was shaking her head, "reporters get two rooms—that's the rule, and we gave you two rooms, including one for your office. So why complain?" It was as if she had heard not a word I said.

Mady could wait no longer. "Madame," she said, trying to control her temper but failing, "my husband is six feet three inches tall. He cannot fit into a small bed. Even I have trouble, and I'm much shorter. Surely you can arrange for us to have a larger bed. That is not too much to ask of a hotel such as the Metropol." Her voice was rising, as she continued. "We won't be here forever. But as long as we live here, and this is our home [sarcasm dripped from the word], I'm sure you want us to be happy."

Madame Borisovna was having none of Mady's plea. "Mrs. Kalb, this is the beginning of a busy tourist season. You are lucky to get two perfectly nice rooms. Two, mind you. I advise you to get used to them. We can do no better."

Speaking in a soft voice and emulating the style of a diplomatic pro I admired, former U.S. ambassador to Moscow, Charles Bohlen, I gently interjected, "Madame Director, just the other day in Paris, I did an interview with Premier Khrushchev. He knows me from my earlier assignment here in Moscow. Interesting, he calls me 'Peter the Great,' because I'm almost as tall as your great tsar, who, by the way, would not have been able to fit into our bed either." I laughed at my attempt at humor, Mady smiled, Madame Borisovna frowned. "Premier Khrushchev told me that he wants better relations with the United States, despite the U-2 problem. I'm sure," I said with a straight face, "that you strongly support the Khrushchev policy. So, let me suggest that you think about our very modest suggestion, which I shall now amend to make it easier for you—we shall keep one room for our office, removing that problem, if you give us a larger room, a suite, for our living quarters. Such a compromise would be in keeping with Khrushchev's policy. I suggest you think about it, and we'll stop by tomorrow before lunch. Would that be acceptable?"

Madame Borisovna cast an unhappy eye at Mady and a withering eye at me. "The only thing that's acceptable," she said, "is that we'll meet tomorrow," at which point she stood up and left. Her associate took advantage of the moment to hand me a note, which I pocketed unread. On our way to the elevator, Mady poked me in the ribs. "Not bad for a beginner," she said, with a big smile.

"Not bad," I said.

For both of us, our exchange with Intourist was a theoretical exercise in power dynamics: who would get the better of the other? So far, stalemate!

"What do you really think?" Mady asked. "Think we'll get a larger room? I don't know if I can manage in the room we've got now. There's no room for anything, not even us."

I tried to sound reassuring but doubt that I succeeded. "We'll check tomorrow. Maybe the Khrushchev reference will produce a minor miracle. We'll see."

When we got to the small room that was our office, I unraveled the note I'd pocketed. It turned out to be a formal, printed invitation to lunch at noon the following day, May 20, with Henry Shapiro, the United Press International bureau chief since 1937. Shapiro was a Harvard-trained lawyer, who first came to the Soviet Union in 1933 to study Russian law but quickly switched professions and became a journalist, covering the great purges of the 1930s, the bloody traumas of World War II, the death of Stalin, and the rise of the Khrushchev era of uncertain reform. Was Shapiro inviting only me? Why? Or was he hosting a special lunch for all of the American reporters? I didn't know, but I immediately RSVP'ed that I'd be there, a newcomer to reporting from Moscow eager to learn from the "dean of Moscow correspondents," a title he'd acquired over the twenty-three years of his reign.

"Was I invited?" Mady asked.

"Nope. Just your esteemed husband," I replied. "No, actually there may be others. I don't know."

Mady was not amused.

Little did Harvard know in the early 1950s that it was hatching a future Moscow correspondent. In my early 20s, I certainly didn't look the part.

Mady and I, even in the winter, enjoyed walking along Moscow's broad boulevards . . .

. . . and in the summer visiting Russia's small, old villages, where things seemed never to change.

In 1938, the concept was revolutionary; now it's taken for granted. CBS's Edward R. Murrow and colleague William L. Shirer initiated "live" radio reporting from a Europe heading into World War II.

Dallas Townsend, always eager for reports from Moscow, anchored the "World News Roundup," CBS's most popular radio newscast.

In the late 1950s, Walter Cronkite began to supplant Murrow as CBS's main anchor and star. He hosted the heralded "20th Century" documentaries, a Sunday feature until displaced by football.

Charles Kuralt, an exceptional TV journalist, leaped to stardom at CBS in months. It took many others years, if they made it at all.

"Ignore the camera. Just talk to me." So advised Howard K. Smith, a rising star at CBS, who anchored my first TV appearance. He soon left for ABC after an argument about how best to cover race relations.

Richard C. Hottelet,

Richard C. Hottelet was an original "Murrow boy." When he anchored the *CBS Morning News* in the late 1950s, he resisted makeup. "Murrow didn't hire me for my looks," he said. Hottelet was brave, honest, and careful.

Lowell Thomas,

Lowell Thomas was one of the most prominent newscasters of his time, making movies, writing articles and broadcasting from around the world. He made news as well as covered it.

Robert Trout,

Robert Trout, born Blondheim, began his seven-decade career in 1932. He was the master of broadcast news with an encyclopedic grasp of names and places, also always a gentleman with a sense of humor.

David Schoenbrun, the man with the golden voice, owned Paris as CBS's bureau chief. Everyone bowed before his command, from ministers to chefs.

David Schoenbrun,

Daniel Schorr,

Daniel Schorr, a terrific reporter, covered the Soviet Union, Poland, and West Germany during the Cold War, amazingly quick at seeing through Communist gambits.

Alexander Kendrick,

Alexander Kendrick knew and appreciated the intricacies of European diplomacy. A superb analyst, he also generously helped younger colleagues, me included.

It was my first *Years of Crisis* broadcast in December 1960, and appropriately I was seated at the end of the table. But, in answer to a Murrow question, I proposed that the United States send its surplus grain to Communist China to feed its starving people, a proposal that made news.

Diplomatic receptions were the places in Moscow where gossip mixed with news. Here Sacha Simon of *Le Monde* whispered a nugget of information to an appreciative colleague.

The "CBS Moscow bureau" sounded large and impressive. It was for a time a desk, a portable typewriter, and copy paper in a dark corner of a hotel room—and, by the way, a correspondent.

No one had a more profound influence on my
career than my brother, Bernie. He was always my
model. He even tried, with only modest success,
to teach me how to use a tape recorder.

Tom Lambert, a superb writer, was an experienced
foreign correspondent for the *New York Herald Tribune*,
always good for a laugh when times were tough.

Not Frances Gary Powers, the captured pilot of the U-2 spy plane, but his father who spoke to reporters and pleaded for his son's life at his Moscow trial in August 1960. In a spy swap, two years later, Powers was released.

Soviet leader Nikita Khrushchev angrily denounced the United States for the U-2 spy plane intrusion. In my first exclusive interview, he demanded an apology from the United States, didn't get it, and then sabotaged the May 1960 Paris summit.

In his long career, Boris Pasternak wrote only one novel, *Dr. Zhivago*; otherwise he created beautiful poetry and translated Western classics into Russian. In 1958, he won the Nobel Prize for Literature, but sadly couldn't accept it.

12

CENSORS, CIRCUITS, AND DOUBLE BEDS

When it was time to return to the Central Telegraph for my 7 p.m. circuit, we decided to walk, but not by taking the most direct route along Moscow's broad boulevards but rather by way of the short, narrow streets that meander through the central part of the city. On one of them sat the historic Moscow Art Theater, which was then featuring Chekhov's Uncle Vanya. We stopped and looked at each other, nodded and happily bought many tickets, launching a run of theater, ballet, and concert-going that was to last for the duration of our Moscow assignment.

Though we might not have loved every show (how could we?), we loved many of them, and with each one, appreciated more than ever the central role of the arts in Russian life.

Mady and I have always loved Russian literature, realizing with each book or poem how the artist tries to maneuver his or her way through tsarist and communist roadblocks to convey the complex reality of their lives. During our time in Moscow, we noticed that theaters, such as the Moscow Art Theater, presented more pre-revolutionary plays than contemporary ones. The reason: it was safer for the actors, the producers, and the theaters to feature the classical works of Pushkin, Chekhov, Dostoevsky, and Tolstoy than to run the risk of offending the ideological gods by showing the works of modern writers and composers whose loyalty to the Soviet state might still be in doubt. Since Stalin's death, Russia was changing, but it had not yet changed.

The Central Telegraph, where we were headed, reflected the split personality of a nation struggling for some form of acceptable change while fearing the loss of its more familiar autocratic mooring. As we entered, we noticed immediately that the newsroom was crowded with as many as two dozen reporters busily writing copy, conferring in different languages, breaking into small groups, sipping coffee or tea, chewing on sandwiches, even arguing pointlessly with the clerks about how much time the censors were taking with their copy.

Five years earlier, shortly after Stalin's death, there had been only four American reporters in Moscow, and they did not argue with the clerks, even though the censors routinely brutalized their copy. They were hounded, their travel severely restricted, and the threat of expulsion hung over them like a daily nightmare they could not shake off.

But now, only a short time later, when Khrushchev began introducing political reform, opening Russia to the world, there were fifteen American reporters, and many more from Western Europe, covering these dramatic changes. Every evening, they would gather at the Central Telegraph to write and file their copy. They had no option—their copy had to be censored, whether they liked it or not, and the Central Telegraph was where the censors wielded their scalpels. Many of the reporters, who spent hours, then weeks and months together, became very good friends, thinking of themselves after a while as family. Associated Press (AP) reporter Angelo

Natale once said: "You don't make friends in Moscow, you make family." Priscilla Johnson, a reporter for the North American Newspaper Alliance (NANA), described the mood among the reporters as "wonderful, just wonderful." They shared the same hardships, shortages, and pleasures. When they traveled, especially within the Soviet Union, they tended to travel together. It was safer. For American reporters, the backyard coffee shop behind the U.S. Embassy was a second convenient spot for exchanging gossip and news tips—and enjoying hot dog, hamburger, and ham-and-egg lunches, which, after a while, Mady and I found to be better than the best at the Metropol, but not quite at the level of the Crillon.

On this particular evening, as we entered the Central Telegraph, we also spotted among the many reporters two old friends, Max Frankel, a *New York Times* reporter, whom I'd met when he was a student at Columbia, and his wife, Tobi. "We heard you were here," Max said, a warm smile on his face. He was typing a story, and didn't stop. Max was seated at one of the round tables. "When did you get in?"

"Yesterday," I replied, sitting down next to him while pulling two scripts, written earlier at the hotel, out of my typewriter. One was the TV script, the other a shorter radio spot. "Max, hang on a sec. My circuit's at 7. I want to get this to the censor."

I gave my copy to one of the clerks behind the long counter. Again, as earlier in the day, the censor had no trouble with my copy, which focused on the U-2 crisis, and returned it quickly. That was the story Khrushchev wanted splashed across the world. Also, as earlier in the day, my circuit was on time. No problem. My lesson for the day: when a reporter's story and a dictator's needs coincide, enjoy the moment. It would not happen often.

When it was time for my 7 p.m. circuit, I found that the line to New York was amazingly static-free, clear as a call on a mountain top. Hal Terkel was again at the other end, and he was in a happy mood. "With you coming up once or twice a day from Moscow, we're going to be better friends than when you were here in New York," Hal joked.

"Well, if the Russians keep shooting down U-2 spy planes," I joked right back, "there will be a lot of news coming out of Moscow."

"I have a feeling," Hal said, more seriously, "that with you in Moscow, there'll be a lot of news coming out of there, with or without the U-2." That was another Terkel compliment, and I appreciated it. "By the way, lots of nice things being said here about your busy first day in Moscow, Dallas [Townsend] and Blair [Clark] especially. Even John Day said something nice, believe it or not."

I thanked Hal and then, after a proper 1-2-3 countdown, broadcast first the TV script, which was essentially a minute-fifteen rewrite of the radio piece I'd done the day before, and then the radio spot, based on a *Pravda* story that caught my eye, basically because it captured the opinion of the Soviet military—namely, that the Americans might be preparing to use atomic weapons against the Soviet Union:

As *Pravda* today reported a Soviet request that the Security Council take up a charge of American "espionage flights" over Russia," the radio piece started, "two Soviet military theoreticians offered some detail of Washington's "spying" activities. "Spy Sputniks," they say, are being developed in the United States to gather military surveillance of Russia. Miniature tape recorders that can be hidden in a spy's hair, or behind his ear, able to record a conversation more than 600 feet away—these too are being made ready for duty. And special reconnaissance troops are being trained, more than capable of carrying a new kind of small atomic bomb that cannot easily be detected. These activities—all inspired by the lesson of Hitler's Germany. Now back to CBS News in America.

"They can't be serious?" wondered Terkel. "Can they?"

"I don't think so," I said. "I think most Russians are using *Pravda* for garbage. They're more frightened of war than we are."

"Okay then, tomorrow at 2 p.m. your time, right?" Hal asked.

"Right, see you then."

By the time I'd finished my broadcast, Max was handing his copy to the censor. "What did you lead with?" he wanted to know. That was a very common question at the Central Telegraph. Journalists wanted to know what other journalists were writing. They feared being scooped. I told Max about our visit to the U-2 spy plane exhibition and also *Pravda* quoting two military theoreticians about the U.S. building atomic bombs so small they could be hidden in tape recorders.

"I saw that," Max shot back, "but it all sounded like bullshit. I didn't touch it."

"You're probably right," I conceded, "but whenever the Russians talk about atomic bombs, I get nervous and think it ought to be reported."

Max laughed. "I'm so glad you're here. I needed somebody I can argue with."

As we walked back toward Tobi and Mady, Max paused here and there to introduce me to a few of the other American reporters. Preston Grover, a distinguished man with graying hair, was leaning into one of the cubicles, whispering something to a much younger reporter typing a story. "Preston," Max said, "meet Marvin Kalb. He's the new CBS reporter. He got here yesterday and is already hard at work, setting a very bad example."

Grover laughed. "Welcome Marvin. I'd heard that you were coming. Welcome." The AP bureau chief spoke softly, conveying the confident air of a southern gentleman, highly experienced and unlikely to be shaken by a Kremlin bulletin. I had read his copy for years. He'd been based in Tripoli during a long tour in the Middle East; he'd also worked in Paris and Berlin.

"I'm honored to meet you, Sir."

"Preston," he said with a warm smile. "Preston. No 'Sirs' here. Whenever you get a chance, please knock at our door. You'll find it always wide open."

I then met two young and friendly United Press International (UPI) reporters, Aline Mosby and Robert (Bud) Korengold, who worked for Bureau Chief Henry Shapiro. Though they both seemed terribly busy, pounding the typewriter keys as though they were rushing stories into print about a new world war, they stopped to shake hands and welcome me to Moscow. Bud looked to be about my age, Aline a little older. "You're going to be working very hard," Bud said. "The truth is, it's enormously frustrating, wearing, and mentally debilitating, but you're also going to love it. I don't know quite why." Bud was to become a close friend.

Another American reporter I met that evening was Tom Lambert of the *New York Herald Tribune*. Though he was Max's direct competition, one New York newspaper going against another, Lambert treated him with respect. No matter the pressure of a front-page story or a late deadline, Lambert always took the time to be friendly to a colleague, younger or older. He loved the English language and embraced it with a special tenderness, especially when he was trying to outwit the censor. One of his favorite stories was how he conveyed the hate Poles felt for Russians, a sentiment the censor would not normally have allowed. Soviet Marshal Konstantin Rokossovsky had just been named defense minister of . . . Poland, though he was a Russian. That night, Lambert wrote that Rokossovsky "was held in the same esteem in Poland as General Sherman in Atlanta." The Soviet censor must not have known much about the American Civil War; he let the Sherman reference slip right through. In a country where news was often hidden like diamonds in a deep, dark mine, Lambert apparently knew how to find the diamonds. A frustrated Khrushchev one day called him "the garbage collector," because Lambert could dig up what Khrushchev would have preferred remain hidden. I liked and admired Lambert the moment I met him.

When Max and I returned to Tobi and Mady, the dinner deal for the night had already been struck. We were to have dinner at the National Hotel, a long block away from the Central Telegraph. Unlike the Metropol, the National had a better dining room with, Tobi insisted, better caviar. As soon as Max's copy was cleared and sent to New York, we headed for the National and dinner with two old friends, each with valuable advice on how to get by in the Soviet capital. Their best advice was "stay cool; tomorrow will likely be worse." Unfortunately, we were to benefit from their advice for only another few weeks. They were finishing their tour in Moscow. Max was going to Washington and would soon be replaced by a former AP reporter, Seymour Topping, highly respected, a veteran of many years in Asia.

By very early Friday morning, I'd learned the hard way that our 5'10" double bed had not grown an inch in the preceding twenty-four hours. It had remained 5'10". I had tried sweet-talking the bed, patting it affectionately on its headboard and reading romantic poetry to it; but the bed, feigning indifference, remained 5'10" long. In desperation, as the sun rose, I dressed, determined to be Intourist's first customer. I was, not that it made much difference.

My "friend" seemed ready for my rhetorical assault. "Good morning, Mr. Kalb," she said. "How did you sleep?"

"I didn't," I replied brusquely.

The Intourist agent was about to smile. "It's not funny," I roared, cutting her off. "Not funny at all. For the second night in a row, I couldn't sleep, nor could my wife, and I demand a larger bed in a larger room. This cannot continue."

The agent had nothing comforting to contribute. "Mr. Kalb, even if I wanted to help you, I couldn't. The summer season is underway. Rooms are scarce. We have given you two rooms. I suggest you adjust."

"Adjust!" I exclaimed. "How can I adjust to a bed that is too small for me. It's 5'10", I'm 6'3"."

The agent shook her head. "I suggest you discuss this matter with the director. I have no authority to do anything. I'm sorry."

I had the impression she would have liked to help, but could not. "When will she be here?"

"She usually gets here at 10 a.m."

"I'll be back, probably late in the afternoon. Please tell her."

I spent the rest of the morning reading newspapers and writing two radio reports, which again focused on the U-2 scandal. Every newspaper was stuffed with similar stories, as though nothing else was worthy of publication. A thought occurred to me: was it possible that the avalanche of news stories condemning Eisenhower and praising Khrushchev reflected Kremlin concern that Khrushchev had suffered not just a diplomatic failure in Paris but also a political setback at home, weakening his position as party leader? Was Khrushchev using the drumbeat of press praise as protection against his political opponents—the Stalinists still in the Kremlin and the Maoist Chinese eager to condemn any Russian effort to improve relations with the West? This line of speculation was not hard news, but it was analysis worthy of a piece for the *World Tonight,* maybe that night or the next.

Before leaving for my lunch with Henry Shapiro, I told Mady about my unsuccessful and infuriating visit with Intourist, my radio reports, the ambassador's weekly 3 p.m. meeting with resident American reporters at the U.S. Embassy, and the planned follow-up meeting with Intourist. A sleepy Mady said she would use the time to try to put Heaven and Earth together in our bedroom and move the excess, of which there was plenty, into our office, using it now as a kind of storage depot. "Great idea," I said, unpersuasively. "See you later."

Shapiro lived in an old, shabby building, 3/5 Ulitsa Formanova, not too far from the once (and now again) fashionable Arbat section of downtown Moscow. He had inherited the apartment from journalist Eugene Lyons in 1935, and he'd lived there ever since. Lyons had arrived in Moscow in 1928, a United Press journalist with decidedly pro-Stalinist sympathies. During seven disillusioning years of living with the reality of Stalinism, Lyons became a passionate anti-communist. Normally a reporter's (or a diplomat's) apartment in Moscow would feature Scandinavian furniture, light, bright, and cheerful. This apartment was quintessentially Russian—in appearance, style, and feel. It was as if nothing had changed on Ulitsa Furmanova since pre-revolutionary days, not the heavy furniture, not the kitchen stove, not the small bathroom, and certainly not his bleak office, lined with bookshelves and lit by a single desk lamp. It was Shapiro's office, but it could just as well have belonged to a Menshevik, plotting in 1917 to topple the Tsar.

After a brief hello, the well-known UPI bureau chief, short, balding, with bushy eyebrows and a thick, dark mustache, invited me into his dining room, where a maid served a delicious lunch of blini with caviar. Shapiro, who seemed in a hurry, got right to the point. There was, among the foreign correspondents based in Moscow, a so-called "alliance system," he explained. According to rules dating back to World War II, the AP and the UPI led two competing news groups. Over the years, the AP tended to combine forces first with Reuters, and the UPI first with Agence France-Presse, and then both wire services would invite any other news organization—a newspaper, magazine, or network—to join one or the other group in a loose alliance designed to help everyone cover the secret world of Kremlin policy and politics more effectively. Shapiro naturally considered the UPI-led group to be better than the AP-led group. He boasted about his broad field of contacts and sources ("I've been here, after all, since the mid-1930s") and, as proof, the number of important scoops he'd achieved in his time in Moscow.

"Look, Marvin," he said, leaning forward as a salesman might, "I don't invite every reporter who arrives in Moscow to join me for lunch. I'm a busy man. I'm inviting you, because I know you are a serious student of Russian affairs. You speak Russian. You taught Russian history. You write books. You could be a big help to me"—he paused—"and I know I can be a big help to you." Another long pause. "So what do you think? Will you join us?"

I knew nothing about the "alliance system," and I was surprised by the speed and bluntness of Shapiro's pitch. "Mr. Shapiro," I replied, "I am flattered beyond words by this offer, and of course I shall give it the most serious consideration." I took a deep breath. "I had no idea such a system existed. Perhaps I should have."

"First of all, Marvin, you must call me Henry," Shapiro insisted. "Everyone calls me Henry. Second, I'm sure Grover will be in touch with you soon, if he hasn't already. When I see someone who can really help us, I move fast. I always have." The UPI was in serious competition with Grover's AP. Then, continuing to play to my ego, he added: "I read *Eastern Exposure*, and really admired it. Ludmilla, my wife, wanted to read it first, but I beat her to it." He flashed a broad grin. "Think about joining us, Marvin, but please do not take too much time. Call me in a couple of days, okay?"

"I shall, and thanks for a great lunch, Henry."

For the next few minutes, we discussed Harvard, our alma mater, he from law school, me from graduate school, and I again thanked him for the "alliance" offer and promised to get back to him "in a few days."

I decided to walk down the Arbat to the Central Telegraph, my next stop. It probably took no more than fifteen minutes, enough time for me to soak up some of the atmosphere of old Moscow and to reach a big decision: I decided not to join Shapiro's alliance—indeed, not to join any alliance. Grover did say something to me when we met about the AP's door always being open, but I didn't think that was a pitch; I thought he was only being polite. The fact is I wanted to maintain my independence. If, months later, I were to change my mind and join forces with any other news organization, it would probably be with the *Times*. Besides, though I respected Shapiro, I also had questions about his long tenure in Moscow: why would any American journalist want to live in Moscow for decades, since the 1930s? Was there no other story, no other country, of compelling interest? During this time, was he not obliged, for family or political reasons, to sell a slice of his journalistic soul? I didn't know, of course, but he left me feeling uneasy. I was soon to learn that a number of American diplomats felt the same way about him.

As I approached the familiar "Entrance 12" of the Central Telegraph, I knew I had made the right decision. I was on my first foreign assignment. I was a free and independent journalist, no matter what Kharlamov said or thought, and I wanted it to stay that way.

I spent less than a half-hour at the Central Telegraph. My copy was cleared quickly. My 2 p.m. circuit was on time. Was this "beginner's luck?" I wondered. Terkel was not on duty in New York. Probably, a day off. I didn't know the editor who recorded my stories. "Good job," he said, as he would also have said even if it was a bad job. "See you tomorrow." He had no messages or questions for me, I none for him.

———————

My next stop was the U.S. Embassy, a large building on another of Moscow's broad boulevards, impressive by Soviet architectural standards. Dirty tan in color, the embassy was divided into three parts: the bottom two stories were the least secure, set aside for visas, cultural and press relations; the top two stories were the most secure, reserved for the ambassador and his close associates; the middle half-dozen or so stories were for apartments. In 1956 I had worked there as a translator, an interpreter, and as a press officer, depending on the embassy's needs. Now, on this Friday, I was joining the other Moscow-based American correspondents for Ambassador Llewellyn Thompson's Friday, 3 p.m., "deep background" discussions about the news from and about Moscow.

My taxi stopped in front of the only large entryway into the embassy. A Marine sergeant stood on guard duty. I said "Hello" as I passed him; he nodded. (In 1956 I knew all of the Marines, because we lived together in America House, not too far from the embassy. Now I knew none of them.) Inside the embassy, behind a large desk, was another Marine. He was chatting with Connie Gagnon, the ambassador's very able assistant. I waited for a moment and then introduced myself, showed my passport, and said I was on my way to a meeting with the ambassador. The Marine checked a list, among many on his desk, apparently saw my name on it, and said, "Okay, Sir, thank you." With a smile, I saluted and headed to the elevator.

Intercepting me, Connie asked, "Can I help you?"

I told her I was going to a meeting with the ambassador. "Follow me, Sir. I'm Connie. I work for the ambassador, and I can assure you, I know the way there."

When we reached her office, adjacent to the ambassador's, a number of reporters were already gathered around her desk, chatting about some tidbit of news. Henry Shapiro was there, and I also recognized Tom Lambert, Preston Grover, and Bud Korengold. "Marvin," said Lambert, trying to look serious, "I can tell you're a good reporter. You've already met the embassy's best source."

Connie laughed. "At least, I know the embassy's best source," she countered skillfully.

It was almost 3 p.m. when a group of other reporters, including Max, entered. I waved at Max and introduced myself to Priscilla Johnson of NANA, Osgood Caruthers of the *Times*, Reinhold "Gus" Ensz of the AP, Peter Kumpa of the *Baltimore Sun*, and Aline Mosby of UPI.

"Okay, lads and lassies," announced Connie, herding the reporters into the ambassador's large, elegant office, "it's roundup time, and the ambassador doesn't like to be late." The ambassador was already seated behind his desk, a cigarette in his right hand. He was slender, graying, distinguished, and blessed with the rugged countenance of a cowboy, the John Wayne of American diplomacy. But since last I saw him, he seemed definitely to have aged.

I remember meeting him briefly in August 1959, when Moscow was one stop on my around-the-world research trip on the Sino-Soviet alliance. At the time both superpowers were exchanging national exhibitions and quietly trying to arrange a four-power summit to settle the vexing problem of a divided Berlin, something Khrushchev had wanted for years. The East-West atmosphere was promising, and Thompson had been active in the negotiations.

Now, Thompson was depressed, like many in Moscow's diplomatic community, who had hoped for an East-West breakthrough but got a Paris breakdown. He later confided to friends that he felt Eisenhower's approval of the U-2 spy flights had severely undercut his efforts to improve U.S.-Russian relations. But, as always, his personal feelings took second place to his professional responsibilities, which he defined as keeping his two "suspicious scorpions" from losing their cool. He would, if he could, maintain his friendly relations with Khrushchev, his close ties with Secretary of State Christian Herter and allied diplomats and his remarkably trusting association with the

American press, which he saw as a valuable asset in educating the public about the ups and downs of U.S.-Soviet relations. He had never been caught in a lie or a leak. At his weekly "backgrounders," he learned as much from the reporters as they from him.

Thompson had been meeting with the Moscow press corps since 1957, when he replaced the irreplaceable "Chip" Bohlen. Unlike Bohlen, who was gregarious and accessible, given even to gossiping if he felt it served his purposes, Thompson was almost always reticent, leaning back and listening, more comfortable asking questions than answering them, rarely engaging in speculation. He was a "Kremlinologist," as his daughters, Jenny and Sherry, described him in their superb biography, a student of Soviet policy and politics, and he considered this job to be a twenty-four-hour-a-day responsibility.

At this Friday gathering, Thompson pulled a surprise on the reporters. Instead of waiting for the UPI's Shapiro, as dean of the Moscow press corps, to ask the first question, he started the backgrounder with a brief analysis of Kremlin politics following the collapse of the Paris summit. Then he asked for comment.

His analysis brought a smile to my face. It coincided with my own thinking. Since the failed Paris summit, Thompson (nicknamed "Tommy") had not yet met with Khrushchev, but his reading of the Soviet press, plus his private conversations with other ambassadors, led him to believe that the Soviet leader had suffered a diplomatic and political setback in Paris. Else, why the thunderous press assault on Eisenhower and the rapturous praise of Khrushchev? Eisenhower had always been seen as a popular figure; now, after Paris, he was suddenly portrayed as evil, a puppet in the hands of "anti-Communist fanatics" at the CIA and the Pentagon. Khrushchev, on the other hand, had always been portrayed in a positive light. That was nothing new for a Soviet leader, but why this seemingly overnight eruption of praise? The U-2 crisis and the Paris meeting had dramatically worsened the international climate. That was obvious. But now what?

The reporters pressed Tommy. Did he believe that Khrushchev had really become vulnerable to political attack? Could he be toppled from power? Who could possibly replace him?

I listened to the questions and Tommy's answers, which were all interesting, but I had an entirely different question in mind: why would an ambassador as cautious as Thompson deliberately raise a question about Khrushchev's political vulnerability, knowing such speculation would likely be a front-page story in Western newspapers? Kremlin officials certainly knew about Thompson's "deep background" sessions on Friday afternoon; and if they saw non-sourced Friday-evening or Saturday-morning stories about Khrushchev suddenly losing a degree of power, would they not logically assume that Tommy had planted this line of speculation—and if so, why? What was Thompson trying to accomplish? More important, what was the White House trying to accomplish, for surely Thompson would not have leaked such a story without its permission?

The hour of give-and-take between a calm ambassador and an animated press corps passed with lightning speed. I deliberately paused while my colleagues rushed from the ambassador's office, each knowing he or she had a really good story. When they had all left, I approached the ambassador and introduced myself. Tommy warmly welcomed me to Moscow.

"I'm pleased CBS is back in the game," Tommy said, "and if I can help, or any of my people can help, please do let us know. Tell Connie. Here in Moscow we are one big happy family."

"A question, Sir?"

"Of course," he replied.

"You seemed eager to volunteer your analysis of Khrushchev's political position. And I wondered why."

"Oh, did I seem eager?" Tommy puffed leisurely on his cigarette, a picture of innocence.

"Yes, and I think the Russians would be interested in knowing why too, wouldn't they?" I continued.

Tommy smiled, his eyes wide open. "I guess they would be."

Connie gently harrumphed from the doorway, a clear signal my time was up.

———

While most of the reporters rushed either to their offices or to the Central Telegraph, I hurried back to the Metropol for another meeting with Intourist, one I was not looking forward to. I didn't think Intourist would be helpful, and I was certain Mady would be unhappy. It was obvious the minute I saw her that she had not had a good day. I found her seated on the only chair in the room, tired and despondent. All day, she'd been packing and unpacking, carrying packages from one of our rooms to the other, trying to find space where none existed.

I kissed the top of her head. "Mady, you don't have to go to this meeting," I said. "I can go by myself. I don't think much will happen."

"No, I want to go." I didn't argue.

When we reached the Intourist office, Madame Borisovna was messing impatiently with some papers on her desk. "Hello, Madame Director," I said, interrupting her, "I'd like to discuss our room problem, if you have the time."

She looked up, and when she saw us, her face crumbled into despair. "How can I help you?" she asked slowly, not meaning a single word.

"Madame Borisovna, we cannot continue to live in that room. It's that simple. Yesterday I offered a proposal to you, a compromise proposal in the spirit of Premier Khrushchev's policy of 'peaceful coexistence.'" I smiled a fake smile. "We'll keep one small room as an office, but we must have a larger room and bed for ourselves."

Mady jumped in, "I tried very hard all day to arrange things so we can stay in that small room, but it just doesn't work. The bed is too small, and there is not even room for our bags. I really tried. It simply doesn't work."

The director was not moved either by my compromise proposal or Mady's plea. "Reporters get two rooms," she repeated, "one for an office, one for a bedroom. And that is what we gave you." She folded her arms, leaned back in her chair and stared at us. "I suggest you accept this arrangement—and adjust." This was exactly the word her assistant had used—adjust!

Mady's reaction was sharp and short. "I just told you," she said, "I tried all day to adjust." She spit out the word, as if it were a deadly virus. "There is simply no room. No room." By this time, she was raising her voice, and I decided not to intervene. In our intellectual tussle with Intourist, I thought at that moment that we might be winning a skirmish, though hardly the war. Every now and then, when dealing with Soviet bureaucrats, the foreigner who loses her cool, raises her voice, and demands action can get her way. I noticed that the louder Mady spoke, the more she attracted everyone's attention in the Intourist office and the more she seemed to embarrass Madame Borisovna.

"We demand action," Mady repeated in a louder voice. "We cannot go on like this. Russia is a large country. Surely it has one large room in this hotel."

I nodded vigorously. "Surely it has one large room in this hotel," I repeated Mady's words as if they were gospel. "There must be one large room." Together we must have made a splendid chorus, because Madame Borisovna, raising both of her hands, seemed to call for a time-out, for us a victory of Pyrrhic dimension. "Let us meet again on Monday," she suggested. "Maybe over the weekend we can find a compromise."

"Why Monday?" I demanded, thinking we were on a roll. "Why not tomorrow? You work on Saturday."

"Yes, we work on Saturday, but we may not have an answer by tomorrow. Monday is better."

I thought Madame Director might be searching for some

kind of face-saving compromise. After all, she used the word "compromise," and she never had before. "Very well, Monday morning at 10 a.m.," I proposed.

"11 a.m.," the director countered. "11 a.m., not earlier. 11 a.m."

I allowed a few moments of silence to enter our negotiation. Everyone else in the Intourist office seemed to be watching us. Why not? I thought.

"11 a.m. then," I agreed. We both swiveled on our heels and exited the Intourist office, holding hands. At a safe distance from the director, Mady hissed, "I'd have insisted on tomorrow. I thought she was wobbly."

"You're probably right," I said, "but who knows? Maybe your little eruption worked. Maybe she is going to try to get us a bigger room. Maybe not. But she did say 'compromise,' which she hadn't before, and I wanted to give her a little space. We'll see."

It had already been a long, tiring day. A taxi to the Central Telegraph probably would have made more sense, but we decided to walk. Our route was by way of small, narrow streets, hidden behind tall, aging buildings fronting on busy boulevards. We were in no particular hurry. My circuit was set for 19:30 local time. We wandered slowly through noisy courtyards with children playing around parked cars. Mothers sat on rickety chairs, smoking and looking out for their children, apparently oblivious to the oddness of a playground serving as a parking lot—or was it a parking lot serving as a playground?

After a while, I realized we were lost. One courtyard looked like another. We were clearly foreigners, and Russians could be excused if they wondered why we were in their courtyard. I spotted a young man, possibly a university student, and asked him for the best way to Gorky Street. Happy for a chance to practice his English, which he had apparently been studying, he pointed to a passageway between two buildings and said,

"Go straight ahead through that . . ." He couldn't think of the word for *passageway.* "Passageway?" I suggested. "Yes, passageway," he repeated, "and through the passageway is Gorky Street." He grinned as though he'd just got an "A" on a final exam. "Straight through the passageway," he repeated to himself, "is Gorky Street."

His directions were perfect. Through the passageway was Gorky Street, and a block away, on the other side of the very wide boulevard, was the Central Telegraph. It still took almost ten minutes to get there, and I gave Mady a quick fill-in on Thompson's analysis of Khrushchev's suddenly shaky political standing—if indeed it was shaky, as Tommy seemed to believe.

"Interesting," said Mady, "but why would he do that? Why push that possibility now? The Russians must know he's the source."

"My question exactly. I asked Tommy why, but he wouldn't answer. Maybe what he's doing is ringing the bell for attention. Maybe he wants a meeting with Khrushchev."

The newsroom at the Central Telegraph was busy, but I found a seat at one of the round tables and wrote an analysis I tagged for the *World Tonight*. In it, I could not identify Thompson, nor U.S. officials, nor even the United States (he spoke to us on deep background), so I copied a style columnist James Reston of the *Times* used in similar circumstances. Often, after a deep background session with the president, the secretary of state, or another prominent official, he'd write, "The feeling here in Washington is . . ." or "There is a large question looming over this capital today."

So, my opening:

The questions many in Moscow are asking tonight are simple to raise but difficult to answer. First, has Nikita Khrushchev lost some of his political clout in the Kremlin following the collapse of the Paris summit and the U-2 crisis? Second, is he still the dominant figure here, or must he now share power; and if so, with whom? And, finally, what effect does this all have on U.S.-Russian relations?

These questions were being raised by "knowledgeable students of Soviet policy," I went on, but they were not accompanied by "knowledgeable answers." Since his return from Paris, Khrushchev had not delivered a speech or given any press interviews; nor had any other senior Soviet official. Where then could one find hints of a possible change in policy or personnel? Based on my 1956 experience as a translator of the Soviet press, I thought there was one place where there might still be an occasional flash of enlightenment, even in a totalitarian state such as the Soviet Union, and that was the Soviet press. In the last few days, I sensed in my reading of the press two shifts of nuance and emphasis. First, President Eisenhower, once popular with the Russian people, was now being attacked as the leader of a "provocative anti-Soviet conspiracy," hatched at the CIA and the Pentagon, and involving the possible use of nuclear weapons. Eisenhower was consistently described as "the hand behind the conspiracy." And second, Premier Khrushchev was either allowing or inspiring his own "personality cult," the boundless adulation accorded Stalin during his worst days. I found that interesting, because Khrushchev was the one who demolished Stalin's personality cult, but now appeared to be standing back and admiring the unmistakable rise of a new one, in which he was being described as a "great and historic leader," "wise" and "experienced," "flawless" and "brave" in the execution of Soviet policy and "admired" and "feared" by friends and foes. Reading these descriptions, I had the feeling Khrushchev tolerated the hyped language of the personality cult in order to retain power but felt decidedly uncomfortable about its excesses.

I continued,

It seemed as though Khrushchev suddenly needed massive doses of public praise to hold off a rise of criticism from Kremlin hardliners, always skeptical of his policy of "peaceful coexistence" with the United States and other Western nations. There has also been running criticism from Communist China, but it's had little effect on Khrushchev's personal power, though it did weaken the Sino-Soviet alliance.

The larger question for me was Russia's relations with the United States, balanced as they were on the head of a nuclear pin. I closed my analysis with this thought:

In the Khrushchev/Eisenhower era, Russia is a dangerous antagonist but one that is well-known. The president thought that he knew what Khrushchev would do in a crisis. But now, given the Soviet leader's wildly flamboyant performance in Paris, Eisenhower may well have questions about Khrushchev—and his policy. And, in a nuclear age, when the Russians are accusing Eisenhower of acting like "Hitler," raising images for Russians of the bloody horrors of World War II, this can lead to dangerous miscalculations. Now back to CBS News in America.

I showed it to Mady before giving it to the censor. She nodded, approvingly, which meant a lot to me. Every now and then, I would feel a rush of insecurity. I would think of myself as an apprentice pretending that he had mastered the art of being a foreign correspondent. Yet, at the very same time, I would recognize that my apprenticeship was over—I was CBS's Moscow correspondent; I was also its bureau chief. I'd made it. Still, on occasion, my self-doubts would surface. Maybe that was a good thing.

For the first time since I arrived on Wednesday, my copy did not wing its way past the censor. Quite the contrary! This time, because I had written about a possible change in Khrushchev's position, I suddenly found myself on slippery, delicate turf, and the censor probably needed guidance from the Central Committee about what a foreign correspondent could, or could not, report on the possibility that Khrushchev had actually suffered a setback in Paris when the Soviet press was filled every day with stories about his success in Paris. The censor needed more time, and took it.

While waiting for the better part of an hour, Mady and I wandered around the newsroom, me introducing her to a number of the reporters whom I had met earlier in the day at the ambassador's briefing. Often, at such times, perhaps as a way of relieving the pressure, everyone would gather around one of the big tables and tell jokes, share anecdotes, exchange gossip, nosh on Russian goodies, or after a while, just start pacing anxiously from one end of the newsroom to the other. Rarely in all this noisy chatter did they talk about the story that was keeping the censor so busy, each still hoping for a competitive edge, which in this case seemed elusive. As soon as the censor cleared one story, though, all of the others quickly followed; and there was a mad dash to the telephone booths or the broadcast "studios" (actually large closets with a table and microphone), as reporters sought to be first with the news, a primordial instinct that has long driven the journalism profession.

In time, my copy was cleared and my circuit opened, quickly linking me to editor Terkel in New York. Minutes before, he'd been reading interesting AP and UPI stories about Khrushchev possibly losing some of his clout and wondered whether I'd be pursuing the same angle.

"And what have you prepared for your breathless listeners today?" he quipped.

"Not much, just a thumbsucker on Khrushchev," I replied.

"Thought so. The AP and UPI are running pretty much the same story. Could you guys have all been to the same briefing?"

"Anything's possible in Moscow."

I realized at that moment how easy it was for the Russians to trace the sourcing of stories. Here was Terkel speculating about a briefing, and he was in New York. Why not the censor in Moscow engaging in similar speculation? Also, if most or all of the American reporters were filing roughly the same story at the same time, they probably got it from the same source. And assuming their source was an American, since no Soviet official was talking, who better a source than Llewellyn Thompson, the American ambassador? Wasn't he the key source for many stories that just happened to break on Friday afternoon?

I did the usual 5-4-3-2-1 countdown, and, when okayed, read my script. Terkel asked me to reread my close. "It's very important," Terkel commented, "and I want you to read it more slowly. No rush. Let the meaning of your words sink in." Hal was always teaching.

I reread the close. "That's better," Terkel said. "You've given your listener something important to think about. Damned good piece."

"Thanks, Hal. Something important is going on here, and we'll try to figure it out."

"I have no doubt," Terkel said, "no doubt at all."

By the time I finished my broadcast, half of the reporters had already left the Central Telegraph—to go home, to a diplomatic dinner, to the ballet or a play. Whichever, the reporter's life in Moscow was not dull. One of those still there was Lambert, who was apparently re-editing his story. The writer in him was never satisfied with his copy. Nearby, reading a book, was his wife, Helen, an artist on a perpetual hunt for the right scene. Seeing me, Lambert stopped for a quick round of introductions, and then asked, "What did you lead with?"

"Questions, really." I didn't want to go into details.

"What questions?" Lambert asked, drilling just a little bit.

"Why now? Why speculate about Khrushchev's position?" I opened up a bit.

"Well, why do you think?"

The gates, having been opened a bit, now opened further. I told him that my reading of the Soviet press suggests Khrushchev was building his own personality cult as a way of strengthening his political standing at home. Why was that necessary now? I asked. Because of rising domestic criticism from Kremlin hard-liners, I thought.

"Fascinating," Lambert said, "really fascinating. You've given me my story for tomorrow." He grinned, Helen laughed, and we promised one another we'd have dinner "real soon."

Which we did, with Tom and Helen, then with Bud Korengold, with Preston Grover, with Osgood Caruthers, and with the small group of embassy officials, who were willing to share information and impressions about Soviet life and politics. One such official was Richard Davies, a political officer, who became a good friend. He had read my book and my articles and considered me, he said, a "serious student" of the Soviet Union. For most of the American reporters based in Moscow, Russia was a terrific story, but it was one of many, and they'd soon be moving on to the others. For a few of us, it was the highlight of our careers. When I was named CBS News Moscow correspondent, I felt I'd reached the pinnacle of my professional aspirations. In time, I too would go on to cover other stories in other countries, but I'd always regard my Moscow assignment as the realization of a dream.

Soon after our arrival, Davies invited me to an office get-together and not long after me and Mady to a dinner in his embassy apartment. We met Jean, his gracious wife, the proud mother of their three sons. "Mr. Davies" soon became "Dick." Jean remained Jean. Dick was amusing, smart, and exceptionally knowledgeable about Kremlin politics. Though he never confided an embassy secret, which I did not want or need, he was very helpful. I could check with him on something I'd heard or surmised, and he would steer me away from what he knew to be questionable or wrong ("Do you really want to get a little pregnant?" he'd joke), leaving me closer to what he knew to be accurate. In this way, he would learn what I had uncovered without ever leaving his office, and I would be left with the added benefit of a diplomatic perspective that made for a better story. It was a good deal for both of us.

BARGAINING WITH BUREAUCRATS

Because I had lived in Moscow before, and Mady had studied the often deceptive ins and outs of Soviet policy, the transition from Gramercy Park South to the Metropol Hotel for both of us was relatively smooth—except for the size of our room and the length of our bed. We could not evade these ubiquitous constraints, though valiantly we tried.

Work came first, of course, and took most of the day. I often met two, sometimes three, circuits a day, diligently read the Soviet press, wrote informative stories, attended any briefing anywhere, went to museums and the theater ("reporting" on Soviet culture, after all), and dropped in on embassy receptions and dinners, whenever possible.

In those early days, I was living on the pinnacle of a new, high-octane assignment. We both acted as though we had an inexhaustible supply of energy, but privately we understood that we desperately needed sleep—six to eight hours a night at a minimum, and I was getting two or three a night, if that, and Mady only a little more. We knew this could not go on for much longer.

One day, a friendly Henry Shapiro, still eager to lasso me into his rodeo, recommended we approach the "Directorate for Service to the Diplomatic Corps"—UPDK, as it was called. "Every now and then," he advised, "they can be really helpful." Though originally set up to help only diplomats, after a while UPDK opened its doors to foreign correspondents as well. In the Soviet mind, the diplomat and the journalist fell into the same category: both were suspected of working for foreign intelligence. Still, on occasion, UPDK did perform a valuable service. If a diplomat or a journalist needed a driver, for instance, he, or she, could turn to UPDK. If a maid or a cook was wanted, again, turn to UPDK. Or a plumber to fix an uncooperative toilet, one could turn to UPDK. If apartment lights suddenly blew, UPDK, of course.

My need was equally urgent: I needed a room and bed I could fit into. Could UPDK help? Yes, I was certain. Would UPDK help? That I didn't know, but had my doubts.

On Saturday morning, I called UPDK, and, lo and behold, someone actually answered the phone and agreed to see me. I jumped into a cab and went to an old, pre-revolutionary mansion on Kropotkinskaya Ulitsa, not too far from the American Embassy. This neighborhood of old Tsarist mansions was being retooled to serve the modern Soviet bureaucracy. Of personal interest to me, the U.S. Embassy had rented one of these mansions years before for its translation service. That's where I worked in 1956.

At UPDK I met with a relatively young official, who was surprisingly friendly, even though the American government and President Eisenhower were being lambasted in the Soviet press every day. I explained my problem. She appeared sympathetic. My heart beat a bit faster. Could I have stumbled upon something? "I proposed a compromise to Intourist," I went on—"that we keep one small room for the CBS office, and acquire a larger room and bed for our living quarters."

"Compromise, you say. Where's the compromise? You'd still be keeping two rooms and expanding one." Her words conveyed the impression of a rigid bureaucrat, but her manner was pleasant. "You'll have your office, and you want a bigger bedroom. Sir, this is the tourist season. Be reasonable."

"Madame," I tried to sound reasonable. I used an example from Russian history. "I am almost as tall as your great tsar, Peter the Great. Could he have slept in a bed only 5'10" long? Of course not. You deal with other American journalists. They have both apartments and offices. I am only asking for comparable space."

My UPDK interlocutor looked up at me, nodded and said, "Yes, you are very tall, but I must say Intourist is following the rules. You were offered two rooms."

"Yes, but can't rules be changed every now and then, depending on circumstance."

"Rules govern our society," she said stiffly. "Rules cannot be changed." But then, switching from rules to possible accommodation, she added, "I'll talk to Madame Borisovna, and then we'll see."

On that ever so slightly positive a note, the UPDK official stood up, shook my hand, and said, "Good luck." I thanked her for her "time and cooperation." She apparently did not like the word "cooperation." She was not "cooperating," she insisted. "Rules are rules, and must be obeyed. Intourist is following the rules."

"Yes, of course," I said and left UPDK. (Over the years, I was to return to UPDK many times.) Would she really try? Would she have the clout to change Madame Borisovna's mind? Could the rules be changed? UPDK was presumed to be part of the KGB and, as such, had more power than Intourist; but would it use that power on our behalf? I did not think so.

On Monday, as agreed, at 11a.m., I met with Madame Bor-isovna, who was, as usual, very busy.

"We have spent a great deal of time on your complaint," she started. "You have gone to other bureaus, I see, and of course that is your right; but we here at Intourist know the rules. We know our job. We gave you two rooms, same as for any other journalist, and again I urge you to adjust to your space. And in time you will."

"Madame Borisovna," I said, thinking I'd raise our negotiation to a higher level, "I think Premier Khrushchev's policy of 'peaceful coexistence' with all nations makes sense. No one, except a mad person, I guess, wants war. Can we not," I smiled broadly, "peacefully coexist? You and I? We'll remain in two rooms, as you insist, but one will be larger. Surely in a hotel of this size and history, such a room can be found."

"You advanced that idea last week, Mr. Kalb, and we rejected it then, and we reject it now," she said, with an air of finality. "I am busy, and I suggest, as I did last week and again today, that you adjust to your situation. You will, after a while."

"After a while?" What did she mean by that? Did she know something we didn't?

I realize now, many years later, that of the two players in this diplomatic contest—me versus Intourist—only one was playing: me. Not for a moment was Intourist playing a game. We were two young, highly educated, but in some ways naïve, Americans trying to adjust to life in the mighty Soviet Union. The Cold War was raging, and the Soviet bureaucracy, with its many unchangeable rules, was clearly winning this battle of the rooms. It had the power; we had the makings of an amusing story for our children and grandchildren.

But I persisted. Why not? When diplomats run into a stone wall, the good ones often choose not to run into it but around it. They try first to keep the negotiation alive and then return to the negotiating table with a better proposal.

I shook Madame Borisovna's hand and held it a bit longer

than usual. "We'll be back tomorrow," I said, "when I hope you and I can continue to try to find a solution to this problem. I'm sure there is one." From the look on Madame Borisovna's face, I wasn't sure she agreed.

Mady and I concluded that what we needed was what Mideast negotiators would later call an "interim solution." After all, we thought we were dealing with a short-term problem. We'd be at the Metropol for a month or so, and then move into an apartment and maintain a separate CBS office. A month or so, no more. That was what we had been led to believe, and, innocent as we were, we believed it. But did Madame Borisovna know more?

In this context, we came up with a possible solution. We might each have thought of it at the same time. It made sense. Would it make sense to Madame Borisovna? The problem, after all, was space. In one room, we did not have enough of it. But if we combined the space of both of our rooms, we would have just enough space for one bedroom. We'd be giving up our office, but for a brief time that seemed like a manageable sacrifice.

The following morning, I returned to the Intourist office. Madame Borisovna paused long enough for me to tell her we had another proposal.

"Mr. Kalb," she said, exasperation in her tone and manner, "we have reviewed your earlier proposal, and rejected it, and advised you to adjust to your two rooms. Please do so."

"Madame Borisovna, we have a new proposal we think you might find appealing. You gave us two rooms. Each room on its own does not have enough space for us. But if we combined both rooms, we would then have enough space for our bedroom."

"Let me understand," she said, a spark of interest in her eyes. "You would give up one of your two rooms for one larger room?"

"Yes," I replied.

"Let me think about it," she said. "I'll be in touch with you, maybe later today or tomorrow."

"Excellent," I said.

Wednesday was a special day for us—the anniversary of our first full week in the Soviet capital, exciting journalism mixed with frustrating bureaucracy. The story appeared with a frantic urgency in the daily press—it was the Kremlin's persistent attack on "U-2 espionage flights," which "exposed" American "perfidy," "violated Soviet sovereignty," and "threatened" international peace, even raising the possibility of nuclear war. The Soviet bureaucracy, on the other hand, operated in darkness, in an unforgiving atmosphere of fear, obfuscation, and deliberate delay. The bureaucrat instinctively distrusted speedy decisions, even if one was easy to make. Change was the equivalent of subversion; it was regarded with suspicion. A slothful resistance would naturally develop, inaction becoming the norm. If you compared the communist bureaucracy with the tsarist bureaucracy, you'd find there was not much difference, except in one area. Fear was a much more compelling feature of communism than it was of autocracy.

Our continuing problem with Intourist was a good example of the irritating power of the Soviet bureaucracy. Another was my dealing with the Bank for Foreign Trade. Because banks were state-run institutions in the Soviet Union, they followed state-imposed rules. There was no such thing as a credit card or a personal check, and I refused to get my rubles on the black market, which, I was told, many foreigners did. The official exchange rates were so absurdly unrealistic. I decided, even before arriving in Moscow, that if I were ever to be expelled from the Soviet Union, I wanted it to be on the basis of what I reported, not what I did on the black market. Therefore,

I exchanged dollars for rubles at the official rate, whatever it was—ten rubles to the dollar in those days. For me, it was the safe way of functioning in Russia.

Of course, I couldn't just call the Bank for Foreign Trade. I had to go there to set up a CBS account for daily expenses, such as cabs, tips, and food, and another to pay for our hotel room, to subscribe to newspapers and magazines, to hire a translator or driver (with UPDK's help), to send cables from the Central Telegraph and make international telephone calls—in other words, for just about everything one could imagine a reporter needed. I asked CBS to send a $3,000 money order to the bank to fund my everyday needs, which CBS did.

That did not mean, of course, that once the bank got the money order, my account was immediately established, or that I could begin to withdraw money for daily use. I had to go to the bank three mornings in a row, starting early Monday, and plead for action, else, I argued, my work would be severely hampered.

Finally, on Wednesday, the Bank sizzled with action, Soviet style. A typically lethargic bureaucrat slowly filled out an endless form. (Of course, first a copy of the form had to be found.) Then I had to wait on long lines to clear a set of totally unnecessary hurdles involving my identity. Showing my passport was not enough. Then, with all the papers signed and stamped, I had to return to the original bureaucrat for his final perusal and approval, which he eventually gave but with obvious reluctance. And only then did I get a small card telling me that I was Marvin Kalb, that I worked for CBS News, and that I was authorized to pay my bills in rubles, exchanged at the bank's rate. Leaving the bank, I could have been depressed by the experience, but the optimist in me cautioned, "Marvin, you have your official card, and it only took three days. Move on!"

And, on this special Wednesday, Intourist, believe it or not, agreed to give us a larger room!

An envelope had been slipped under our door. Inside was a brief note on Intourist stationery. "Please come see me," it read. No name, but, I assumed, who else but Madame Borisovna?

Wasting not a minute, I sprinted to the elevator and then to the Intourist office. "Good morning, Madame Borisovna," I said, interrupting her absorption with an official document. "You wanted to see me?" I tried to contain my excitement but almost certainly failed.

"Yes, Mr. Kalb," she said, looking relieved for the first time in our negotiation. "I was able this morning to liberate a small suite on the fifth floor, room 570. It was booked for the whole summer, but I was able to arrange for the other guest to go elsewhere, to be moved to another hotel. You can have it for as long as a month or two or longer, at least until you get an apartment. But I must know immediately."

Why did I suddenly feel that the rug was being yanked from under my feet? This was what we wanted—indeed, what we proposed; so why this uneasy feeling? "May we look at the room first?" I asked.

With an impatient wave of her hand, she grunted, "I thought that's what you wanted."

"It is, Madame Borisovna, but surely my wife has a right to see the room before I agree."

She glanced at her wristwatch. "All right," she murmured, "but I can hold it for only a half hour." She added, "I suggest you hurry."

Why the big hurry? I wondered.

I picked up Mady, told her the news, and together, with a mix of promise and concern, we entered room 570, which was to be our home, office, and "warehouse" for the rest of the year, although at the time that was a pessimistic projection beyond our gloomiest calculation. We'd been told, time and again, that we'd have an apartment "in a month or so."

Room 570 was the literal coming-together of two small bedrooms, except by becoming one larger room, it lost a bathroom and a window in the process. But it did satisfy our request for a larger bedroom, and the bed seemed to be larger, too, though that might have been an optical illusion. "Mady," I said, seeing her furrowed brow, "this is hardly ideal, but it is what we asked for."

"Yes, it is what we asked for," she repeated. "But . . ."

"And it's only going to be for a month or so," I broke into her thought. "I think we can manage."

"I guess we'll have to," Mady smiled. She returned to our room and began packing once again, and I returned to Intourist and Madame Borisovna. She had already filled out the proper forms for hotel occupancy for a month or longer. They were on her desk. "Mrs. Kalb and I," I announced, "will move into room 570 this afternoon. Thank you for your assistance."

Gracelessly, she did not respond with a parallel "You're welcome." She simply pushed the forms toward me, and said, in a commanding tone, "Please sign forms," adding a moment later, "We can arrange help for your move." Though she was finally finished with the Kalb problem, she seemed dissatisfied. And, oddly, so was I.

I signed the forms, shook her hand, and left. Having wrangled a larger bedroom out of Intourist's inventory, I should have felt satisfied—I had achieved my goal.

Years later, Henry Kissinger, no stranger to tough negotiations, told me that the best agreements left both sides feeling slightly dissatisfied. The rocky negotiation for room 570 was no Camp David, but Borisovna gave us two rooms and got one back, and we got a larger room, which, as it turned out, was to become our living and work space for the next seven months.

Most of the time we managed reasonably well, but early in our occupancy of room 570 we lived through a nightmare. The circumstances were so miserable that Mady was reduced to tears and I had to resort to threats in an effort to stop what turned out to be daily, even hourly, harassment.

Soon after we moved into 570, people, unidentified but malicious, started to pound on our door, day and night, threatening that if we didn't leave the Metropol, "immediately," they would take certain unspecified action against us. "Like what?" I would shout through the closed door. "You'll see," they would answer. Officials, again unidentified, telephoned our room every five to ten minutes, night and day, yelling epithets and again demanding that we leave the Metropol. Or else.

This pressure was unrelenting. On June 3, after a week in our new quarters, I felt I had no option but to complain bitterly to Kharlamov, warning him that I would have to close down CBS operations in Moscow if this "rampant hooliganism" and "overt discrimination" did not come to an immediate stop. I also warned that if this activity did not stop, I would broadcast the news of "anti-press hooliganism" to the world. I then stated, accurately, that other foreign correspondents based at the Metropol were given a suite plus an office. Why not CBS?

I also wrote a letter to John Day, which I never actually sent, outlining our unfortunate experiences and urging him to write to Kharlamov, demanding "respect" and "civilized behavior" toward CBS and me, else I would have to leave Moscow and the CBS bureau would again be shuttered. After writing the letter, I deliberately left it on my desk, knowing the KGB would read it while we were out of the room. I wanted both the KGB and Kharlamov to know that neither I nor CBS would be intimidated by this "anti-press hooliganism."

A few days after my direct appeal to Kharlamov and my "letter" to Day, the annoying calls and the frequent door-pounding stopped, as if an order had come down from above. Apparently, in exchange for the relative silence, I got a note from Madame Borisovna informing me that our apartment would become available not in "one month or so," as she had earlier forecast, but in three or four months. Was this her way of exhibiting her power? Maybe, but then she had us as her guests for that much longer.

Communication in the Soviet Union took many odd forms. Some worked. Harrison Salisbury, the *Times* correspondent in Moscow in the early 1950s, had an awkward but effective way of communicating with communist officials. Whenever he met a stonewall in the press department, which was often, he would get his message or complaint through to higher communist officials by speaking to the microphones he assumed were in his hotel room's chandelier. The KGB was always listening. Salisbury did not always get what he wanted, but he did get his messages through to higher authorities. My experience several years later was similar. Not much would really change in the Soviet Union until the whole structure of communism collapsed in 1991.

THE "PIGEON" LOST IN MY PASTERNAK ADVENTURE

From the first days of my Moscow assignment to the last, few stories touched me as deeply as the death of Boris Pasternak, the Russian poet and author of Doctor Zhivago who won the Nobel Prize for Literature in 1958.

Pasternak happily accepted it, but then, a few days later, had to double back and reject it because of fierce opposition from many communist critics. He died two years later on the evening of May 30, 1960. He was 70.

There was no official announcement. Word reached me and other journalists the next morning at the Central Telegraph. Pasternak was buried two days later in a small cemetery in the shadow of the Church of the Transfiguration in the writers' colony of Peredelkino in suburban Moscow.

Though I had never met Pasternak, I felt as though I knew him. The story of his passing saddened me, but the story of his life inspired me. I had read some of his poetry and, of course, *Doctor Zhivago*, his remarkable novel about life and love during and after the Russian Revolution. I admired his lonely insistence on creative independence in a political environment that demanded conformity. "I am alone," he wrote in a poem called "Hamlet." "All 'round me drowns in falsehood."

For me, as a journalist with a story to tell, Pasternak's death fell into three parts: first, my visit to his dacha in Peredelkino; then, the unforgettable scene at his funeral; and finally, the "pigeon" who wouldn't or couldn't fly.

One of my pleasures, early on in Moscow, was meeting a number of very impressive western European foreign correspondents. Among them was Michel Tatu of *Le Monde*, for whom Kremlinology was a fine art. He instinctively knew when a comma in a *Pravda* editorial was misplaced, and since commas were not normally misplaced in such editorials, what that could mean. On Saturday, May 28, during a brief chat at the Central Telegraph, Michel raved about an article in *The Paris Review* by Olga Carlisle about her recent visit to Pasternak's home in Peredelkino. He gave me his copy. "I've been there, but you ought to go," Michel said. "Maybe you'll even get an interview."

"Can I? Do I need special permission?"

"Technically, yes, but not really. Peredelkino is in the forty-kilometer zone that we're allowed to travel in. Have fun."

While waiting for my circuit, I read the Carlisle article. Michel was right. It was beautifully written, and it contained valuable insights. It described a Pasternak who was "handsome," looking like an "Arab," she wrote, "youthful" in his manner, walking with "long, loping strides" across the snow and ice, and delightfully accessible, perhaps, she guessed, because he knew her parents.

Moved by her description, I decided that I'd go to Peredelkino the next day, a Sunday. If I could get an interview, that of course would be a huge professional benefit; but even if I could just meet and talk to him for a few minutes, I'd be thrilled. It would be worth the trip. Also, Russians generally visit on Sundays, family and friends getting together for a favorite snack of sliced fresh cucumbers soaked in vinegar and washed down with vodka. I wasn't family, but I was his friend. He just didn't know it as yet.

I canceled my Sunday circuit and to avoid asking Intourist for a limo, which seemed inappropriate, though I wasn't sure why, I negotiated the cost of a ride to and from Peredelkino with a cab driver, one of those waiting for a customer in front of the hotel. Thirty rubles each way, we both agreed, plus a hefty tip for waiting. The drive took about forty minutes. We went from the heart of the city to the suburbs along roads that became narrower and bumpier, until they became dirt roads.

The driver, a nice man named Sasha, probably in his late forties, asked many questions, mostly about American cars. His favorite was Chevrolet. He had difficulty believing that many American "workers" could afford one. I assured him many did. He also wanted to know about President Eisenhower—why he had become such a "warmonger," when only recently he had seemed like a "peace-loving president." That gave me an opening to ask him about Khrushchev at the Paris summit. He said he wasn't interested in such "big questions." I asked him instead about his life, his job, his family, and he was perfectly willing to tell me he was married, had two children, and lived in a suburb.

"But what do you think about Premier Khrushchev? Do you like him?" I persisted.

The driver looked at me through the rearview mirror, paused as he pondered a reply, and finally said with a sigh, "He's okay. He does his job." He then went silent. Clearly he felt he had said enough.

When we reached Peredelkino, a community of prominent writers and artists living in traditional wooden dachas, Sasha drove directly to Pasternak's home, as if he'd been there before, which raised a question in my mind about Sasha, but I didn't choose to pursue it. Pasternak lived in a weathered two-story dacha on Ulitsa Pavlenko, on a hill covered with apple and lime trees, lilac bushes, and fir trees, with an old wooden gate that was slightly ajar. Could I just walk in? That was what Carlisle said she had done. Why not? Leaving my tape recorder and camera in the cab, I pushed the gate open all the way and walked up the hill to the house. But before I could get there, a heavyset woman and three young men suddenly appeared, blocking my path. They were pleasant but preoccupied and quite insistent that Pasternak was not able to see me or anyone at that time.

"Is he not well?" I wondered.

The woman, smoking a cigarette, replied, "Boris Leonidovich is simply not able to see anyone at this time. He is . . .," she paused, "occupied."

One of the young men, who looked like a young Pasternak, possibly a son, added, "Did you call? Who are you? Did he know you were coming?"

"Forgive me," I tried to explain, "I'm Marvin Kalb, an American reporter. I did not call, but like so many others, I am a great fan of Pasternak and just wanted to meet him. It would be a great honor."

The woman, wanting me to leave, repeated, "Boris Leonidovich cannot see anyone at this time. We are very sorry."

"No, no," I stammered, "I am very sorry. I did not mean to intrude. If you could just give him my card and tell him I'd be honored to return to see him whenever he wishes. I'm staying at the Metropol in Moscow. Thank you."

The young man shook hands with me before I turned to leave. He looked especially sad.

Passing through the gate, before I got into the cab, I noticed, on the other side of a broad field of springtime flowers, the austere Church of the Transfiguration sitting on a small hill, its blue and white, onion-shaped domes glistening in the sunshine. I would soon be seeing the church, the flowers, the field, and Pasternak's home again.

The ride back to the Metropol was comparatively quiet. I was absorbed with many unanswerable questions, most particularly Carlisle's description of Pasternak as "youthful," which led me to presume he was in good health. Why then did everyone at his home look so sad? Why was "Boris Leonidovich" not able to see anyone "at this time?" With these questions, my visit came to an end.

Though the news of Pasternak's death on May 30 was big news in the rest of the world, in Russia, his home, it merited only a small item in two literary newspapers—*Literature and Life* on June 1 and *Literary Gazette* on June 2. The major newspapers made no mention of it. But, in a daring show of what would later be called *samizdat*, the underground publishing of controversial books, word of his funeral appeared in unofficial posters pasted on buses, trains, and in the Moscow underground. Thus word was spread that Russia had lost one of its greatest writers.

In Russia, most writers live in a special world. Novelists are revered, many spoken of with the respect the ancient Greeks reserved for their gods. Poets attracted the popular adulation of Hollywood stars. I once heard Yevgeny Yevtushenko recite one of his poems before a hushed audience of 20,000. And, in America, I could not help but wonder, how many would watch, admire, and listen to a poet?

By the time I returned to Pasternak's dacha on Thursday afternoon, June 2, the day of his funeral (in this telling of the story, I've italicized many phrases and sentences from radio reports I wrote over the next few days), it was already crowded with many hundreds of Russians, young and old—maybe many more, for they seemed to spill over into the field between his dacha and the church. They had come to mourn Pasternak as much for his exceptional talent as for his love of Russia, which he once described as *"the incomparable Motherland—famed far and wide, martyred, stubborn, extravagant, mad, irresponsible, adored—with her eternally splendid and disastrous and unpredictable adventures."* Pasternak was born a Jew in a thoroughly assimilated, secular family, his father a renowned artist, his mother a concert pianist. He converted to Orthodoxy, in part because he felt that by embracing the faith, he would be bringing himself closer to his "incomparable Motherland."

With my tape recorder rolling and camera in hand, *I made my way slowly through the crowd toward the dacha, passing many in tears, some carrying flowers, a cluster of young Russians with books of Pasternak's poetry and his exceptional Shakespeare translations and more than a few security men in mufti, looking totally out of place, as they took pictures of Russians they suspected of harboring "bourgeois sentiments."*

The mourners moved slowly, silently through the dacha. *The floor of the veranda was covered with pine needles. All of the mirrors were veiled, as Russian custom demanded. A yellowing Pasternak lay in an open wooden coffin, his head on a large white pillow with roses, lilacs, and narcissuses running down the side of his legs. His arms were crossed over his stomach. Mourners would occasionally pause, say a prayer and cross themselves in Orthodox fashion, before moving on into the living room, where the only sound, aside from the rustling of feet, was a Chopin nocturne played on a dilapidated upright piano by Sviatoslav Richter, probably Russia's most renowned pianist,* who was there in clear defiance of a communist injunction to ignore Pasternak's funeral. From the kitchen came the unmistakable aroma of *pirozhki*, Russian meat pastries, prepared apparently for the evening's post-funeral feast. *Outside, beyond the living room, was a garden, splendidly vibrant with pine trees, bushes in blossom, and dozens of Russians sitting on the grass listening raptly to a young poet, Andrei Voznesensky, who read from Pasternak's poetry and referred to him as "my mentor and muse." Remembering their many lengthy walks and Sunday get-togethers, Voznesensky said Pasternak had given his life "magi-cal meaning and a sense of destiny." The presence of Richter and Voznesensky alone attested eloquently to Pasternak's place in the pantheon of Russia's notable artists.*

From the moment I approached the dacha, I started film-ing the entire spectacle, hesitantly at first, then with no inhibition—the mourners, the veranda, the coffin with Pas-ternak, the Chopin nocturne with Richter, the garden with Voznesensky—and no one, not even the security men, made any effort to stop me. If there were other American networks recording the scene, I did not see them. It was as if Paster-nak, although now from beyond life, had ordered a distinctly un-Soviet openness to his musical, poetic, and very Russian departure.

And it was not yet over. *At 4 p.m., as the church bells rang, six Russian men slowly hoisted the coffin to their shoulders and carried it out of the dacha and down to the dirt road, passing hundreds of mourners, who instinctively pulled back, like the Egyptian seas for Moses. Many crossed themselves while others reached for the coffin just to touch it, their last contact with the poet they felt best represented them. Then, very carefully, the six pallbearers walked slowly down the winding dirt road that led to the church yard, followed by a thick phalanx of mourners, who threw bouquets of flowers at the open coffin, while sing-ing church hymns.* They seemed indifferent to a cloud of dust that swirled over the coffin and to the broiling late afternoon sun. With many others, I took a shortcut directly across the hot flowering field, anxious to reach the gravesite before the hushed procession. *On top of the hill was the striking Church of the Transfiguration, which dated back to the fifteenth century. Half-way up, in the shadow of three white birch trees, was the gravesite that was to be Pasternak's final home.*

A brisk breeze blew across the field and up the hillside, no doubt reminding some of the mourners of a favorite Pasternak poem, called "Wind."

"*I have died*," the poet wrote, "*but you are still among the living. And the wind, keening and complaining, makes the country house and forest rock.*" *Pasternak respected nature's awesome power; for him, Peredelkino was a wondrous pantheistic paradise. Before his coffin was finally lowered into the grave, his lover, Olga Ivinskaya, kissed his forehead,* which she later described as "already cold," *while his wife, Zinaida, the heavyset woman I first met on Sunday, stood to one side, smoking, staring coldly at the scene, probably simmering with hurt and anger.*

No religious service accompanied his burial, no priest said goodbye. Maybe that should not have been surprising. Pasternak was not observant, and if he represented anything, it was a lonely independence of spirit. I heard only one brief eulogy, delivered by a friend, later identified as Valentin Asmus, a professor of philosophy. *He praised Pasternak but also criticized his "mistakes." A few young Russians wanted to offer their eulogies. One spoke in glowing terms about Pasternak. "Over the poet's open grave," he proclaimed, "his verse shall resound." At that moment, when others could have joined to honor Pasternak, a big man, almost certainly security, interrupted them, shouting, "Enough! Enough! It's over. Go home!" Most of the mourners, having paid their respects, actually left, but quite a few remained, gathering around the simple Pasternak gravesite, covering it with flowers, reciting his poems, singing prayers, feeling the need on this overwhelmingly sad occasion to bond with one another for the loss of a giant.* They stayed for hours.

I could easily have joined them. Pasternak's death moved me deeply. But I had to return to Moscow, write and broadcast my story and then, somehow, find a "pigeon" for the film, which I considered precious.

Webster's Collegiate Dictionary defines *pigeon* as "any of a widely distributed family of birds with a stout body, rather short legs and smooth and compact plumage." That's one definition.

But if you were an American correspondent in Moscow with exposed footage of a major news event, and you wanted desperately to get the footage to New York, where it would be developed and then be broadcast on the *CBS Evening News*, you would first have to rush to Sheremetyevo Airport, no matter the time of day or night, to find a "pigeon," who would be kind enough, or naïve enough, or brave enough, or foolish enough, to carry your film past customs, without declaring it, knowing it was illegal to do so, and then onto the plane heading for any Western city for transshipment to New York. As a correspondent, you had to have known (and I did) that the shipment of exposed film out of the Soviet Union by a foreign correspondent was illegal. You needed official permission, and that took time and was rarely granted. So, I sought a pigeon—usually a tourist, a diplomat, or another journalist—who was leaving Russia for a trip to the West. Whether the pigeon was a man or a woman, whether they had a stout body, or a slim body, or fat legs or slender legs, or plumage such as a stunning hat or a luxurious fur coat, meant absolutely nothing to the correspondent as long as the exposed footage eventually made its way past Moscow customs and to New York. That this illegal system occasionally worked was a tribute to both advance planning and pot luck.

On the evening of the Pasternak funeral, I did not have the time or foresight to plan a safe escape for my footage. I had to rely on pot luck, and soon after arriving at Sheremetyevo, after an exhausting but exciting day, I thought I'd hit the jackpot, even though, from all objective appearances, the odds were stacked against me. The terminal building looked almost empty. There was only one flight westward, but it was to a desirable destination—London. (There were many flights from London to New York.) The Moscow-London flight was still a few hours away, leaving, I hoped, time to catch a pigeon. With fixed determination, I made my way to the waiting room where twenty-odd passengers were reading, chatting, or nibbling on peanuts. It took only a quick glance around the room for me to realize that I'd spotted a likely candidate.

Fussing with a huge carry-on bag was a well-dressed, middle-aged woman, who was talking amiably to a younger woman seated next to her. They looked American, but I was unsure. Could they be mother and daughter? Perhaps. Teacher and student? Possibly. Could they be CBS listeners? I hoped so. I sat down a seat or two away from them and pretended not to be listening to them, although I was listening very intently. They were definitely American, probably New Yorkers. The older woman was boasting about a photo she had taken of a Kremlin guard earlier in the day. She wondered aloud whether she would have trouble clearing customs, since she and her daughter—yes, it turned out to be her daughter—both carried cameras with exposed footage.

"No," I said, intruding into their conversation, "you shouldn't have any trouble. After all, you're here as tourists, aren't you? Tourists take pictures. That's understood."

"Yes," Mother replied, nodding with relief. "We should be fine." Then, a moment or two later, she asked, "By the way, do you live here? You sound like an American."

"I do live here, and I am an American. I work for CBS. I'm Marvin Kalb."

Daughter, who had been staring at me, broke into a broad grin. "I thought so," she exclaimed. "I thought so. I recognized your voice. Sure, Marvin Kalb. You've heard him, Mom, haven't you?"

Whether she had or not, she said she had, smiled broadly, and we got into a pleasant conversation about subjects ranging from Russia to CBS. What had they seen in Moscow? Had they been anywhere else? Did I really know Edward R. Murrow? Daughter was especially interested in knowing whether Eric Sevareid was really as handsome in person as he was on air? We got along so well I thought the time had come to ask the key question: would they take my exposed film with them to London?

"I was at the Pasternak funeral today," I said, genuinely excited. "It was a fantastic story, beautiful, very moving, and," holding my small package of exposed film in my hands, "my film is about the funeral. It would be great if I could get this footage to London as soon as possible. It would be for the *CBS Evening News*." A long pause preceded my question. A plaintive look spread across my face. "Will you help me? Will you take it to London?"

Before she could respond, a brainstorm suddenly struck me. "You know what? I'll ask Eric Sevareid to pick it up from you at the airport." In truth, I did not know whether Sevareid was in London; and even if he were in London, he would not have gone to the airport to pick up and transship film, no matter how important the story. After all, he was Eric Sevareid. But, playing on Daughter's obvious attraction to Sevareid, Mother's apparent desire to help an American reporter, and my keen interest in getting the footage out of Moscow, I promised Daughter that Sevareid himself would meet them at the London airport to pick up the film. Hearing my promise, Daughter leaped into Heaven, but Mother, though tempted to help, was still suspended between Heaven and Earth.

"Why don't you just ship it?" Mother asked, suspiciously. "Isn't that the way you would normally do it?"

"Yes," I admitted, "but it's very late, and, according to the rules, I'd have to process the film here in Moscow before it could be shipped, and that would take forever." I looked beseechingly into her eyes, hoping her maternal instincts could be aroused to see and appreciate my dilemma. "So will you help me?" I pleaded. "It's a terrific story, and I'd like to get it on air as soon as possible."

Mother was clearly hesitant; Daughter just as clearly enthusiastic about the challenge.

"But it's illegal, right?" Mother wanted to know.

"Yes, but so is your exposed film." I was being disingenuous: there was a big difference between a tourist taking pictures of a Kremlin guard, and a correspondent shooting film of a major news event. "All exposed footage is illegal, but most of the time nobody pays any attention, and you sail right through."

"Think so?" Mother was tilting toward Daughter's willingness to run the risk. "I don't want any trouble."

"I don't think you'll have any trouble." I tried sounding persuasive but knew my conscience was beginning to intrude into my salesmanship. "But I can't swear," I mumbled. "Life is funny, and Russia is crazy, but I think you'll both be fine. Really, I do. Will you help me and take my film, please?"

Daughter, with decisiveness, nodded yes, and Mother, with reluctance, looked down at her carry-on bag, slowly opened it, and, before she could change her mind, I dropped my small package of exposed CBS film into it. Realizing what had just happened, Mother quickly zipped up the bag and placed it protectively under her knees. The three of us then resumed our conversation about CBS, as though nothing had happened. By the time their flight was called, we were great friends. I'd written their name (Field), address, and phone number into my notebook and promised, crossing my heart, that I'd call the next time I was in New York. They in turn promised to listen to me every morning. It was the perfect deal. As they headed toward their dreaded encounter with customs, I shouted, "Have a great flight, and give my best to Eric." Daughter smiled and Mother waved, as they slipped behind a security barrier, my film snuggled securely in Mother's bag. My first adventure with a pigeon had gone well. But would it fly?

I waited on tenterhooks for the flight to be airborne before I dared to leave Sheremetyevo and return to the Metropol. Once there, I sent a telegram to Paskman. It was artfully crafted:

"Pigeon" Londonward BA 617 arrival 22:15 local Stop Give "Pigeon" note signed "Sevareid" saying "best regards" but had "urgent" broadcast Stop Best Kalb.

Knowing nothing more I could do to get my first big television story to New York, I went to bed.

I rarely dream, but that night I had a dream that mixed wild fantasy with wilder desperation. I dreamed that Sevareid actually went to London's Heathrow Airport, met Mother and Daughter, gave both a signed autograph, graciously stood for a photo with Daughter, took possession of the Pasternak footage, then transshipped it to New York, where it just made the *CBS Evening News*, beating the competition, and then he, John Day, and Paskman sent me a joint telegram of congratulations. "Great job," it read. "Beat NBC by miles."

And then at 7 a.m. I woke up. My dream now only a dream, I quickly dressed, eager to learn whether the film had ever reached London and then New York. Sadly, there was no morning telegram to that effect. I sent a telegram to the CBS office in London and New York asking if British Air 617 had in fact reached London and if anyone had been there to get the film. Yes, as it turned out, the plane had reached London. It got there on time. A CBS courier with a "Sevareid" note stood at the gateway asking one arriving passenger after another whether she was Mrs. Field. No one acknowledged his appeal. When the last passenger had left the plane, the courier rushed to the British Air counter and asked for a loudspeaker announcement that a Mrs. Field arriving from Moscow on BA 617 please come to the BA counter. No one came. He waited for an hour, he later told CBS in London, but there was no Mrs. Field and therefore no film of one of the most remarkable stories I would ever cover. All day, while on my circuits to New York or in my telephone calls to London, I appealed for any information about BA 617 and about Mrs. Field or her daughter, and I learned nothing.

I was crushed, disappointed, and bewildered. What had happened? Had customs confiscated the film? Had she chickened out at the last moment? Had she been questioned about her conversation with an American reporter at Sheremetyevo and, frightened, decided to drop the film into the nearest wastepaper basket before even boarding the plane? Why had she not acknowledged the CBS courier? She must have heard the announcement. Whatever the reason, the film never got to New York. My first experience with a pigeon had been an unmitigated disaster. CBS viewers never got to see the extraordinary Pasternak funeral, at least not on CBS. And, though I got the story, and did several long descriptive, analytical pieces for radio, which generated rave reviews, I never got to report the story on television. My disappointment was deep, lasting not just years but decades. I remember it to this day.

Fourteen years after Pasternak's death, Nikita Khrushchev said what no other Soviet leader would ever have said—that he was sorry that when he had the chance to greenlight the publication in Russia of *Doctor Zhivago*, he "failed to act." Khrushchev admitted a failing. In the second volume of his remarkable memoir, *Khrushchev Remembers: The Last Testament*, published in the United States in 1974, the then former Soviet leader said simply, "I did nothing, and now I regret it." The manuscript had been "put in cold storage" by the police, meaning the powerful KGB, leaving a "bad aftertaste for a long time." Still, if Khrushchev, as party leader, had wanted to overrule the KGB, the book would have been published, and Russia would have been able to avoid the global condemnation that accompanied the book's suppression.

Why did he do "nothing," yet feel the need for a public, though belated, "regret"? One possible explanation was that in 1956, when *Zhivago*'s publication in Russia was a hot question, a literary grenade seconds away from a political explosion, Khrushchev was still living with the dangerous consequences of his famous speech at the 20th Party Congress. This had demolished Stalin's god-like legacy and ignited the fiery Hungarian Revolution, which threatened to destroy Russia's grip over Eastern Europe. Overnight, it seemed, Khrushchev's political position had become vulnerable. Could he, so soon after that speech, again confront the KGB and other party hardliners and allow publication of a highly controversial book with explosive potential? Apparently, not.

In his memoir, surreptitiously composed and secreted out to the "capitalist" West, no different ironically from what Pasternak himself had been forced to do, Khrushchev imagines a self-satisfying, reformist scenario, according to which he actually approved publication. He might have been driven by a belated sense of guilt. "Let's go ahead and publish the book," he hypothetically posits, "so that Pasternak will be able to go abroad and pick up his award. We'll give him a passport and some hard currency to make the trip." Though a reformer, Khrushchev could not abandon the autocrat's inclination to lie. "Then, quite unexpectedly," he continues, with feigned innocence, "Pasternak let it be known through a statement in the newspapers that he had no intention of going abroad and that he wasn't even going to raise the question."

In fact, when Pasternak was awarded the Nobel Prize, he would have been delighted to accept it in Stockholm; but when the Kremlin opened a brutal propaganda campaign against him and his novel, threatening even to expel him from his beloved "motherland," Pasternak sent an urgent, personal appeal to Khrushchev not to expel him, sweetening his appeal with the promise that he would never consider leaving Russia under any circumstance. Khrushchev, the autocrat, could have rejected his appeal and sided with the hardliners. He could easily have forced Pasternak's expulsion from Russia. But

Khrushchev, the reformer, chose simply to ignore Pasternak's appeal, knowing the effect would be that Pasternak would not be expelled.

For the next two years, Pasternak lived under a loose form of "house arrest" in Peredelkino—not dissimilar, as it developed, from the way Khrushchev lived in the Moscow suburbs after he was unceremoniously ousted from power in October 1964. Neither was executed, neither put in chains. (Footnote to an era: *Doctor Zhivago* was not published in Russia until 1988, exactly thirty years after it had become a bestseller everywhere else.)

"DO SVIDANIIA"

After covering the Paris summit and the Pasternak funeral, I found that the balance of my first year as Moscow correspondent flew by at warp speed, punctuated by two wholly unanticipated events—the arrival of our bed and the departure of a broadcast legend.

From June to December, Khrushchev was my story—whatever he said, wherever he went. His politics, policies, and personality fascinated me. He was raucous and unpredictable, pushy and aggressive, tough as his peasant background, but when the occasion arose, he could also be charming, flashing a smile as wide as the Siberian plain. Always, it seemed, he was testing the limits of his ability to win the day in his running confrontation with the United States.

Khrushchev rewrote the script for a Soviet leader. He was so unlike Stalin, who was remote, untouchable, rarely appearing in public. Khrushchev enjoyed projecting power, even if much of it was pure propaganda. He stimulated a rush of nationalist pride, he produced an avalanche of dramatic copy—and he knew it.

At diplomatic receptions, routinely frequented by Western reporters as much for the food as the story, one would often find Khrushchev holding forth for diplomats and reporters alike, joking, taking questions, boldly attacking Western policies. He loved being the center of attention. His Politburo cronies, including the powerful Politburo comer, Leonid Brezhnev, who ultimately replaced him, stood off to one side, laughing when their leader laughed, serious when he scowled. It was in this setting that I met Brezhnev, who occasionally offered me a grudging answer to a question, but rarely one that made news.

For a reporter, Khrushchev was obviously the best show in town—and on the road. Like the eighteenth-century tsar, Peter the Great, Khrushchev loved to travel, especially to the West, which he both envied and spurned. When he had occasion to hit the road, he always had a ready suitcase, as did I and most other resident Moscow correspondents.

After a while, I came to realize that by covering Khrushchev, I was also covering the confused and complicated history of the Soviet Union. It was a fascinating assignment—to my way of thinking, the best outside of Washington, D.C.

Unlike most of my colleagues, who had apartments, offices, and a comfortable bed, Mady and I had the austere grimness of room 570 in the Metropol Hotel. The bed and I were plainly incompatible. It remained 5'10" in length; I remained 6'3" in height. I didn't fit.

And then on one wonderful day in early July 1960, everything changed. Our large double bed arrived from South Orange, New Jersey, thanks to the generous spirit and magical maneuverings of Ralph Paskman, the same foreign editor who had roughed me up during the Paris summit. When I discovered that the bed had made its way to the Metropol, I belatedly realized that Paskman must also have had a heart. In those days in Moscow, I was known as the reporter who worked every angle to get a larger bed, but failed, until the "Paskman" miracle happened.

I used to stop every morning at the Intourist office and, depending on my mood, begged, complained, yelled, argued, and pleaded—"I need a larger bed" was the core of my appeal. Madame Borisovna, after a while, would hide when she saw me entering her office. She'd had enough of Kalb.

On my daily visits to the Central Telegraph, I appealed to any correspondent who would listen that I was in desperate need of a double bed—as I put it plaintively, "a nice, simple, normal double bed." "Sorry," they'd say.

I checked at the U.S. Embassy, where there might have been an extra double bed, but my request was considered so unusual that the maintenance officer figured he'd get into trouble if he found such a bed. He took the easy bureaucratic route: he simply declared there was none.

And, of course, I objected to the press department's Kharlamov that we were promised an apartment, but weeks had passed without one. "When will we get our apartment?" was my frequently asked question; his answer, never directly from him, was, "You will get an apartment and an office soon."

"When?"

"Soon," I was told; and the phone would click, line disconnected.

I even wrote nagging letters to my boss, John Day, complaining about this persistent problem, but my appeals had little impact, perhaps because my work product suggested I had no problems at all. I did radio broadcasts almost every day, and though I had no cameraman, I also did television pieces based on the film that I shot and shipped. I urged Day to write a letter to Kharlamov, pleading on our behalf for an apartment. He said he did. Whether he did, I never knew. I never got a carbon.

At wit's end, in desperation, I sent a letter to Paskman. I did not really expect an answer. He'd shown little to no sympathy for me in Paris. I assumed that if he did answer my letter, he would not be helpful. He would pass the buck. He would say only Day could do something, not he.

But, from Paskman one morning in late June came a telegram with a totally unexpected question. "Please be specific," it read. "How can we help with bed problem?"

I was astonished. Paskman, sounding reasonable? Paskman, sympathetic? I decided to reach for the stars. Why not?

"Could you please send our bed?" I asked. "It's at my in-laws in South Orange, New Jersey."

If Paskman regarded my request as an example of youthful chutzpah, that would not be surprising. It was. In fact, I suspected that by sending my request, phrased as it was, I had only worsened an already shaky relationship.

Days passed with no Paskman response. I was not surprised by the silence. But, unbeknownst to me, my usually unsympathetic foreign editor was, during this time, getting Day's reluctant approval to send my bed to Moscow. Expeditiously, as it turned out. It reached Moscow a week later. How could it have arrived so quickly?

CBS *airmailed* our bed from South Orange to Moscow. That's right! The bed was *airmailed*, wrapped like a big holiday gift, including sheets, pillows, and pillowcases, from a small town in New Jersey to the capital of the Soviet Union.

And Paskman made the arrangement. Unbelievable!

Again the proud possessor of a double bed, I was able to get five or six hours of sleep a night, sometimes more, and Mady was able finally to enjoy one of the comforts of home, though 4,664 miles from home. No Superman was I, for sure, but I was able with the extra sleep to recharge my energy cells and cover the footloose Khrushchev for the rest of the year, no matter where he went. The restless Soviet leader certainly maintained an active schedule.

With great fanfare, Khrushchev went to Austria in early July, a goodwill mission designed to prove that the Soviet Union was nothing more than a friendly neighborhood bear. The big story on this trip was not a new trade agreement, which was expected, but rather the embarrassing sight of dozens of large bags and boxes, stuffed to overflowing with consumer goods, waiting in front of the Imperial Hotel for the return flight to Moscow. Apparently, what Khrushchev and his family could not find or buy in Moscow, they found and bought in Vienna, even if the sight of the bags and boxes undercut Khrushchev's propaganda boast that the Soviet Union would very soon "catch up and surpass" the West in overall production. These were the ingredients of a good television story.

On August 19, Khrushchev stage-managed the U-2 spy trial of Frances Gary Powers, who was accused of violating Soviet sovereignty. A death sentence was possible, even likely. But, with Khrushchev's eye on bigger game, namely the troubled future of U.S.-Soviet relations, Powers was given a much lighter sentence, and within two years he was freed in exchange for a Soviet spy. With the help of my colleague, Sam Jaffe, he of the lavish cocktail parties on the east side of Manhattan, I managed to get an exclusive interview with Powers, which, even though exclusive, contained little new information.

On the same day as my interview with Powers, Khrushchev announced triumphantly that two Soviet dogs had just returned safely from a space flight and would be available for "interviews" later in the day. Dogs in space? That was a big story. I was not the only foreign correspondent who raced from the conclusion of the Powers trial to a science center for a chance to meet the two dogs, Belka and Strelka, who charmingly barked a propaganda message of Soviet scientific superiority to the world.

In early September, Khrushchev traveled to Helsinki, Finland, a small, courageous nation that successfully resisted a Soviet invasion in 1939, proving it could maintain its independence even though it lived on the rim of Soviet power. Soviet leaders, including Khrushchev, learned it made more sense to coexist with Finland, however uneasily, than to fight it. I was delighted to report on Khrushchev's visit to Finland, because it was one of my favorite countries. I admired its style and spunk, or what the Finns might call its "sisu."

Over the years, whenever I journeyed by train from the Soviet Union to Finland, or back again, I was always amazed by one extraordinary sight, among many others: on the Finnish side of the border, the grass grew tall and green; on the Soviet side, it was always scruffy, if it grew at all. Yet the climate was the same on both sides of the border.

Later in the month, Khrushchev flew to the United Nations in New York, where, for almost a month, he exploited this well-known backdrop for a riveting display of personal diplomacy. From morning till night, he was on the run, not wasting a minute. He courted the newly independent nations of Asia, Africa, and Latin America, rarely missed a chance to denounce the United States and the North Atlantic Treaty Organization (NATO), threatened to organize his own United Nations, and in a final act of defiance, he negotiated a new and dangerous alliance with Castro's Cuba that proved to be a preamble to the October 1962 missile crisis. The sight and story of Khrushchev hugging the bearded, jubilant Castro in a Harlem hotel should have been proof that they were hatching a strategic plan that in time would bring the world to the edge of a nuclear conflagration. Many suspected problems; few suspected problems of that magnitude. In retrospect, it proved that the Khrushchev-Castro duo was the definition of big-time trouble.

In November, back in Moscow, Khrushchev had trouble of another sort, closer to his Marxist heart. He hosted an extraordinary summit meeting of eighty-one Communist Party leaders that brought his ideological differences with China's Mao Tse-tung to the surface, fracturing the Sino-Soviet alliance. This story played to my strengths as a student of the Sino-Soviet alliance. It also reconfirmed the value and importance of the round-the-world trip Mady and I had made in the summer of 1959.

Much to my surprise and delight, my reporting from Moscow also attracted attention and admiration, and in November, the *Sunday Times*, a highly respected British newspaper, asked me to be its Moscow correspondent, filing a weekly analysis of Soviet affairs. CBS had no objection, and I agreed. This new assignment added a European perspective to my news analysis, which enriched my copy.

As I traveled with Khrushchev and watched him perform on a global stage, catching a brief interview with him when I could, my coverage became absorbed with two questions: one that seized my attention and never let go; and the other that seemed constantly to preoccupy Khrushchev.

First, could a reformer such as Khrushchev succeed in changing a dictatorial system of government?

That was the question that gripped my interest and imagination from my first days in Moscow. I could see his efforts at reform even in the lobby of the Metropol Hotel. There I met a few of the thousands of political prisoners released from Siberian jails in 1956. They tried, not often with great success, to recapture the strands of their ruptured lives. Those with industrial skills went to their old factories seeking jobs. Those who were teachers went to schools. Those who were writers returned to the magazines or newspapers where once they worked and asked if they would be welcomed back. Those few who spoke English and had the courage to go to a hotel lobby in downtown Moscow met with foreign journalists, who were in the market for Russian-to-English translators. I spoke with a number of them and found to my surprise that their familiarity with American literature was truly impressive.

Khrushchev had also demonstrated his commitment to reform by denouncing Stalin at the 20th Party Congress and cutting the military budget while boosting consumer spending. I wondered, how far could Khrushchev's reforms go? Could they evolve into a more democratic form of government? Could he, in the final analysis, change Russia?

Whenever I had the chance at a diplomatic reception to discuss politics, foreign policy, or even basketball with him, I could not keep these questions from popping into my mind. Probably because I was a student of Russian history, I tried to find answers in books about Russia and in my own experience in Russia. Khrushchev was plainly part of the answer. His face was a map of Russia, his personal background a study in the rise of communism in a vast country stretching from the Baltics in Eastern Europe across the Siberian plains to the Pacific Ocean.

The answer, I thought, had to lie somewhere in Russian history, which was hybrid in nature, tied as much to the West as to its own Muscovite blend of "Orthodoxy, Autocracy and Nationality," as formulated by Sergey Uvarov, the conservative nineteenth-century theoretician who was the subject of my unfinished PhD dissertation.

Russia's imprint on global history and culture has left its distinctive mark everywhere. Its composers and writers have produced some of the world's great music and literature. Concerts in New York or Paris regularly feature the works of Tchaikovsky and Mussorgsky, and no Western university can ignore the classics of Tolstoy, Dostoevsky, or Chekhov. Eighteenth- century tsars Peter and Catherine were strongly influenced by Western military technology as well as by French and German philosophy. Throughout the nineteenth century to the start of the Russian Revolution, a political and intellectual battle raged between "Westerners" and "Slavophiles" about whether Russia should align its future with the West or go its own way. The battle was called "Whither Russia?" Even communists such as Lenin and Trotsky measured their success in part by whether Germany and other Western industrialized nations would follow the example of their 1917 revolution.

Yet, although there were undeniably powerful connections between Russia and the West, one of them unfortunately was not the importation and subsequent flowering of democracy. A number of Russian writers, such as Herzen and Turgenev, dreamed of democracy but experienced its pleasures only on their trips to the West. Never at home did they breathe the promise of democratic rule.

But still the question lingered in my mind: could Khrushchev's rupture with Stalinism and his obvious program of reforms succeed in the Soviet Union? I wanted so much to believe that the answer would be yes, but the evidence everywhere was that it was much more likely to be no.

The Soviet Communist Party remained the dominant political power in the country, and dissidents were easily contained and, if necessary, eliminated. More important, the reformer himself, Khrushchev, was a totally committed communist, who sincerely believed in the Marxist-Leninist system of government, in which power devolved from top to bottom. He saw reform as a necessary step toward improving the system, not toward replacing it. Moreover, the ruling party elite, though divided on budgetary priorities, was united behind a shield of fierce patriotism, convinced that Russia was surrounded by real or potential enemies and, right or wrong, had to be protected against all enemies, foreign and domestic. Russia, in their minds, would always be "Mother Russia," with a Teutonic twist, Russia *uber alles*, or in today's vernacular, "Russia First."

If Khrushchev's role as a reformer in Russian history absorbed me, the 1960 American presidential election was the issue that captivated Khrushchev. It seemed always to be on his mind, wherever he was. Who would be president of the United States after the election in November? Who would be the person in position to inflict devastating damage on Mother Russia? Would it be the Republican, Richard Nixon, who would likely pursue President Eisenhower's policies on Berlin, or would it be the Democrat, John F. Kennedy, who might at least consider a new approach to the problem?

Like everyone else in Moscow, Khrushchev had to wait for an answer, and that was no easy thing for him to do. He was impatient. He summoned a troika of "America" experts—his foreign minister, Andrei Gromyko; Soviet ambassador to the United States, Mikhail Menshikov; and his son-in-law, Alexei Adzhubei, editor of *Izvestia*—and he posed very specific questions to his experts and demanded answers.

Would Nixon follow Ike's U-2 policy?

Would Nixon be a rigid hardliner, or might he be a surprise and accept détente as the backbone of U.S.-Soviet relations?

Might Kennedy change Ike's U-2 policy? Could he buy into the concept of East-West détente?

Of course, none of his experts could go beyond speculation. None was a specialist on American affairs. Still, Gromyko told Khrushchev that, according to his foreign ministry specialists, Kennedy would probably have apologized for the U-2 mission, which was good, but they also thought Kennedy would favor a "belligerent" military buildup on Berlin, which was bad.

Khrushchev was dissatisfied. He wanted to know more about Kennedy, the man. Gromyko explained that Kennedy was the scion of one of America's richest families, that he'd studied at Harvard and had "an acute, penetrating mind capable of quickly assimilating and analyzing" information. He was no lightweight, Gromyko emphasized. According to biographer William Taubman, Khrushchev received "less flattering assessments" of Kennedy from Adzhubei and Menshikov. The former disparagingly described Kennedy and his brother, Robert, as "little boys in short pants." The latter, thinking he was accurately conveying the opinion of the diplomatic corps, dismissed Kennedy as "an inexperienced upstart."

Khrushchev had met Kennedy once during his brief 1959 visit to Washington's Capitol Hill. He told Kennedy he thought he looked "too young" to be a senator. Khrushchev actually had a much better sense of Nixon. He had spent many hours with the vice president during Nixon's 1959 visit to the American Exhibition in Moscow, and Khrushchev considered him an "unrepentant hardliner."

Khrushchev, after a while, came to the unsatisfying conclusion that "Kennedy is an unknown quantity" and therefore wished "Nixon would win because I'd know how to cope with him."

But not really. During his trip to Austria, I asked Khrushchev whether he preferred Nixon or Kennedy. He jokingly replied, "Roosevelt."

———

I clearly had a terrific year. 1960 was good to me. I went from one satisfying story to another, and, on December 29, to the most personally and professionally satisfying of them all.

Though I'd been a foreign correspondent and bureau chief for only seven months, John Day, who had questioned my ability to be a Moscow correspondent, arguing I had no prior experience, invited me to join a panel of senior CBS foreign correspondents in New York for the eleventh annual edition of the highly acclaimed, one-hour, year-end broadcast, *Years of Crisis*, a jewel in the CBS crown.

I greatly admired the broadcast. It was one of Murrow's finest programming ideas. He imagined reporters gathering around a bar after a busy day covering a big story, shooting questions at one another, and then arguing about answers—so, what really happened?, who said what to whom?, anything unusual, funny, important?—always with a serious undercurrent of pride in what they'd discovered, whom they'd met, and what it all meant. On television, the bar in Murrow's vision became a studio, the drinks became microphones, and the network provided an hour of primetime television. It was Murrow's way of informing the public about what was happening in an increasingly complicated and dangerous world. It was CBS's way of boasting that if you were really interested in serious news and analysis, you'd come to the right network.

We "band of brothers," as Murrow described us, an accurate and politically acceptable term in those days, met briefly on December 28 to discuss the program. Day told us not to "make speeches," and though Murrow, as moderator, could have a note or two in front of him, we could have none in front of us. I left the meeting feeling my stomach slowly turning into a knot.

On December 29 we all gathered in Studio 41 two hours before the 10 p.m. broadcast for make-up and the shortest pep-talk I'd ever heard. Av Westin, a good friend whom I'd met early in my time at CBS, was director, and all he said was "Break a leg, guys." At 9:45 p.m., we were seated around a large rectangular table, four of us on one side, four on the other, and Murrow at one end, an ashtray and a clean pad of paper in front of him. We knew where to sit because notecards with our last names had been placed on the chairs.

To Murrow's immediate left was Winston Burdett, the Rome correspondent, who'd spent most of the year reporting from Africa. To his left, Richard C. Hottelet, an experienced foreign correspondent who had covered the United Nations for many years. And then a pipe-smoking Dan Schorr, who was based in Bonn, West Germany, responsible for the chronic crisis of a divided Berlin and the seething unrest in Eastern Europe; and finally, Peter Kalischer, based in Tokyo but an energetic explorer of the vastness of Asia, always with an eye on communist China.

To Murrow's immediate right was Howard K. Smith, who had covered World War II, then Western Europe and was now the network's chief Washington correspondent. To his right, David Schoenbrun, based in Paris but in 1960 absorbed with the anticolonial rebellion in North Africa, especially in Algeria; then Alexander Kendrick, London bureau chief responsible for covering Great Britain's shrinking but still influential empire; and finally, me, the new Moscow bureau chief, as far from Murrow on the right side of the table as Kalischer was on the left.

At exactly 10 p.m., the floor director, acting on a cue from Westin in the control room, snapped his right index finger at Murrow, who looked up at the camera through hazy cigarette smoke, as he'd done hundreds of times before, and, after an opening "Good evening," briefly introduced the program, making the point that we'd been at this job of reporting world news for a long time (excluding me, I thought), that we'd be "unrehearsed," and that we had a lot to discuss. But before we plunged into the substance of our reporting, he wanted us to introduce ourselves, starting with Burdett. Fortunately, I was at the end of the line. My throat was dry, my right foot tapping an unknown tune. When my turn finally came, I managed to say, "I'm Marvin Kalb, and my beat is Moscow," after which I leaned back, took a few deep breaths, and hoped I was ready for the intellectual combat I'd seen on earlier broadcasts of this year-end classic.

Murrow's first question: what was, in our judgment, the most meaningful event on our beat? Smith said the election of Kennedy. Burdett spoke of the independence movement in Africa. Kalischer invoked the rise of communist China. As they spoke, I searched my mind for an event both important and yet hardly recognized, and found it, seconds before Murrow turned to me. "The Pugwash Conference," I said, explaining that while East-West tensions escalated, and nuclear weapons proliferated, Russian and American scientists quietly gathered in Moscow for another meeting to explore ways of containing the spread of nuclear weapons. Pugwash was the name of the Nova Scotia town where these annual get-togethers began in 1955. The Moscow meeting was hopeful and especially interesting, I added, because four Chinese communist scientists, including three educated in the United States, had also joined the discussion. I noticed Burdett nodding with genuine interest and Hottelet smiling approvingly.

We then discussed the global phenomenon of "neutralism," the balancing of a nation's loyalty between East and West, a concept the Eisenhower administration regarded with suspicion. Burdett, Hottelet, Schoenbrun, and Kalischer argued that neutralism was changing, and we'd better appreciate and adapt to the changes. Schoenbrun and Hottelet clashed about what should be the proper American response to the civil war in Algeria. Schorr stressed the danger of a divided Berlin sucking Russia and the United States into an unwanted, unplanned confrontation.

Another Murrow question: what should the new Kennedy administration do? Smith, Schoenbrun, Kendrick, and Schorr all suggested different approaches. Smith proposed that the United States work with the UN to keep Africa from becoming a new center of East-West conflict. Kendrick hoped for an atmospheric nuclear test ban treaty, Schorr for some imaginative way out of the Berlin crisis, Schoenbrun for a lasting solution to the Algerian war, respecting both rebel and French needs.

"Avoid another U-2 disaster," was my contribution. "It was a major goof in U.S. diplomacy." It led to the collapse of the Paris summit. What was critical at the moment, I stressed, was that the Kennedy administration "earn the respect of the Soviet leadership." One way was quickly to arrange U.S.-Soviet negotiations for a nuclear test ban; another was to sponsor a superpower UN aid package for the developing world. Schoenbrun immediately objected, saying "our European allies" would oppose any suggestion of superpower "hegemony." Not distracted, I argued, "We should seize the initiative" in order to generate "respect." The Russians were always "absorbed with respect."

Kalischer then raised one of my favorite subjects—the troubled Sino-Soviet alliance. It was crucially important, he said, and had already opened a "rift between Russia and China," complicating international relations not just in Asia but in Europe too. I agreed, adding that proof, if any were needed, was the recent meeting of eighty-one Communist Party leaders in Moscow. Covering the meeting, I said, I came to two conclusions: first, communist China was now "an alternative center of communist inspiration and leadership," a position once held exclusively by Russia; and second, just as Chinese diplomacy had played a key role during the Hungarian Revolution in 1956, China now had the clout to lead a "diplomatic mission of reconciliation" anywhere in the communist world, again a power once enjoyed exclusively by Russia. I stressed that China was "rearranging" global relations, and the United States, in not formally recognizing China, was only hurting itself.

Toward the end of the hour, Murrow asked an intriguing final question: if you had the chance, what would be the most original recommendation you would make to the new president? He started with Burdette and ended with me. The recommendations were excellent but not very original. They ranged from recognizing communist China to launching a new diplomatic effort in Latin America, from sending emergency assistance to the Congo to strengthening America's traditional ties with Western Europe. I was challenged by Murrow's use of the word "original." I thought about an interesting article I had read earlier that day, and suddenly I knew what I wanted to recommend.

"We learned today that half of China's arable land, what could be cultivated, was in drought, resulting in mass starvation in China," I observed. "The United States should send some of our excess wheat to China to feed the people of China." My proposal was admittedly controversial and raised immediate objections from Schoenbrun and Hottelet. But we had run out of time, and Murrow gracefully stepped in to conclude the broadcast. For a few moments, while the announcer identified the network, we all sat silently around the table, each with his own thoughts.

When the studio lights dimmed, Day, Westin, and other CBS bigwigs entered the studio, shook hands with the correspondents, and congratulated Murrow on another superb broadcast. He seemed subdued but responded politely with a smile, lighting up another cigarette, one of sixty-to-seventy that he smoked in a day. Drinks were served and everyone wandered over to a swiftly arranged table of hors d'oeuvres, talking and arguing about ideas that had not been fully explored during the broadcast. I struck up a conversation with Kalischer about China's rapid rise in the communist world, telling him about my round-the-world journey the year before. I also chatted with Hottelet, Smith, and Burdette, all of whom, in different ways, expressed admiration for my performance during the broadcast. Smith was especially interested in my China proposal.

I noticed Murrow drifting off to one corner of the studio. He was alone. That was not unusual. Many times, after an important broadcast, he'd be a silent bystander in the studio. He'd had his say on air. Because we had always enjoyed a friendly relationship, he calling me "Professor" and I calling him "Sir," I followed him, eager to tell him how much it meant to me to be on this broadcast with him.

"Sir?" I started.

Murrow looked at me but did not respond.

"I just wanted to tell you how excited I was to be with you tonight. I've been watching *Years of Crisis* for a long time. This, for me, was very special. Thank you so much."

I was expecting some response, but Murrow said nothing. He again looked at me, then down at his shoes.

Awkwardly, I continued, "I hope this will be the first of many broadcasts that we can do together." I meant every word.

Murrow slowly shook his head, took a deep drag on his cigarette, still said nothing, and walked away, his head lowered.

I felt awful. Had I said anything wrong? Had I offended him

somehow? Or maybe, in his eyes, I had been a total flop, and he didn't want to tell me. Or, was he not well? I had heard that in recent months he had been seeing a medical specialist on some problem.

Unhappy, confused, I left the studio and headed toward the elevator. Dan Schorr was waiting there. I told him about what had just happened with Murrow.

"Oh, didn't you know?" Dan said. "That was his last broadcast."

His words didn't register. "What do you mean, his last broadcast?"

"Yes, Ed's leaving CBS. He's joining the Kennedy administration. He's going to be head of the USIA, running the Voice of America and such things. I'm sorry, I thought you knew."

I was dumbstruck. "You're not kidding me?"

"No, I'm sorry to put it this way, but you were on Murrow's last broadcast. It hasn't yet been announced, but he's finished as a CBS broadcaster. His era is over." I heard Dan's words but couldn't quite process them. It would be a while before I could.

In the Murrow era, after a major broadcast, everyone in TV news waited for the judgment of Jack Gould, the TV critic of the *New York Times*. He was read as the gold standard of criticism. He could make or break programs and careers. On December 31, he wrote that NBC, which had watched Murrow's *Years of Crisis* broadcasts with envy for years, decided to run one of its own, and in this new year-end competition, in Gould's view, NBC "had much the best of it," bringing "detail, zest, informality, and personality" to its presentation of world events. CBS covered the "same range of topics," he went on, but "not so interestingly or with as much bite." In the last paragraph of his critique, he wrote that "the bright spot on the CBS panel was a newcomer to the year-end session, Marvin Kalb, the correspondent in Moscow. He, for one, spoke with attractive naturalness and his thinking was the most provocative of the hour." Gould especially appreciated my "feed the people of China" proposal, expressing the hope that the new Kennedy administration would at least consider it.

Gould's comments were read at CBS with different degrees of interest, disappointment, and envy. I was thrilled, of course, but I felt bad that he had been less than enthusiastic about Murrow's performance. He probably did not yet know about Murrow's decision to leave CBS. When the news broke a week later, he praised Murrow without reservation as a "trailblazing giant" in broadcast journalism.

Murrow was that and much more to me. He'd been the one who welcomed me to CBS News. He wanted someone who knew about Russia and spoke Russian. He was intensely curious about Russia—its politics, its literature, its people. More than anyone else, Murrow had given me the chance to be CBS's Moscow correspondent. Early on, he encouraged me to write several of his radio commentaries and then after a while to broadcast my own analysis of Soviet affairs in my own voice on his program. He had opened the door, and I'd walked through it.

Now Murrow was leaving, just as I was settling into the Moscow assignment he probably had in mind for me from the very beginning. I vowed to myself that no matter the story or challenge, I would always conduct myself as if Murrow were still at CBS, a towering reminder that a reporter's job was not to make news but to cover it—with honesty and humility, with fairness and dignity.

I was honored to be on his last broadcast. He left a legacy unmatched by any other broadcast journalist. Though he walked with many, he walked alone. There would never be another like him.

16

SAYING NO TO MURROW?

In mid-March 1961, a few months after Mady and I returned to Moscow from the *Years of Crisis* broadcast in New York and the stunning news of Murrow's switch from CBS to President Kennedy's United States Information Agency (USIA), I attended a Friday afternoon briefing in Ambassador Llewellyn Thompson's office. The big story was the Soviet military buildup in Cuba and the Congo. Khrushchev's Russia was clearly on the move, and the new American president faced a major challenge. Thompson acknowledged the Soviet buildup, but dodged all questions about what would constitute a proper American response.

When the briefing ended and the reporters filed out of the ambassador's office, his secretary, Connie, caught my eye. "The ambassador would like to see you," she whispered, "if you have a moment."

"Of course," I replied.

Thompson's desk, as always, was covered with files, and from one he extracted a letter.

"Here," he said, handing it to me. "It's from your friend,

Edward R. Murrow." He used Murrow's full name, as if, in his mind, there was no other way of referring to him.

I was surprised. Why would Murrow be writing to me?

It was a short letter, stamped "Secret" and signed "Ed," asking if, at my earliest convenience, I could call him about a "matter of a confidential nature." In our last conversation, he had not said a word to me. Now he wanted to have a "confidential" talk. What about?

"Mr. Ambassador," I asked Thompson, "have you any idea what this is all about?" I assumed he had read the letter.

"No," he answered, "but," with a smile, "I wouldn't make the call from the Metropol or the Central Telegraph," alluding to the likelihood that the phones there would be tapped.

"Could I make it from here?"

"No, you're not cleared to use an embassy phone." He stood up, signaling the end of our meeting. "Have a nice weekend in Paris," he said with a broad grin, as he left the office. I followed him, placing the letter in the inner pocket of my jacket. "By the way," he added, catching a glimpse of the letter's journey, "leave the letter with Connie. It's secret and can't leave the embassy."

I wanted immediately to inform Mady about this rather startling development, but first I raced to the Central Telegraph to broadcast a few radio reports on Cuba and the Congo. Then, by pre-arrangement, I met her at the National Hotel for an early dinner. But before entering the restaurant, I suggested we go for a walk. The restaurant, always catering to foreigners, was bugged, and I needed the security of fresh air.

On our way to Red Square, as unlikely a destination for discussing secrets as any other in Moscow, I told Mady about the letter containing Murrow's request for a "confidential" talk, and then about Thompson's jocular suggestion that we "have a nice weekend in Paris." Her eyes lit up at the thought of Paris, but she too was baffled about Murrow's real intent in sending this secret missive. What could be so secret that it had to be sent through diplomatic channels?

The only way to clear up the mystery was to call Murrow, and Paris, we both agreed, had a superb collection of secure phones. First, though, I had to inform Paskman and Day. I couldn't just leave Moscow without their permission. They would want an explanation, but what could I tell them that would justify a weekend in Paris? That Murrow had asked me to call him about a "confidential" matter and I needed a "secure" line, one the Russians could not easily bug?

I expected them to pepper me with questions, and I had little to tell them. After all, Murrow was no longer with CBS. Also, why would a senior administration official, which described Murrow at the time, send a secret letter to the CBS correspondent in Moscow requesting a "confidential" call? Was he going to leak a big story and wanted to give it only to Kalb? Highly unlikely, in my judgment. So why the letter?

Much to my surprise, neither Paskman nor Day raised a single objection to my proposal for a Paris weekend. After a broadcast the next day, I told the editor in New York to tell them that I had to go to Paris for the weekend on an urgent matter, leaving Friday and returning Sunday night. That's all I said. I then asked for their explicit approval. In a few hours, both sent me telegrams approving of my weekend in Paris, Paskman's even adding, "Have a good trip." Day, usually a tightwad on budgets, did not raise a question about cost. By implication, CBS would pay, and it did.

Maybe, by this time, I'd been in Moscow too long and suspected conspiracies even on a clear day, but I could not help but wonder why CBS management was so understanding and generous. Could they already have known what Murrow had in mind?

The flight to Paris was swift and uneventful, and because we were traveling light, a small suitcase for each of us, we were able to get through customs without any delays, and taxied not to the Crillon but to the Plaza Athénée, located only a few blocks from the CBS office.

During a late lunch, we discussed possible strategies for my call to Murrow but quickly realized that only Murrow knew the reason for the call, and we would soon know it too.

Back in our room, I placed the call. From Paris to Washington, there were usually no problems, and there was none that day either. In less than a minute, I was through to Murrow's office. A soft voice announced, "Director's office."

"I'm Marvin Kalb. I'm calling from Paris. Is he in?"

"Yes, Mr. Kalb. He told me you'd call one of these days. Just a minute, please."

I had not seen or heard Murrow since the *Years of Crisis* broadcast and felt reassured to hear his strong, familiar voice.

"Hi, Professor," he said, still sounding as if he was on air, "happy they let you out of prison for a weekend." For the next few minutes, we chatted about CBS and Paris. He also flattered me about a broadcast I'd done on the Congo, and then got down to business.

Murrow told me that since his arrival in Washington in early February, he'd been busy learning first about the USIA, his new home, and then about the equally new Kennedy administration, specifically, where he fit, what to know, whom to call. Murrow stressed he had much to learn. His job, as he put it, was to "sell" American policy to the world, "as honestly as possible." He said he needed "good people close by" to get the job done. Murrow paused, probably to light a cigarette. Most important, he continued, he needed someone who knew about the Soviet Union, a massive nuclear power posing a chronic threat to America's national interest; someone who knew Khrushchev; who spoke Russian; who could sense from the language of *Pravda* whether Khrushchev was faking or serious about a diplomatic or military move.

Then, Murrow explained why he had sent the secret letter to me in Moscow requesting a "confidential" conversation. "I'd like you to be at my side," Murrow said, choosing his words carefully, "helping me understand Russia, and China, and probably the rest of the communist world too."

I heard what Murrow said, but what he said left me speechless.

"Professor, you there?" he asked.

"Yes, Sir," I responded. "Forgive me, but I don't know what to say." A few seconds of silence followed. "I think what you're saying is you want me to quit my CBS job in Moscow and join you at USIA and move to Washington. Am I right?"

"Right you are," he countered. "Look, give it some thought. I know it would be a big decision for you. You're finally in Moscow, where you've always wanted to be, and now I'm asking you to come here. In these parts, everyone says, 'the country needs you.' I know I need you." Another long pause followed. "Discuss it with Mady, and call me back tomorrow. Okay?" He gave me his home number.

After I'd hung up the phone, dazed by the opportunity Murrow had just placed before me, I turned to Mady, who had been hovering over me throughout the whole conversation. "Wow!" was all I could say.

"Wow, indeed," echoed Mady. "I think we better go for a walk and think this one through."

The embankment along the Seine has been the scene of many private conversations. Ours added to its romantic legend. We walked and talked for what seemed like hours, at one point crossing the historic river into the Left Bank, stopping for a coffee, visiting an art gallery, enjoying the scenery but always dancing around the key question Murrow had posed: would I leave CBS in Moscow to join my mentor in Washington?

It was, for me especially, an extremely difficult decision. I had dreamed about becoming the CBS correspondent in Moscow, arranged my studies to be properly prepared, learned the language, did the research and started writing my PhD dissertation, wrote two books (one published to excellent reviews, the

other soon to be published), traveled around the world for information and insight into the Sino-Soviet alliance, learned the
business of radio and television news, and finally had reached
the pinnacle of foreign assignments for a broadcast journalist during the Cold War: I was CBS's Moscow correspondent
and bureau chief and had reached the top only three years
after Murrow hired me, presumably with this assignment in
mind. And now he was asking me to leave CBS and join him in
Washington.

Could I leave Moscow? As important, could I say no to
Murrow?

I knew Murrow's offer was a great honor. The job was also
a stellar opportunity for me to serve my country at a tricky,
anxious time in the Cold War. I considered myself a patriot.
I wanted to help the United States survive the Cold War with
its dignity and principles in good shape. Indeed, it could be
argued that my extensive academic preparation for the CBS
Moscow assignment was equally applicable to the job of adviser on Soviet affairs to the director of the USIA, perhaps
even more so. When CBS management was considering my
appointment to Moscow, Murrow described me as "our kind
of guy." Apparently I did not disappoint him or management.

What to do?

While it was an agonizing decision for me, it was a simple
one for Mady. She listened sympathetically, but, as we returned to the hotel, she said, "You are now where you have
always wanted to be. And you're only just starting."

"Yes, I know, but working with Murrow on Soviet affairs
would be real and exciting, especially now with a new administration coming into power." I tried to persuade Mady (and
myself apparently) that the Murrow job might be a once-in-a-
lifetime opportunity for me to see, from a high inside perch,
how the U.S. government really worked. I could probably then
use the experience to teach at a university or return to jour-

nalism. Besides, how could I say no to Murrow, who had done so much for me? That was always a key question.

Mady understood my reasoning and sympathized with my dilemma, but strongly believed I should reject Murrow's offer, difficult as that might be for me. "You've now proven to Murrow, John Day, everyone, that you are where you should be—CBS's Moscow correspondent. Why leave when you're just beginning?"

I called a truce. I couldn't make the decision just yet; I needed more time.

"Let's go out," I proposed. "No more Murrow, no more Moscow. Not tonight. Let's just enjoy a delicious dinner. Let's be sure to drink too much wine. And then let's walk around the Champs. We're in Paris. Let's enjoy ourselves." And we did indeed enjoy ourselves on this memorable night in the beautiful French capital.

The next morning, I was up early. I had made up my mind at some point during the night that I would decline Murrow's offer. I would remain CBS's Moscow correspondent. I thought that it would be a 51–49 decision, a very close, painful decision to remain a journalist, but it was closer to a 75–25 call. I was meant for the Moscow assignment. It had been my dream job, and I must have been doing very well at it, or why would Day have invited me to join his best foreign correspondents for a *Years of Crisis* broadcast, and why would a distinguished British newspaper ask me to write a weekly column?

I woke Mady and told her of my decision. "It won't be easy saying no," she cautioned. "But I'm sure you'll do it well."

I did not wait another minute. I called Murrow and told him that Mady and I had spent many hours discussing his "fantastic offer" but decided that, at this point in my career, it made sense for me to remain CBS's Moscow correspondent. I had diligently prepared for the job, and though I'd have been thrilled and honored to work at Murrow's side, the thought of leaving

Moscow and journalism now, in the middle of the Cold War, seemed wrong.

Murrow did not interrupt me. When I finished, there were a few seconds of dead air, and then he said, in a soft voice, that I had been doing a "masterful" job of reporting from Moscow, that my career was at a "take-off point," and that he "fully understood my decision." When I again stressed that the decision was "difficult" and "painful," he assured me that "explanations" were not necessary. "Our friendship will remain solid, untouched," he assured me.

"Please understand, Sir," I stressed, "I want to remain a journalist. As you were."

"I understand, Professor," he was bringing our conversation to a close. "Good luck, and warmest best wishes to Mady."

When I hung up, I found myself in tears. At least, I felt as though I was in tears. Murrow had been so kind, helpful and understanding to me, and I had just said no to him.

Mady and I could have spent another day in Paris, but I was not in the mood for Paris now, and we decided to return to Moscow that afternoon. There was reporting to be done.

The following day, I wrote a letter to Murrow, again explaining my decision. "At the end of the day, I wanted to remain a journalist, and I pray that you understand. It was you who set an example not only for me but for every journalist in radio and television. . . . You embodied radio-TV news with a dignity that is awesome. You gave CBS News life and the Murrow tradition, and I want to follow in that tradition."

A few weeks later, on April 3, I got a letter from Murrow, thanking me for my letter to him. "It is one of the few letters that I shall keep," he wrote. "It will serve to warm me when the chill winds of criticism begin to blow. . . . Thank you for the kind words, and I cannot but agree with your decision." It was signed, "Warmly, Ed."

No matter the story, time, or place, I hoped that my reporting from Moscow over the next two years, including such stories as the Berlin crisis and the Cuban Missile Crisis, justified my Paris decision. I worked in the Murrow "tradition" of fairness, decency, and unafraid, honest journalism. He remained my mentor, he set the example, though I was in Moscow and he in Washington.

INDEX

In this index, sublevels use "MK" to indicate Marvin Kalb.